LIBRARY OPERATIONS
RESEARCH

LIBRARY OPERATIONS RESEARCH

by
Robert J. Daiute
Kenneth A. Gorman

1974
OCEANA PUBLICATIONS, INC.
Dobbs Ferry, New York

Library of Congress Cataloging in Publication Data

Daiute, Robert James.
    Library operations research: computer programming
of circulation

    Includes bibliographical references.
    1. Library use studies. 2. Libraries and readers.
3. Sampling (Statistics) 4. Electronic data processing
--Library science. I. Gorman, Kenneth A., joint author.
II. Title.
Z711.3.D33   028.7   73-20303
ISBN 0-913338-01-X

©Copyright 1974 by Oceana Publications, Inc.

All rights reserved. No part of this publication may be reproduced or
transmitted in any form or by any means, electronic or mechanical, including photocopy, recording, xerography, or any information storage
and retrieval system, without permission in writing from the publisher.

Manufactured in the United States of America

028.7
D132e

To Ellie, Rob and Ria

and

To Pat, Nancy and Susan

TABLE OF CONTENTS

PREFACE

This book represents three to four years of thinking,
planning and work by the two of us. It has been subjected
to review and evaluation by many other persons who have had
wide experience in the library field. The sampling methods
described in this book generally are consistent with what is
considered necessary by leading researchers on the subject of
book usage. Also, it can be noted that the sampling methods
described can be applied to any type of individual library
and to a system of libraries.

The data-collection phase of research on book use inside
the Rider College library was financed by a grant from the
U.S. Office of Education, to whom we wish to express our
gratitude.

We owe a real debt to Bob's wife, Ellie, for her typing.

R. J. D.

Lawrence Township, N.J.   K. A. G.

LIST OF TABLES

LIST OF FIGURES

Summary of Book

Library Operations Research attempts to fill a lacuna in information on the use of library books. The gap has the form of a lack of data on in-library book use. Up to now, there has been no fully empirical method for measuring book readership inside a library.

This book explains how statistical sampling theory can be applied in a practical sampling method for collecting data and analyzing the data on in-library book use at any library. The sampling schedule and route for conducting interviews are derived from the requirements of the sampling theory. The method's feasibility is proven by its successful application at the library of Rider College.

Student interviewers were employed to conduct interviews of book readers inside the library. Other students served as validators of the interviews. Sampling was used in this validation.

The results of the interviews were combined with information from a computer data bank about reader characteristics. The data on book characteristics and reader characteristics have been analyzed. The rationale of computer methods has been formulated so that a computer could be used to facilitate the processing and analysis of the data. The Chi-Square test and the Student-t test are the tests that have been applied in the analysis of results.

It can be said, now, that it is entirely feasible to measure empirically, by means of sampling, book readership inside of a library. There are important implications of this conclusion for the solution of significant problems which face library administrators. For example, such sampling can round out the complete description of readership of library books. Thus, an academic library would be in a position to determine more effectively the relationship between library book use and the academic curriculum.

Similarly, a systems approach to a group of libraries would draw upon the sampling of in-library book readership. Readership, once ascertained, would indicate utilization and would help to evaluate the effectiveness of individual libraries in a library system. Furthermore, the sampling of readership would serve as a basis for allocation and reallocation of books among libraries to meet demand and conserve funds.

The sampling technique can be extended to the sampling of library staff personnel and to the auditing of book loss. By this means control would be achieved of the two largest items of library costs. Finally, the basic concept of library standards would be revised in light of the sampling of in-library book use; that is, the method of measuring library use would be generalized and inadequate quantitative standards of the past would be abandoned.

Serious students of library administration find that sampling methods for library use studies often are poorly conceived. They call for statistically sound random sampling methods to be used.

A review of 700 studies that use sampling in library use studies found that two types of methods are employed. One samples all books in the collection to determine past usage from library records. The other method samples books being checked-out of the library, during a period of time. Both of these methods would determine book use for books in circulation.

In-library book use has been determined by: (1) noting the books subject to reshelving after having been left on tables and other surfaces; (2) sampling areas of the library to determine monographs which have been left on tables; and (3) user opinion questionnaires.

It is apparent that there does exist a gap in knowledge about library use, especially with respect to the empirical basis for finding who is reading what books inside the library. The main purpose of this book is to explain an improved method for sampling book use inside of a library. The method is explained step-by-step, as are the results of the study at Rider College which demonstrated the feasibility of the method.

When data on in-library book use is combined with data on books in circulation, there are important uses of such information. Examples are: long-range and short-range planning; book acquisitions; assignment of library staff personnel; and evaluation of library effectiveness. The results of the in-library book use study can be extended in order to formulate a simulation of book use and carrel utilization in the library. Selected problem areas of library administration, such as control of personnel cost and control of book loss, will yield to well-designed methods of sampling and analysis.

For methods of sampling to be well-designed, they must be derived from pertinent sampling theory. The sampling theory for both means and proportions is relevant to the design of sampling methods for measuring in-library book readership.

Sampling makes use of partial observations to make general judgments. One can estimate population averages or proportions or totals from sample results at hand. For sampling to serve such a purpose, the sampling must be random. That is, every element in a stratum must have the same opportunity of appearing in the sample.

Random numbers tables can be used to get a random selection, when the population is small. When the population is large or infinite, it is impractical to use random numbers. Systematic sampling might be used, in that event. Under systematic sampling every k^{th} element is chosen for the sample; however, systematic sampling can introduce a bias if the population is arrayed according to a pattern.

The sample mean permits one to obtain an unbiased estimate of the population mean. The sample mean is the arithmetic average of the values of a sample. The population mean is the arithmetic average of all the values of a population. The average of all possible sample means is the population mean. However, any single sample mean can differ from the population mean. This error is subject to measurement in order to enhance the precision of the estimated population mean.

One way of measuring the precision of the estimate is to take all possible sample sizes and average out the error. But this method requires us to know the population mean in advance. And that's the very thing we are trying to estimate.

Fortunately, there is a relationship between the variance of the sample mean and the variance of the population values themselves. The square root of the sample mean gives the standard error of the sample mean. A single sample permits the calculation of the variance of the sample mean. The sample variance is the sum of the squared deviations about the sampled mean, divided by the sample size less 1. Only when the subtraction 1 is made, is there an average obtained of all possible sample variances equal to the population variance.

A more commonly used measure of variation is standard deviation. Standard deviation is the square root of variance. Again, it is vital to subtract 1 from the sample size when calculating variance in order to measure precisely the variance in the population values.

A discussion of standard deviation should note that there is less variation among the sample means than among the population values. For simple random samples the standard error of the sample mean is:

$$\frac{\sigma}{\sqrt{n}} \qquad \sqrt{\frac{N-n}{N-1}}$$

If the population size is large and the sample size is small we can drop the finite multiplier and calculate the sample mean as follows:

$$\sigma_{\bar{x}} = \frac{\sigma}{\sqrt{n}}$$

The standard error of the sample mean permits us to measure the precision in estimating the population mean. The degree of confidence one would have in the estimate is measured by the standard error of the sample means in conjunction with the Central Limit Theorem.

The Central Limit Theorem can be explained in the following terms. If sampling is repeated for large-size samples, the sample means approach a normal curve with a mean which is the population mean and a standard deviation which is the standard

5

error of the sample mean.

In other words, one can be 68 percent certain that the population mean differs from the sample mean by no more than 1 standard error, and 95 percent certain that the population mean differs from the sample mean by no more than 1.96 standard errors.

But the normal approximation holds only when the population standard deviation is known. When the standard deviation must be estimated, using sample results, the theoretical distribution of sample means follows a Student-t distribution rather than a normal distribution.

The Student-t distribution is a family of curves that depends on the number of degrees of freedom in the sample. The latter is the number of variables in that sample that are free to wander.

The Student-t-curves are symmetrical about the mean and bell shaped. For the Student-t-curves the peaks tend to be flatter and the tails wider than for the normal distribution curve. When the sample size is larger and the number of degrees of freedom greater the Student-t approaches the normal.

Stratified sampling can reduce the sample size needed for estimating the population mean with no loss of precision. This is possible if partitioning of population values can be accomplished so that in at least some of the strata there is less variation among the values than for the population as a whole. Sampling within each stratum is random. It is necessary to determine the amount of sampling for each stratum. The two most common methods are called proportional allocation and optimum allocation. In proportional allocation the amount of sampling is proportional to the relative size of the stratum. When optimum allocation is used, sampling is proportional to the relative variation of the stratum.

According to proportional allocation, the standard error of the sample mean would be

$$\sigma_{\bar{x}} = \sqrt{\frac{\sum\limits_{h=1}^{S} W_h \sigma_h^2}{n}}$$

where σ_h^2 is the variance of the hth stratum

S = number of strata

n is the overall sample size

W_h is relative size of the hth stratum

the finite multiplier is omitted

The finite multiplier must be included if the population is finite.

Under optimum allocation the sample estimate of the population mean is

$$\bar{x} = \sum_{h=1}^{S} W_h \bar{x}_h$$

The standard error of the sample error is

$$\sqrt{\frac{\left(\sum\limits^{S} W_h \sigma_h\right)^2}{n}}$$ if the population is arbitrarily large

The sample is allocated according to the relation

$$n_h = \frac{n\ W_h \sigma_h}{\sum\limits^{S} W_h \sigma_h}$$ where n_h = the number of units to be sampled in the hth stratum

Stratification can bring about savings in sample size compared to simple random sampling. However, care must be taken in stratified sampling. To use it, there must be known the relative sizes of strata and the standard deviation of values within the strata.

Often it is not an average value that is of interest, but a proportion. A unit of interest is called a target unit. There is a proportion of target units in proportion to total number of units in population, just as there is a proportion of target units in sample to total units in sample.

The sample proportion is used as an estimator of the population proportion. The standard error of the sample proportion measures the expected variation in sample proportions. The formula for the standard error of the sample proportion can be derived from the formula for the standard error of the sample means.

The standard error of the sample proportion is given by

$$\sigma_{p'} = \sqrt{\frac{PQ}{n}} \quad \text{when the population is infinite}$$

The population proportion is needed in order to compute $\sigma p'$. But it is the population proportion that is being estimated. An estimate of the population proportion of a previous study, or drawn from a preliminary sample, or the proportion .5 can be used to calculate σp.

The Central Limit Theorem gives confidence limits for the estimate of the population proportion. When the sample size is small, the Student-t distribution is used to get confidence limits. A proportion is a form of means.

In stratified random sampling, the estimate of the population proportion is

$$p' = \sum_{h}^{S} W_h P_h$$

where S is the number of strata, W_h the relative size of the hth stratum and P_h the population proportion of the hth stratum

The standard error of the sample proportion is given by

$$\sigma p' = \sqrt{\frac{\sum W_h P_h Q_h}{n}} \quad \text{for infinite population}$$

Formulas are available for optimum allocation, as well.

In cluster sampling the population is partitioned according to some characteristic. In cluster sampling, sampling takes place only in a randomly selected number of clusters. Thus, cluster sampling is more convenient and less costly than stratified sampling. However, there can be a greater error in estimation, for cluster sampling. Formulas are available to measure the two sources of variation in cluster sampling, "within" and "between" clusters.

What is needed is a general formula for the maximum magnitude of these two variances in advance of sampling itself. The following formula can be derived to measure the maximum variance of the variance proportion.

$$\text{Max V} = \frac{.25}{M} \left(\frac{1}{k} + 1 \right)$$

where M = number of clusters selected at random

k = number of units in each cluster that are to be sampled.

In stratified sampling, the maximum variance would be $\frac{.25}{Mk}$.

In addition to the forms of sampling discussed up to this point, other forms of sampling will be discussed as they arise in the course of analysis of other topics.

The foregoing sampling theory for means and proportions underlies the plan for sampling book readership inside the Rider College library. The sampling method which is described here we believe to be the first fully empirical method for determining who is reading what books inside a library.

The origin of the Rider study is to be found in the activities of a faculty committee on the library. That committee defined its interest in the library to be confined to academic uses. It was concerned with explaining how academic departments of the School of Business Administration could draw upon identified sources of information, in order to audit academic uses of the library.

From this origin, a professor of Management and a professor of Quantitative

9

Methods combined their talents to plan studies that would sample library operations and uses. The first project undertaken was that of sampling a bibliography of Management books to see what proportion of the bibliography would be found in the library collection.

A random numbers table was used to select a sample of 100 books out of the 696 items in the bibliography. Forty-two of the 100 were found in the library catalog. Thus, it was concluded that 42 percent of the 696 books are in the library collection, with 95 percent certainty that the error of the estimate is no more than $\pm$ 9 percent.

After that step was completed, a random sample was taken of 10 books out of the 42-book sample. Again, a random numbers table was used to select the sample. The circulation record of the 10 books was examined. On the average, each had been borrowed 8 times; the standard deviation was 10. For those books that had been borrowed as many as 20 to 30 times, a preliminary check indicated that they had been included in required reading assignments for students.

The scope of the professional interest in book use then was shifted to include only book use inside the library building itself. It was recognized that random sampling could be adopted to measure book readership inside the library. The sampling attributes of unobtrusiveness and economy of data collection would make sampling an excellent instrument for purposes at hand. It was seen that randomness should have the two dimensions of random time and random place. Time and place are simple yet basic.

A sample size of 600 for sampling in-library book use was considered an optimum size. With that sample size, the estimated error would avoid too much distortion in the smaller percentages which are common to some categories of students and books. Extra precision would not be worth the extra cost of a larger sample.

For each sample time selected, it was planned that the interviewer would be prepared to visit several reading locations in sequence, each place having been selected at random, until the interviewer did find a book reader. The interviewer would be directed to obtain two types of information from the interviewee: the name of the book reader and the full bibliographical description of the book being read. The several characteristics of each reader could be determined by reference to records of the school.

It was planned that the results of the sampling would be analyzed to determine the statistically valid inferences which could be drawn about book readership inside the library. The Chi-Square test was recognized as a useful statistical test to serve that purpose.

In implementing the sampling plan, there was a need for managing the interviewers and the data collection process. Two student organizations participated in the interviewing and the validation of the interviewing program. One is the Alpha Phi Omega fraternity of men at Rider. The other is the Phi Chi Theta fraternity of women at Rider. It was considered desirable to make use of such organizations because by so doing we were demonstrating that students could participate effectively in an important phase of academic planning and evaluation. The women served as validators of the interviews conducted by the men.

In addition to the two organizations mentioned above, there was an organizational context in which this institutional research was conducted. It was necessary to obtain cooperation of many different departments of the school -- fundraising, controller's, printing office, for instance -- to carry through the research project to a successful completion. This required the ability to motivate by explanation, a generous amount of tact and diplomacy and, in one or two instances, a clear line of administrative communication to higher authority.

The procedures for data collection proved to be an interesting exercise in translating sampling theory into operational behavior of interviewers. The final plan called for selecting sample times at random from some 8,900 5-minute intervals which made up the time the library would be open during the 60-day period of interviewing. Random numbers tables were used to select the 700 sample 5-minute intervals. The interviewers were required to refer to a special clock in the library to determine when the interview attempt should begin.

Also, the interviewers were told of the sequence of five reading locations to visit, each place having been selected at random, until the interviewers found a book reader at one of the locations. The interviewers were told how to determine if a reader is reading a book. There were 397 reading places, in the immediate vicinity of the open stacks, that were covered in the survey.

In validating the 700 interviews attempts, a sample of 50 sample times was selected at random from the 700 interview occasions. The women validators followed the standard interview procedure on those 50 occasions.

The data obtained from the interviews of book readers and the data bank on student characteristics were coded and punched into cards for processing and analysis at the IBM 1130 computer. The computer print-outs furnished results which are summarized below. There are seven classes of results:

1. General results
2. Reading of library and nonlibrary books by type of book
3. Characteristics of book readers
4. Matrix analysis
5. T test analysis
6. Profile of student
7. Use of library carrels by time of day and day of week.

Each of these topics will be discussed in turn. Of the 661 interview attempts actually conducted, interviews were completed of 64 readers of library books and 204 readers of nonlibrary books. There were no interviews completed for 393 of the interview attempts; no book reader was found at any of the five alternative reading locations. In general there is low utilization of the library for the reading of library books. Three times as many readers sampled were reading non-library books as library books in the sample of book readers.

Types of books being read in the library were duly classified. The relative frequency (50 percent) of reading Social Science books is significantly higher than for any other type of library book. The lowest three percentages of reading are in Pure Science, Technology, and the category of Geography and History (running between 3 and 6 percent).

The distribution of textbook reading in the library was found. For the total of 174 textbooks found being read in the sample, 58 percent were required textbooks in Liberal Arts courses; 38 percent, Business Administration; and 4 percent, Education.

Turning to the measurement of relative frequency of book readership by Major Field of Study of the reader, Business Administration majors read relatively more frequently than any other field of study. Liberal Arts majors stand next and Education majors last. Education majors, in addition, read significantly less than their proportionate share in the population.

The mean cumulative average of the readers of books in the library is significantly higher than the cumulative average of the daytime undergraduate population at Rider. Whether the cumulative average is a valid measure of scholastic achievement is a question which is outside the scope of the immediate research study.

It has been found that dormitory students read in proportion to their share in the population, while commuters read more than their proportionate share. Sorority and fraternity members read books in the library less than their proportionate share of the student population.

Freshman students read books in the library less than their proportionate share; Sophomores more; and Juniors and Seniors the same as their proportionate share of the student population. For men and women together, men alone, or women alone no significant difference exists between the sample's mean class year and the population's mean class year. Men students read books in the library with about twice the frequency of women students. Also, men students read more frequently than their proportionate share, while women read less than their proportionate share in the student population.

The results of the Chi-Square test are summarized next. The only relationship between reading of library books or not and the several characteristics of the reader is in connection with student or nonstudent readers. The null hypotheses was rejected with respect to that relationship.

Secondly, no relationships were found to exist between the kind of library book being read, on the one hand, and any other characteristic of the reader, on the other hand, where the Chi-Square test was possible. Thirdly, only one relationship was found to prevail between Major Field of Study of the reader and the other several characteristics of the reader. That relationship was to sex of the reader.

Fourth, a relationship was found between residence of a reader and the reader's sex, class year, day of week of reading, and time of day of reading. Finally, no relationship existed between weekday reading and any other characteristics of the reader, where the Chi-Square test was possible.

The Chi-Square test was supplemented by the Student-t test. The Chi-Square test gives a single test result for a whole matrix. The T test can be used to test for significant differences between cells within a matrix.

The detail of the T test results is so rich and diverse that it is not possible to summarize the T test results beyond the treatment given to these results

14

in Chapter 5. However, some examples can be given.

Library Book or Nonlibrary Book By Cumulative Average

Students who have the highest cumulative averages read non-library books with greater relative frequency than do those who have middle and lowest cumulative averages. However, the students who have the highest cumulative averages read library books relatively less frequently.

Students who have middle cumulative averages read library books more frequently than nonlibrary books. The reverse holds for the students who have the highest cumulative averages. For the lowest students there is no significant difference.

Library Book By Major Field

Education majors read Other library books more frequently than do Business majors.

Business majors read Technology books more frequently than either Literature or Other library books.

Major By Library and Nonlibrary Book

Library books are used more frequently by Education majors than nonlibrary books. No significant difference is found for any other pairing.

Nonlibrary books are read more frequently by Liberal Arts majors than by Education majors. There are no significant differences for any other pairing.

Library books are read more frequently by Education majors than by Liberal

Arts majors. There are no significant
differences for any other pairing.

A profile was prepared of the typical man student and woman student library
reader. The typical man student library reader is a first-semester Sophomore
whose cumulative average is 2.48. He lives in a dormitory and his major is Business Administration. He prefers nonlibrary to library books but when he does read
a library book he prefers a Social Science book. He prefers to read in the library
on a Tuesday afternoon or morning.

The typical woman student is a second semester Freshman whose cumulative
average is 2.55. She lives in a dormitory and her Major Field of Study is Liberal
Arts. She prefers nonlibrary to library books, but when she reads a library book
it is not in the Social Science area. She prefers the library on a Monday evening
or afternoon.

On the basis of the sample results, it has been possible to simulate the complete utilization of carrels, hour-by-hour and day-by-day. The simulation indicates that the highest percent of hourly carrel occupancy is between 8:00 p.m. and
9:00 p.m. with an average occupancy of 27 percent and a 95 percent confidence interval of 12.9 percent. The lowest percent of hourly carrel occupancy is between
8:00 a.m. and 9:00 a.m. with an average occupancy of 3.6 percent and a 95 percent
confidence interval of 5.9 percent.

The highest percent of daily occupancy is Sunday with an average occupancy of
20 percent; the lowest percent of daily occupancy is Saturday with an average occupancy of 5.6 percent.

The overall percent of occupancy is 12.2 percent.

Next, the rationale for computer methods is summarized. The logic of the computer methods is presented at an abstract level to make them applicable to any type

of computer, whatever the required computer language. The computer programs, pre-pared for the Rider research, made use of FORTRAN IV language.

The first of the methods to be explained is the program for print-out of data, internal validation of data and random check. This program identifies transcription errors and duplication errors. Also, it determines whether data have internal consistency. A number of cards are chosen randomly. They are cross-checked against the original interview forms to verify proper transcription. The cards are com-pared to see if there are duplicate cards. When a duplicate is found it is identi-fied by line number. Cards with other types of errors are identified, as well.

Internal consistency is tested to determine whether

> code numbers assume valid values
>   pattern of numbers is consistent
> a cumulative average has been recorded
>   for a matriculated student
> inconsistencies among column entries
>   have occurred.

The program gives a print-out of the number of cards read and the number of errors detected.

With respect to the rationale of descriptive statistics and simulation, data cards are read, tabulated and analyzed to yield an output of descriptive statistics and simulation of library use. The descriptive statistics include:

1. Counts on interviews attempted and interviews completed
2. Relative frequency of reading
        library books
        types of library books
        other than library books
3. Relative frequency of reading by
        time of day
        day of the week
        class year
        residence
        major field
        male readers
        cumulative average

4. Average reader by
   cumulative average
   class year
   sex.

Standard errors and 95 percent confidence intervals are given for virtually all categories.

The simulation of library use is an hour-by-hour, day-by-day simulation of in-library reading.

The third rationale of computer methods to be summarized is that of testing a matrix of sample results for independence between row elements and column elements. In this method, characteristics of the sampled readers are examined to see whether the results indicate a relationship between these characteristics in the population of all library readers at the library studied.

What kinds of questions can be answered? Examples are: Do the sample results indicate a relationship between the day a person reads in the library and his sex? Do the results indicate a relationship between the day a person reads in the library and his major field? Is there a relationship between the day of reading and the reader's residence status? Is there a relationship between a reader's major and his class year?

All of these questions amount to the same basic query: Is there a relationship between paired characteristics of the reader? A matrix is a convenient device for arraying paired characteristics of a reader.

The null hypotheses is basic to the statistical testing of data arrayed in a matrix format. The null hypotheses states that no relationship exists between the two paired characteristics. The null hypotheses can be tested by sample results and accepted or rejected at some stated level of significance. A 5 percent level of significance, for example, means that in rejecting the null hypotheses we run a 5 percent risk of being wrong.

Expected cell frequencies can be calculated that would obtain if the null hypotheses is to be accepted. Actual cell frequencies and expected cell frequencies are compared. If the magnitude of these differences is such that they cannot be explained by random sampling variation, the null hypotheses is rejected. The Chi-Square statistic and the Chi-Square distribution are used to determine what kind of differences are acceptable.

There are four major groups of matrices. They are: Major Field of Study Group; Day of Week Group; Kind of Library Book Group; and Residence of Reader Group. To illustrate the groups, the Major Field of Study Group contains five matrices. They are: Major Field by Sex Matrix; Major Field by Library Book or Not Matrix; Major Field by Residence Matrix; Major Field by Class Year Matrix; and Major Field by Cumulative Average Matrix. For each of these matrices, the Major Field is the column heading; the other five characteristics are the respective row titles.

A separate program is written for each of the four matrix groups. Matrices are printed, one at a time, and tested by means of the Chi-Square test subprogram.

Significant differences between pairs of cells are not detected by the Chi-Square test. A more precise test is needed for this. The Student-t statistic provides the means for testing pairs of cells for significant differences.

The four major groups of matrices, referred to above, that earlier were tested for by Chi-Square are now analyzed by the computer, cell-by cell, to see where significant differences exist. In each matrix the data are analyzed by row, then column.

Each matrix is adapted to a form which makes it possible to treat any combination of two cell proportions in a given column as though they were sample proportions from two populations. These sample proporations can be tested for significant differences using the Student-t test. For each column, the Student-t statistic is computed for differences between two proportions, for every combination of proportions, two at a time. The computer prints-out the results of the testing of all combinations of row proportions, two at a time, for each column.

The rationale of the analysis by columns is much the same as that by rows. In each row all combinations of proportions, two at a time, are tested for significant differences. The computer print-out the results of the testing of all combinations of column totals, two at a time, for each row.

One must rely on a computer to perform the large number of calculations involved in running these tests. The analysis of the Major by Residence matrix alone involves 18 compares and the Major Field group requires 156 compares.

It can be demonstrated how selected problem areas of library operations will yield to the effective application of sampling methods and analysis. Five problem areas are discussed. They are: controlling time use and activities of library staff personnel; auditing book loss; relating the academic curriculum to effective use of the library; controlling a system of libraries; and the nature of library standards.

Some background discussion is in order before one treats the topic of time study of library staff personnel. Time study enjoys a fairly long history in the history of Management. It was a leading technique of Scientific Management and continues to be an integral part of industrial engineering today.

Time study of the operative worker involves subdividing the job cycle into elements, repeatedly timing with use of a stopwatch the time taken for the subject worker to complete each element. The average times for each element are added together to get the average actual time for the cycle. To get the standard time for the task cycle, allowances are introduced for such factors as rating of speed of subject worker, unavoidable delays, and so forth.

Statistical sampling has been adopted in work sampling to establish a basis for time-delay allowances. Work sampling has been found to be both reliable and valid.

One might have thought that sampling of time use would have been extended to managerial personnel on a wide scale. Such has not been the case, however. Some students have argued that managerial work is intangible and nonrepetitive; thus, it is not suitable for time study. Nevertheless, there are some cases of time study of managerial personnel, especially at the supervisory level.

At the same time there have been developments in Management theory which point the way for the empirical time study of executive behavior. Chester Barnard redefined bases of specialization to incorporate an operational definition of executive behavior in terms of place where work is done, time at which work is done, persons with whom work is done, things upon which work is done, and method or process by which work is done.

In 1951, Sune Carlson conducted a time study of executive behavior, adapting Barnard's scheme of classification of behavior. Carlson directed attention to communication behavior of the executive, its place, time and technique.

Thus, it can be said that the statistical methods and Management theory are available for application to time study library staff personnel. A sampling of communication activities of the chief librarian, for example, would show the frequency with which he resorts to different forms or techniques of communication, and how much time he devotes to each form. A random sample of 600 occasions would provide a standard error on the order of 1 percent to 2 percent for some four types of communication activities. The results can be used for self-evaluation by the chief librarian.

Sampling methods can be devised to measure the portion of their time subordinate library administrators are devoting to administrative activities as opposed to other types of activities. Such a survey would show whether there is a need for a greater degree of delegation of authority by the chief librarian to subordinate administrators. Furthermore, the proportion of time devoted to subprofessional activities by professional librarians would be revealed.

Finally, sampling could be applied to clerical employees at the library. Such a study would measure the proportion of their time devoted to nonproductive activity versus productive activity. Library administrators would use such information to determine whether corrective action is needed.

The large portion of the library budget devoted to personnel costs calls for the adoption of sampling techniques to control and evaluate library personnel activities.

The cost of books is second only in importance to personnel costs of libraries. Sampling can be used to audit the book collection of a library. It can be employed in determining the loss of books from the collection.

A master shelf list is recorded on some suitable form of computer storage. A number is assigned to each book. The computer can be programmed to generate random samples. An operational definition is given to books overdue and presumed lost. The computer itself checks all books lost because of overdue. The actual handiwork in the sampling is limited to the checking of sample books which should be on the shelves.

Sampling can be used to check the checkers who have checked by hand the sample books that should be on the shelves. A random sample of 100 books can be selected. If one or more errors by checkers turn up in the sample of 100, do a complete recheck of all the books that were supposed to be on the shelves in the main sample.

A similar procedure can be followed for checking errors in source documents.

What is the proper size for the main sample in auditing the collection? If the library collection contains 200,000 books, and we wish to be 95 percent certain that the error is no more than 1 percent, then a sample size of 1,809 is indicated. This sample size also assumes a book loss of 5 percent.

Simple random sample seems appropriate. Stratification does not decrease the sample size appreciably.

The sample furnishes important information from which can be derived:

an estimate of the average annual loss rate

a projection of the annual dollar loss for
future years

an evaluation of the feasibility of alternative methods for dealing with the book loss.

On this last point, a comparison can be made of alternatives such as these three:

1. accept the losses, do nothing to reduce
   losses
2. install an electronic detection system
3. close the shelves to access by readers.

Capitalized cost can be used as the criterion for choosing the most feasible alter-native. The capitalized cost method requires the use of a discount rate to take into account the time value of money.

Library use studies appear to have identified a close relation between teaching practices and the curriculum, on the one hand, and library use, on the other hand. For example, Patricia Knapp in 1954 found that over 90 percent of withdrawals from a college library were for academic course purposes.

Knapp related student characteristics to the borrowing of library books. She found that smaller class size and more advanced classes were associated with greater use of books, particularly for problem-solving purposes. She classified the small, advanced course as library-dependent.

Knapp concludes that the three-part use of the library-- using books, using information resources of the library, and using the library for problem-solving-- can be achieved when there is a (1) conscious analysis of the total curriculum to see the relevance of library resources and (2) specific designing of courses to bring about different levels of use of the library. Knapp regards the problem-solving use as the highest use of the library.

The Knapp study of library use in comparison to our study of library use suggests the following comments:

> Individual differences in readership are to be expected among libraries; hence, there is a need for sampling many libraries in order to find variations in library use
>
> The Knapp study could serve as the basis of a model to predict library use; course structure would predict library usage and book needs
>
> The sampling plan for determining book readership inside a library can be adopted to identify course purpose of reading and to correlate in-library and out-of-library use of books.

Richard W. Hostrop has extended the Knapp approach to the community college level. He found that borrowing of books for course purposes came to 87 to 89 percent of total book loans at the junior college library studied. A survey questionnaire indicated that 59 percent of book reading inside the library consisted of the study of their own books by the students.

Hostrop concluded that: "Student use of library materials at College of the Desert is largely course stimulated and somewhat comparable to the circulation figures of senior institutions..." And "...the Library at College of the Desert and the public libraries as well are used, in the main, as a place to do homework out of textbooks."

A recent study reported by Kenneth Allen of three community colleges in Illinois measured library utilization by means of a questionnaire. The most frequently mentioned primary reason for entering the library was "to study without using library materials." Sixty-two percent gave that reason.

In examining the studies discussed in this chapter, as well as the Rider sampling study of in-library book use, a pattern is found to exist. Most library use, which includes in-library use along with books used in circulation, is directly related to course work by students. If the course design and content allow or encourage it, the use of the library by the student will take the form of study hall where he reads his textbooks. On this point, it does appear that measurement of library use at a college can serve as a barometer or index to measure and evaluate the effectiveness of curriculum and faculty.

Sampling the library system in order to achieve better control and coordination is an important topic in library operations. In general, a system consists of interrelated parts. The concept of a system is a loose-knit one which can treat systems at different levels of abstraction. Management planning and control can be fitted into a systems approach, contributing improved coordination among the parts and enabling the overall system to achieve its purpose.

The DuPont system of control of divisional performance can be regarded as an example which a library system could well emulate. By sampling, comparisons can be made among the individual parts of a library system, to introduce economies and improve the service of the whole system.

The forecasting of book use and the allocation and reallocation of books among libraries would be illustrative of how a system's parts can be coordinated better with one another to improve performance of the system as a whole.

The problem of book acquisition and allocation can be dealt with in terms of book use. A method of forecasting demand is needed. The simulation of carrel occupancy hour-by-hour and day-by-day can be used. It can be translated into the number of in-library readers. Tables of relative strength of arrival can be prepared and used for this purpose.

Only a minimum amount of information is required. On the basis of a single hour's arrival count estimates can be developed of in-library reading by type of book. Of course, weekly estimates derived from a sample of one hour's activity are subject to wide error. The impact of these errors can be reduced by applying to the weekly estimates of in-library usage the device of exponential smoothing, a widely used tool in inventory control.

In exponential smoothing, the projected demand for the n + 1 period is a weighted average of all past demands. The weights assigned to those demands decrease exponentially with their age. If necessary, a correction for trend can be added to the exponential average. In connection with in-library book usage, the exponential average is used to put confidence bands on the estimate of a book usage gained from the single hour's count.

If one were concerned with controlling allocation of books among the 15 libraries of a state system of colleges, one would conduct a sampling of book usage at each library. This method furnishes a frequency distribution of books used.

Cluster sampling then would give the picture of demand in absolute numbers for a week. The cluster sampling would be applied for each successive week. Exponential smoothing would be used to adjust forecasts for book use in the succeeding week in light of errors in earlier weekly forecasts. Books would be allocated and reallocated to the libraries on the basis of these week-by-week forecasts.

Probably, the most authoritative statement of college library standards is the statement promulgated by the American Library Association in 1959. It outlines

a hierarchical formal organization for the library with the college librarian at

the apex. Planning and controlling functions on behalf of the library are included

in the duties of the chief librarian. The statement indicates the status of the

professional librarian and clerical employee of the library within this organization.

Quantitative standards describe the number of professional librarians re-

quired. Also, quantitative standards stipulate that at a minimum the college li-

brary should be allotted 5 percent of the total educational and general budget

of the college. Furthermore, the statement calls for salaries of library employees

to be about twice as great as the amount of the expenditures on books for the li-

brary.

It should be noted that the 5 percent budgetary standard would be subject to

upward or downward revision in light of results of library use studies by sample

methods as described in this book. In addition, the allocation of the total

budgeted amount among competing library uses would depend in part on library

utilization studies.

The ALA statement devotes a section to the library collections. Qualitative

phrases are used; such as:

> there should be a strong and up-to-date
> reference section
>
> the library holdings should be compared to
> standard bibliographies.

Quantitative standards on the collection are influenced by selected variables,

it is recognized in the statement, and are minimal. They state that a college li-

brary should have a minimum of 50,000 volumes. For each additional 200 students in

the student body beyond 600 students, there should be added 10,000 volumes, accord-

ing to the statement.

In addition to quantitative statements on the library building and facilities, the statement maintains that there should be seating capacity in the library for one-third of the student body, and that provision should be made for future growth of the library over the next 20 years. Quantitative standards are given, as well, on shelf space, floor space per staff worker, and table space per reader.

In the discussion of the evaluation of the quality of library service, the ALA statement recommends analysis of book circulation records, surveys of reading in the library, and other methods.

The concluding topic in the 1959 statement is the topic of "Inter-library Cooperation." While planned purchasing of materials to avoid duplication is recognized as a source of economies from interlibrary cooperation; nevertheless, the statement notes that one library should not borrow from another library those things that are basic to the college program of the first library.

A review of the impact of the 1959 statement, some five years after the statement's original publication, provided at least two conclusions of special interest: (1) there is a need for an improved objective basis for quantitative standards and (2) there is no one set of quantitative standards that could be applied universally.

Unlike the statement of college library standards, a 1966 statement of public library standards gives great emphasis to the importance of a system of libraries so as to enable the relatively small local library to provide greater service to users. The statement indicates that the centralization of selected functions should be adopted where appropriate. Perhaps, the topic of "Sampling the Library System" would have special relevance here, in explaining how to sample a system of libraries and gain an improved basis for evaluation and the achievement of a synergistic effect in book allocations.

As a basic proposition, what appears to be needed in the matter of quantitative standards for libraries is the _methodology_ of measurement and analysis which can be generalized and standardized. However, whichever concept adopted for quantitative standards they would not and could not supersede the exercise of judgment by professional librarians.

INTRODUCTION

Need for Library Data

It is appreciated by many librarians that there is a need for improving the relevance of statistics which are used in library evaluation.[1] More specifically, in use studies of libraries, sampling methods and data-gathering techniques often are poorly conceived. Salverson recommends adopting a standard methodology in order to determine with precision just what is the extent of book use at libraries.[2] Along the same lines, M. Carl Drott proposes the adoption of statistically sound random sampling methods in determining how to cope with the important aspects of library use and user satisfaction.[3] He gives examples of purposes of random sampling in libraries. Random sampling of a book collection can be conducted to determine whether a complete inventory should be taken to identify missing books. Random sampling can be used to survey users' opinions about library services. Thirdly, random sampling can be used to determine categories of little-used books which might be removed from the shelves.

Methods of Sampling

A. K. Jain has described his methods and results in applying statistical samp-

---

1. See Carol A. Salverson, "The Relevance of Statistics to Library Evaluation," College and Research Libraries, July, 1969, p. 354.

2. Ibid., p. 360.
   For a 21-page bibliography on library use, see "Use, Mis-Use and Non-Use of Academic Libraries, ed. by the Committee on Requirements of the Academic Library User, New York Library Association, Woodstock, N.Y.

3. M. Carl Drott, "Random Sampling a Tool for Library Research," College and Research Libraries, March 1969, p. 119.

ling at Purdue University.[4] He tells of his review of some 700 studies that make use of sampling to determine library book use. There are two basic types of these studies. One type is a sampling of books found in the total book collection in order to determine past usage from library records. The other type samples all books checked out for out-of-library use, during a period of time.[5] However useful they might be for other purposes, it should be noted that neither one of these two types of methods is directed toward determining in-library book usage. However, McGrath has developed an approach for deducing in-library usage of library books from out-of-library book use of the library's collection.[6] First, it is necessary to establish correlations between out-of-library and in-library book use. McGrath calculated such correlations, making use of a count, over a four-week period, of books left on tables, desks and other surfaces. These books were subject to reshelving by student reshelvers. The count of these books served as the means of measuring in-library book usage.[7] McGrath did find a high degree of correlation between out-of-library and in-library use for selected categories of books. McGrath calculated an overall 2:1 ratio as the ratio of out-of-library to in-library book use at the Library of the University of Southwestern Louisiana. However, other sources indicate three, four and as high as nine times as much book use inside the

---

4. A. K. Jain, "Sampling and Short Period Usage in the Purdue Library," College and Research Libraries, May 1966, p. 211.

   A. K. Jain, "Sampling and Data Collection Methods for a Book-Use Study," Library Quarterly, July 1969, pp. 245-252.

5. A. K. Jain, "Sampling and Data Collection Methods for a Book-Use Study," p. 245.

6. William E. McGrath, "Correlating the Subject of Books Taken Out of and Used Within an Open-Stack Library," College and Research Libraries, July 1971, p. 280.

7. Ibid., p. 281.

library as outside, for books in the library's collection.[8] Once the correlations are computed, the records of books in circulation can serve to estimate or predict with a specified precision subsequent in-library book usage, or in-library use can serve as a basis for estimating in-circulation use.

Jain's method of determining in-library book use is similar to McGrath's. Limiting the scope of his study to monograph usage at the Purdue Library, Jain subdivided the library into areas. The sampling of monographs left on tables in the morning was conducted by selecting at random the sequence of areas to be visited.[9] Jain recognizes the need for determining in-library use and the difficulty of devising suitable methods.

Behling and Cudd tell of the results of the questionnaire survey of user opinion conducted at the main library of Ohio State University.[10] They found, for example, that there was progressively less use of the library for study purposes from Freshmen to Sophomores, Sophomores to Juniors, and from Juniors to Seniors. Of all the major fields of study, History majors were found to be using the library the most. The afternoon hours were most popular for library use among users in comparison to morning and evening hours of use.

---

8. For references to in-library book use being much greater than books used in circulation, see Herman H. Fussler and J.T. Simon, _Patterns in the Use of Books in Large Research Libraries_ (Chicago: University of Chicago, 1969).

9. A. K. Jain, "Sampling and Data Collection Methods for a Book-Use Study," p. 249.

10. Orlando Behling and Kermit Cudd, "A Library Looks at Itself," _College and Research Libraries_, November 1967, p. 416.

Usefulness of User Surveys

Behling and Cudd have no doubt of the practical value to library administration of the conduct of such library user surveys. Their results can be used in long-range and short-range planning, in staffing assignments by areas and types of services, and to reorient library operations, for example, in meeting demand for study facilities.

On the basis of the foregoing review of the literature on the subject, one can conclude that there should be appropriate statistical methods employed in sampling library usage. When this is done, valid statistical inferences about library users and library usage can be drawn. Furthermore, one can see that there is a gap in knowledge about library usage, particularly in the matter of in-library usage of books. However, some methods have been devised for sampling in-library use of library books directly and for inferring in-library book use on the basis of out-of-library use of books.

Purpose of Book

The purpose of the present book is to explain improved methods for sampling and analyzing book readership inside a library. The feasibility or practicability of the methods has been demonstrated in firsthand experience. Random sampling is used, and the technique and the rationale of the sampling are described in full. Next, the organization for data collection is explained. There is a vital need at this step to assure that the procedures of data collection properly implement the sample design.

Once the data are collected on book readers and on books being read, the next stage is to analyze and process the data so as to achieve accuracy and economy. A computer should be used for this phase. For the computer to yield its full benefits,

34

a good deal of quantitative analysis and programming must be brought to bear on library operations. The programs incorporate this quantitative analysis to give step-by-step instructions to the computer in processing the data.

This book explains in detail the quantitative analysis of the data. The analysis consists of: (1) listing characteristics of book readers and books being read in the library (within measured limits of sampling error); (2) finding relationships among the several characteristics by means of the statistical tests of the Chi-Square test and the Student-t test, and (3) preparing a statistical model of book readership inside the library to simulate in-library book use, hour-by-hour and day-by-day. The simulation determines high and low periods of use. This information furnishes a high specificity of detail that can be helpful in such administrative matters as setting library hours, scheduling work loads, and preparing the library budget.

The programming of the computer entails translating the statistical analysis into FORTRAN IV computer language. The FORTRAN language can be understood by the computer which will carry out the analysis dictated by the program. The FORTRAN programs themselves have been included in Appendix I. Other computer language could be used just as well - for example, BASIC AND COBOL. The logic of the programs together with flow charts are to be found in Section III of this book.

Given the computer methods described in this book a systems analyst and a computer programmer can proceed (after making the necessary adjustments) to prepare programs for any computer in order to analyze sample data on book readership inside the library, for any library. Of course, the full statistical significance of results would remain to be determined by those who have professional competence in Statistics.

There can be no doubt that the valid statistical inferences have great value for administrative planning and decision-making on behalf of libraries. Accurate information on book use inside a library would contribute to greater effectiveness in dealing with such topics as: ascertainment of library standards, library building design and architecture, library facilities, book acquisitions, cost effectiveness in budgeting, staffing assignments, control of usage and loss of books in the book collection, relating the individual library to other libraries in loan service and book storage, and so forth.

In other words, it is difficult to see how truly effective decisions can be made on a wide range of library problems in the absence of accurate and comprehensive information on usage of the library's collection. Well-designed statistical sampling of book usage within the library is essential to a complete description of book use at libraries. Library administrators are confronted by the opportunity to adopt sampling methods of great significance to library administration. Statistics cannot be used independent of the competent librarian's judgment and expertise. Where there appears to be a conflict between judgment based on professional experience and what is suggested by the results of the quantitative analysis, the two must be integrated by the librarian.

Selected Topics Considered

In addition to explaining the need for, methods of, and use of results of sampling in-library book use, this book also considers selected topics in the library field to which sampling can be applied to the end of yielding productive results for library administration. The topics are: sampling used in time study of library staff personnel; auditing the book collection for loss of books; the curriculum and library use; a systems approach to libraries; and, finally, library standards.

The sampling and time study of library staff personnel brings to bear sampling for control of managerial, professional and clerical activities in a library. Control, here, is no Big-Brother gimmick which in fact intrudes into personal privacy and denies individual freedom. Only a small proportion of a staff member's activities would be sampled and observed. Control must be self-control to a great extent. It is vital to control staff activities since salaries and wages - that is, costs of personnel - make up the largest single cost item in the library budget.

A sampling method has been devised and is explained for auditing the book collection. Auditing is used here in a manner that is parallel to that used in business accounting practice. The sampling serves to measure historical rates of book loss. It also serves as a means of tracing those responsible for theft and mutilation.

In the chapter on the curriculum and library use, leading studies on that subject are reviewed. It is apparent that an accurate measurement of in-library use must be conducted in order for the relationship between curriculum and over-all library use to be determined. The methodology used in this book, however, has never been used before to determine in-library use.

The systemic approach to libraries also follows lines which can be regarded as being parallel to established practice in business management. Thus, decentralized operations and selective centralized control are illustrated in the discussions of how a library system permits evaluation of performance of individual libraries. Furthermore, an extended discussion is provided of the forecasting of book use among libraries so that books can be allocated and reallocated among individual libraries to better meet local demand. Finally, the use of a system of libraries to conduct controlled experiments is illustrated. Such experiments permit an evaluation of innovations and help to assure that change is carried out in a responsible and effective fashion.

The last chapter of this book treats the topic of library standards. The 1959 statement of the American Library Association on college library standards is summarized. It is clear that there is a recognized need in the library field for an objective basis for quantitative standards. The adoption of appropriate sampling methods, library-by-library, will enable libraries to meet that need.

PART I

SAMPLING THEORY

Introduction to Part I

Part I contains two chapters on sampling theory--Chapter 1 and
Chapter 2. Chapter 1 presents sampling theory for means, while
Chapter 2 summarizes the sampling theory for proportions. This
sampling theory was applied to determine the sampling methods to
be used in sampling book readership inside a library. Furthermore,
this theory was applied to other selected topics dealt with in
this book, such as sampling library staff personnel and auditing
the book collection.

CHAPTER 1

SAMPLING THEORY FOR MEANS

Purpose of Sampling

The purpose of sampling is to make general judgments on the basis of partial observations. Typically, we are concerned with estimating population averages, or proportions or totals based on sample results.

The important thing in connection with these results is that the sampling must be random. This means in the case of simple random sampling that each element in the population has an equal chance of being included in the sample. If the population is stratified then every element in a given stratum must have an equal chance of appearing in the sample allocated to that stratum.

Random selection is sometimes difficult to achieve. If the population is small, random numbers tables can be used to get a random selection. A table of random numbers is an array of digits in rows and columns such that every digit 0 through 9, inclusive, had the same chance of appearing in any row and column. The numbers are arrayed in the following fashion

```
20   34   26 . . . .

91   73   23 . . . .

45   61   45 . . . .

 :   07   32 . . . .

 :    :   94 . . . .

 :    :    : . . . .

 :    :    : . . . .
```

Suppose we want to choose three students at random from a group of eight Students using random numbers. Assign a one digit number to each student as follows:

Name	Assigned number
Smith	1
Jones	2
DeLuca	3
Spinoza	4
Church	5
Greenberg	6
Loo	7
Snyder	8

Turn to any page and any column of the random numbers tables and begin reading numbers. If an unassigned number is encountered or if a duplicate number appears, skip it, and continue reading until the third eligible number has been read.

Suppose we read random numbers from column 5 in the array of random numbers that appears above.

We get

Random numbers	Eligible	Name
2	ok	Jones
2	skip	
4	ok	Spinoza
3	ok	DeLuca

Therefore, we choose Jones, Spinoza, and DeLuca.

When the population is large or infinite it would be impractical to use random numbers in selecting a sample. An alternative might be systematic sampling. If it is fair to assume that the elements in the population are independently arrayed we could choose every k^{th} element for our sample. The danger here is the question of independence. If the elements of the population are arrayed in some kind of pattern systematic selection may introduce an appreciable bias.

Estimation of the Average Value of a Population in Simple Random Sampling

The population mean, indicated by the Greek letter μ, is the arithmetic average of all the values of a population.

Suppose a population consists of the values: 1, 9 and 5.

$$\mu = \frac{1 + 9 + 5}{3} = 5$$

The sample mean $\bar{x}$ is the arithmetic average of the values of a sample, and is used to estimate μ. There are other ways of estimating μ, but the sample mean is generally preferred because it is an unbiased estimate of μ; that is, the average of all possible sample means is the population mean.

Suppose we take all possible samples of size 2, allowing repetition, from the above population. The samples together with their means are:

Samples Values	Sample mean
1, 1	1
9, 9	9
5, 5	5
1, 9	5
9, 1	5
1, 5	3
5, 1	3
5, 9	7
9, 5	7

If we average the nine possible sample means we get

$$\frac{1+9+5+5+5+3+3+7+7}{9} = 5 = \mu$$

Although the sample mean $\bar{x}$ is an unbiased estimate of μ, any one sample mean can be expected to differ from μ. Consequently, the use of $\bar{x}$ to estimate μ involves an error. In order to have confidence about the precision of our estimate we must have some way of measuring this error.

44

One way of measuring the precision of our estimate is to take all possible samples of size 2, calculate the sample means $\bar{x}_i$ for i = 1, 2, . . . 9 and average out the errors.

That is, in our illustration, compute:

$$\frac{(\bar{x}_1 - \mu) + (\bar{x}_2 - \mu) + \ldots + (\bar{x}_9 - \mu)}{9} \quad \text{which}$$

in terms of a summation symbol, can be written

$$\frac{\sum\limits_{i=1}^{9} (\bar{x}_i - \mu)}{9} = \frac{(1 - 5) + (9 - 5) + (5 - 5) + \ldots + (7 - 5)}{9} = 0$$

This kind of averaging will always give 0 because the + and − deviations will cancel one another out.

To avoid this canceling process, square the errors and average. That is, compute

$$\frac{\sum\limits_{i=1}^{9} (\bar{x}_i - \mu)^2}{9} = \frac{8}{3}$$

This statistic is called the variance of the sample mean and is denoted by the symbol $\sigma_{\bar{x}}^2$

Take the square root. The result is called the standard error of the sample mean or standard deviation of the sample mean and is denoted by the symbol $\sigma_{\bar{x}}$. In our illustration

$$\sigma_{\bar{x}} = \sqrt{\frac{8}{3}}$$

In other words, the variance of the sample mean is the average of the squared deviations of the sample means about the population mean; the standard deviation of the sample mean $\sigma_{\bar{x}}$, is the square root of the variance of the sample mean. Obviously, we need an alternate way of calculating the variance of the sample mean, for this averaging method **requires that we take all possible** samples and calculate the corresponding sample means. Moreover, it **requires** that we know the population mean and this is the thing we are trying to estimate in the first place.

Fortunately, there is a relationship between the variance of the sample mean and the variance of the population values themselves. And knowing the population variance or an estimate of it, we can calculate the variance of the sample mean by taking a single sample. Once we know the variance of the sample mean we simply take the root to get the standard error of the sample mean.

Population Variance σ^2 and Sample Variance σ

Just as the variance of the sample mean $\sigma^2_{\bar{x}}$ measures the variation of the sample means, the population variance σ^2 measures the variation in the population values themselves. It is the average of the squared deviations of the population values about the population mean.

For our illustration

$$\sigma^2 = \frac{(1 - 5)^2 + (9 - 5)^2 + (5 - 5)^2}{3} = \frac{32}{3}$$

In general, then

$$\sigma^2 = \frac{\sum_{i=1}^{N} (x_i - \mu)^2}{N}$$, where N = population size
μ = population mean
x_i = for i = 1, 2, . . ., N are the population values

When the population variance is unknown we estimate it using the sample variance $\hat{\sigma}^2$. $\hat{\sigma}^2$ is not to be confused with $\sigma^2_{\bar{x}}$. $\hat{\sigma}^2$ is the variance of the sample values; $\sigma^2_{\bar{x}}$ is the variance of the sample means.

The sample variance is the sum of the squared deviations about the sample mean divided by the sample size less 1.

That is,

$$\hat{\sigma}^2 = \frac{\sum_{i=1}^{n} (x_1 - \bar{x})^2}{n - 1}$$, where n = sample size
$\bar{x}$ = sample mean
x_1 = sample values taken from the population

The sample variance takes nearly the same form as the population variance except for the denominator, where 1 is subtracted from the sample size in the averaging process. This subtraction of 1 matters little in large samples, but in small samples it is imperative. The reason for the subtraction is that only in this form is the sample variance an unbiased estimate

46

of the population variance. Only then is the average of all possible sample
variances equal to the population variance.

Using our illustration, the sample variances of all possible samples are:

Sample values	Sample mean	Sample variance
1, 1	1	0
9, 9	9	0
5, 5	5	0
1, 9	5	32
9, 1	5	32
1, 5	3	8
5, 1	3	8
5, 9	7	8
9, 5	7	8

Average of sample variances $= \dfrac{3\ (0)\ +\ 2\ (32)\ +\ 4\ (8)}{9} = \dfrac{32}{3} = \sigma^2$

Standard Deviation

Although Variance is a measure of variation a more commonly used measure
is standard deviation, which is simply the square root of variance.

Thus, the population standard deviation is

$$\sigma = \sqrt{\frac{\sum\limits^{n}(x_i - \mu)^2}{N}} = \sqrt{\frac{32}{3}}$$

for the population consisting of the
values 1, 9 and 5.

and the sample standard deviation is

$$\hat{\sigma} = \sqrt{\frac{\sum\limits^{n}(x_i - \bar{x})^2}{n - 1}}$$

Again, to further emphasize the importance of subtracting 1 from the
sample size when calculating variance, and consequently, standard deviation,
take the following production line situation. Example: Production of
couplets is considered to be under control if 95% of the diameters of the

couplets are within the range 2 $\pm$ .06 cms. A random sample of 6 couplets is taken from the line and the diameter of each couplet is measured. Suppose the measurements are

   2.04, 1.97, 2.03, 1.96, 2.00 and 2.02

On the basis of this sample is production under control?

Here, we are not concerned with estimating a population mean. Rather, we want to know if the variation exhibited by these sample values indicates the overall variation in diameters is such that 95% of all diameters will fall within the acceptable range.

Assuming normality of measurements 95% of them will fall within 1.96 standard deviations of the mean. Thus, for production to be under control, we must have

$$1.96 \ \sigma \leq \quad .06$$

or

$$\sigma \leq \quad .031$$

Calculate the sample standard deviation and see if it indicates that $\sigma \leq .031$.

$$\hat{\sigma} = \sqrt{\frac{(.04)^2 + (.03)^2 + (.03)^2 + (.04)^2 + (0)^2 + (.02)^2}{5}}$$

$$= \ .033$$

Since $\hat{\sigma}$ is greater than .031, the sample indicates production is out of control. Had we divided by 6 we would have found $\hat{\sigma}$ = .03, which would indicate, improperly, that production is in control.

Relationship between Standard Deviation of the Sample Mean $\sigma_{\bar{x}}$ and Population

Standard Deviation σ

In our illustration dealing with a population of the three values 1, 9, and 5, we saw that

$$\sigma_{\bar{x}} \ = \ \sqrt{\frac{8}{3}}$$

$$\sigma \ = \ \sqrt{\frac{32}{3}}$$

Two things should be noted

1. $\sigma_{\bar{x}} \ < \ \sigma$ That is, there is less variation among the sample means than among the population values

48

themselves. (We could have equality if all the values in a population are the same or if we take a sample of size 1.)

2. And more precisely

$$\sigma_{\bar{x}} = \sqrt{\frac{N-n}{N-1}} \cdot \frac{\sigma}{\sqrt{n}}$$

For instance, in the case of our illustration we have

N = 3

n = 2

$$\sigma = \sqrt{\frac{32}{3}}$$

$$\sigma_{\bar{x}} = \sqrt{\frac{3-2}{2}} \frac{\sqrt{\frac{32}{3}}}{\sqrt{2}} = \sqrt{\frac{1}{2}} \sqrt{\frac{32}{3} \cdot \frac{1}{2}} = \sqrt{\frac{8}{3}}$$

If the population size N is large and the sample size n is small relative to N, say 5% of N or less, then

$$\sqrt{\frac{N-n}{N-1}} = \sqrt{\frac{N-.05N}{N-1}} = \sqrt{\frac{.95N}{N-1}} \approx \sqrt{\frac{.95N}{N}} \approx \sqrt{.95} \approx 1.$$

Thus, in the expression for $\sigma_{\bar{x}}$, we can drop the factor $\sqrt{\frac{N-n}{N-1}}$ called the finite multiplier, and use for the standard error of the sample mean:

$$\sigma_{\bar{x}} = \frac{\sigma}{\sqrt{n}}$$

Hence, for simple random samples the standard error of the sample mean is given by:

$$\sigma_{\bar{x}} = \begin{cases} \frac{\sigma}{\sqrt{n}} \sqrt{\frac{N-n}{N-1}} & \text{if the population is finite of size N} \\ \qquad \text{or} \\ \frac{\sigma}{\sqrt{n}} & \text{if the population is infinite or arbitrarily large and } n \leq .05N \end{cases}$$

Analogous formulas hold for stratified samples, i.e., samples drawn from a subdivided population. These will be taken up later.

The standard error of the sample mean gives us the tool to measure the precision of the sample mean $\bar{x}$ as an estimate of μ. Next, we need some means of measuring the degree of confidence we might have in our estimate. That is, how

49

certain are we that μ is in some specified neighborhood of $\bar{x}$? The standard error of the sample mean $\sigma_{\bar{x}}$ gives us a way to set up the neighborhood. The Central Limit Theorem gives us a way of measuring our certainty.

Central Limit Theorem

If the sample size is large and sampling is repeated the distribution of the sample means $\bar{x}$ approaches a normal curve with mean μ and standard deviation $\sigma_{\bar{x}}$.

The shape of the population distribution from which the sample values x are drawn does not matter. They might appear as shown in Figure 1.

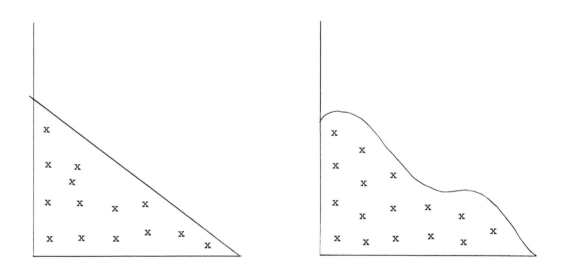

Figure 1

If we repeatedly draw large samples from each of these populations and make frequency distributions of the sample means, in every instance, the distributions of the samples means will follow a normal pattern as shown in Figure 2.

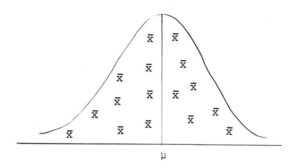

Figure 2

In operational terms, we can say the following: if the sample size is large, say 25 or more, and the sample values x are randomly chosen and if the population standard deviation is known, then the certainty we can have about the precision of $\bar{x}$ as an estimate of μ is shown graphically in Figure 3.

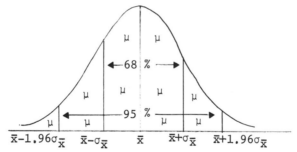

Figure 3

In other words we are 68% certain that the population mean μ differs from the sample mean $\bar{x}$ by no more than 1 standard error, and 95% certain that μ differs from $\bar{x}$ by no more than 1.96 standard errors.

Example: We want to estimate the average diameter of couplets coming off a production line. Assume an infinite population and that the standard deviation of diameters is σ = .03 cms. How large a sample must we take in order to be 95% certain that our estimate of μ is off by no more than .01 cms.

Since 95% certainty corresponds to 1.96 standard errors, we want to choose the sample size n so that

$$1.96 \; \sigma_{\bar{x}} \; = \; .01$$

Henceforth in our illustrations, in order to simplify the arithmetic, we will take 95% certainty to correspond to 2 standard errors, rather than to 1.96 standard errors.

Thus, we choose n so that

$$2 \; \sigma_{\bar{x}} \; = \; .01$$
$$\sigma_{\bar{x}} \; = \; \frac{.01}{2} \; = \; .005$$
$$\frac{\sigma}{\sqrt{n}} \; = \; .005$$

or

$$n = \left(\frac{\sigma}{.005}\right)^2 \; = \; \left(\frac{.03}{.005}\right)^2 \; = \; 6^2 \; = \; 36$$

Here, in choosing our sample of 36 we might use a systematic approach. Randomly choose a sampling time and pick out, say every 5th couplet until we have our sample of 36. Or perhaps, randomly choose 6 sampling times, and pick out 6 couplets at random each time.

Suppose $\bar{x}$ turns out to be 1.98 cms. Then one can be 95% certain that the true average diameter of couplets is somewhere in the interval:

$$\bar{x} \pm 2\sigma_{\bar{x}} = 1.98 \pm .01$$

This means that 95 times in 100 the sample average $\bar{x}$ based on 36 observations will be within .01 of the true average μ.

Inventory Estimation

Suppose we have 100 shelves of books of various kinds and we want to estimate the total dollar value of the books. We take a random sample of 25 shelves, count the books, cost them, and average the cost per shelf. Suppose the sample average value of a shelf $\bar{x}$ is

$$\bar{x} = \frac{\text{total value of books on 25 shelves}}{25} = \$480$$

Estimate the standard deviation of the dollar value of the 100 shelves in the population, using the sample standard deviation:

That is, calculate

$$\hat{\sigma} = \sqrt{\frac{\sum\limits^{25} (x_i - \bar{x})^2}{24}}$$

Here a problem arises. The normal approximation in connection with sample means holds only when the sample size is large and when we know the population standard deviation σ. If we know σ then a sample of size 25 can be considered large and we can apply the normal approximation. But when σ must be estimated using sample results, the theoretical distribution of the sample means follows a Student-t distribution, rather than a normal distribution.

Student-t Distribution

The Student-t distribution is a family of curves that depends upon the number of degrees of freedom (d.f.) in the sample. The number of degrees of freedom in a sample is the number of variables in that sample that are free to wander.

In our case, given a sample of size 25 and a sample mean of 480, any 24 of the 25 values could be of any magnitude, whatsoever. Once these 24 values have been fixed, however, the 25th value is automatically determined.

For

$$\bar{x} = \frac{\sum\limits^{25} x_i}{25}$$

53

or

$$\overset{25}{\underset{}{\Sigma}} \; x_i = 25\bar{x} \; = \; 25 \; (480) = 12,000$$

Thus if 24 of the values are known, say the first 24, the 25th

value is automatically determined, since we have

$$x_1 + x_2 + \, . \, . \, . \; x_{24} + x_{25} = 12,000$$

or

$$x_{25} \; = \; 12,000 \; - \; \overset{24}{\underset{}{\Sigma}} \; x_i$$

Hence the degrees of freedom are 24, i.e., 25-1. And in general,

for estimations of this kind, the number of degrees of freedom is n-1,

that is, one less than the sample size.

Like the normal curve, the family of Student-t-curves is symmetrical about

the mean and bell-shaped. The difference is that the peaks tend to be flatter

than the normal and the tails, wider, though as the sample size increases

and with it the degrees of freedom, the Student-t curves approach the

normal curve.

For example, for 24 degrees of freedom the Student-t curve for the

distribution of sample means would be as depicted in Figure 4.

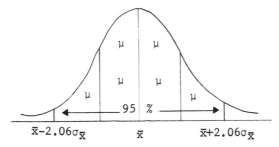

Figure 4

For 120 degrees of freedom the Student-t is practically the normal.

Returning now to our problem of estimating the dollar volume of

the books on the 100 shelves.

$$\bar{x} \; = \; 480$$

and suppose $\hat{\sigma} \; = \; 20$

When $\hat{\sigma}$ is used to estimate σ 95% certainty corresponds to 2.06

standard errors of the sample mean. Thus, using the finite form for

$\sigma_{\bar{x}}$, we have

54

$$2.06 \ \sigma_{\bar{x}} = 2.06 \ \sqrt{\frac{N-n}{N-1}} \ \frac{\hat{\sigma}}{\sqrt{n}}$$

$$= 2.06 \ \sqrt{\frac{100-25}{99}} \ \frac{20}{\sqrt{25}}$$

$$= 2.06 \quad (.87) \ (4) \ = 7.17$$

Hence, we are 95% certain that the true average value of a shelf is in the range

$$\bar{x} \ \pm \ 2.06 \ \sigma_{\bar{x}}$$

$$= \ \$480 \ \pm \ \$7.17$$

And therefore we are 95% certain that the total dollar value of the 100 shelves of books is within 100 (480 $\pm$ 7.17); that is, between $47,296 and $48,717.

In selecting our sample here we might use random numbers. Assign the number 01 to the first shelf, 02 to the second, and so on. Read two-digit random numbers until 25 shelves have been selected. If a random number is encountered that has been read already, or if an unassigned number is encountered, skip it and go on reading.

Validating Accounts Receivable (Simple Random Sampling)

The book figure of a firm's accounts receivable is $150,000, and there are 2,500 accounts. We are to validate this figure by sampling, accepting it only if we can be 95% certain that the figure is in error by no more than 2%.

Put the stipulated total dollar value into terms of an equivalent average dollar value of an account μ.

Thus,

$$\text{Stipulated } \mu = \frac{\text{Total dollar value}}{\text{Number of accounts}} = \frac{\$150,000}{2,500} = \$60.$$

We will accept the firm's claims if the sample results indicate that we can say with 95% certainty that the firm's figure is off by no more than 2% total.

Now a 2% total error corresponds to an average error per account of .02μ or $1.20.

Hence, we will accept the firm's claim if the stipulated average value 60 is within ± 1.20 of our sample average value $\bar{x}$.

The question is: How large a sample should we take? In order to be 95% certain that our error in estimating the true μ is no more than 1.20, we must choose the sample size n so that

$$2 \; \sigma_{\bar{x}} \; = \; 1.20$$

or

$$\sigma_{\bar{x}} \; = \; 60$$

Using the finite form for $\sigma_{\bar{x}}$ we have

$$\sqrt{\frac{N-n}{N-1}} \; \frac{\sigma}{\sqrt{n}} \; = \; .6$$

Since we don't know σ, take a preliminary sample of, say, 25 accounts, calculate the sample standard deviation $\hat{\sigma}$, and use it as an estimate of σ. Suppose it turns out to be 10. Then, substituting into the above expression, we get

$$\sqrt{\frac{2500 - n}{2499}} \; . \; \frac{10}{\sqrt{n}} \; = \; .6$$

$$\sqrt{\frac{2500-n}{2499n}} \; = \; .06$$

$$n \; = \; \frac{2500}{9.996} \; = \; 250$$

Suppose the sample mean $\bar{x}$ turns out to be 62. Reject the receivables since the stipulated mean μ is not within the interval

$$\bar{x} \pm 1.20, \; \text{i.e., within the interval } \$62 \pm \$1.20$$

Note: Technically, we should have used the Student-t distribution instead of the normal, since we had to use the sample standard deviation to estimate σ. However, for a sample size of 250 the Student-t distribution and the normal are practically the same.

In practice before actually taking a simple random sample of 250 accounts, one would see if stratification would reduce the sample size.

Stratified Sampling

If a population of values can be partitioned into parts, called strata, so that the variation among the values in some or all of the strata is less than the variation among the values in the population as a whole, then stratification will reduce the sample size needed for estimating μ with no loss in precision.

Sampling in each of the stratum will be random. The amount of sampling to be done in each of the stratum can be allocated in several ways. The most commonly used allocations are proportional allocation and optimum allocation. In proportional allocation the amount of sampling in a stratum is proportional to the relative size of the stratum; if optimum allocation is used, sampling is proportional to the relative variation of the stratum.

Proportional Allocation

When proportional allocation is used in estimating the population mean μ, the sample estimate of μ is

$$\bar{x} = w_1\bar{x}_1 + w_2\bar{x}_2 + \ldots + w_s\bar{x}_s$$

where S = number of Strata

w_h = relative size of the hth stratum, for h = 1, 2 ..., S

$\bar{x}_h$ = a sample mean taken from the hth stratum

and the standard error of the sample mean $\sigma_{\bar{x}}$, omitting the finite multiplier, is

$$\sigma_{\bar{x}} = \sqrt{\frac{\displaystyle\sum_{h=1}^{S} w_h \, \sigma_h^2}{n}}$$

where σ_h^2 is the variance of the hth stratum

and n is the overall sample size.

If the population is finite the finite multiplier must be inserted as a factor on the righthand side.

The sampling in the strata is allocated on a proportional basis, i.e.,

57

$n_h = w_h n$, where n_h = number of units to be sampled in the hth stratum.

Optimum Allocation

When optimum allocation is used in estimating the population mean

again the sample estimate of μ is

$$\bar{x} = \sum_{h=1}^{S} w_h \bar{x}_h$$

and the standard error of the sample mean is

$$\sigma_{\bar{x}} = \sqrt{\frac{(\sum^S w_h \sigma_h)^2}{n} - \frac{\sum^S w_h \sigma_h^2}{N}} \quad \text{if the population is finite}$$

or

$$\sqrt{\frac{(\sum^S w_h \sigma_h)^2}{n}} \quad \text{if the population is arbitrarily large}$$

The sample is allocated according to the relation:

$$n_h = n \frac{w_h \sigma_h}{\sum^S w_h \sigma_h} \quad \text{, where } n_h = \text{the number}$$

of units to be sampled in the hth stratum

Validating Accounts Receivables (Stratified Sampling)

Return to the previous illustration dealing with the validation of

accounts receivables:

Summary of the pertinent facts:

Number of accounts = 2,500

Stipulated dollar value = $150,000

Stipulated average value = $60.00

Error allowance = 2% total or $1.20 per account, on the average.

To validate the firm's claim at a 95% confidence level the sample

58

size was chosen so that

$$\sigma_{\bar{x}} = .60 \quad \text{which yielded}$$

$$n = 250$$

Suppose 500 accounts are for amounts over $100 and the rest are $100 or less. The question is: For the same precision and certainty as before, what reduction in sample size would stratified sampling bring about; using over $100 as one strata and $100 or less as the other? Whether proportional or optional allocation is used the estimate of the population average value is:

$$\bar{x} = \sum_{h=1}^{2} w_h \bar{x}_h = w_1 \bar{x}_1 \times w_2 \bar{x}_2$$

where $\bar{x}_1$ = sample mean of the over $100 accounts

$\quad w_1$ = proportion of accounts that are over $100

$\quad \bar{x}_2$ = sample mean of the $100 or under Accounts

$\quad w_2$ = proportion of accounts that are $100 or less

Now for sample size. In order to have the same certainty and precision as we had in the simple random sampling case, we must choose n so that

$$\sigma_{\bar{x}} = .60$$

If proportional allocation is used, then this implies that n must be chosen so that

$$\sqrt{\frac{\frac{1}{5}\sigma_1^2 + \frac{4}{5}\sigma_2^2}{n}} \sqrt{\frac{2500 - n}{2499}} = .60$$

Suppose σ_1, the standard deviation of the over $100 accounts is 7 and σ_2, the standard deviation of the $100 or less accounts is 5, then we get

$$\sqrt{\frac{\frac{1}{5}(49) + \frac{4}{5}(25)}{n}} \sqrt{\frac{2500-n}{2499}} = .60$$

Solving for n, we get n = 81, a substantial reduction in sample size. The sample is allocated as follows: 1/5 of the sampling, or 16 accounts, will be drawn in the over $100 stratum; 4/5, or 65 accounts, in the $100 or less stratum.

59

Optimum allocation will reduce the required sample size **slightly more:**

Substituting the standard error formula for optional allocation into the expression

$$\sigma_{\bar{x}} = .60, \text{ and solving for n we get}$$

$$\sqrt{\frac{(\Sigma \, w_h \sigma_h)^2}{n} - \frac{\Sigma \, w_h \sigma_h^2}{N}} = .60$$

$$\sqrt{\frac{\left(\frac{1}{5}(7) + \frac{4}{5}(5)\right)^2}{n} - \frac{\frac{1}{5}(49) + \frac{4}{5}(25)}{2500}} = .60$$

which gives n = 79

The sample is allocated as follows:

The number of over $100 accounts to be sampled:

$$n_1 = \frac{n \, w_1 \sigma_1}{\Sigma \, w_h \sigma_h} \qquad = \frac{79 \, \frac{1}{5} \, (7)}{\frac{27}{5}} = 20$$

The number of $100 or less accounts to be sampled:

$$n_2 = \frac{n \, w_2 \sigma_2}{\Sigma \, w_h \sigma_h} \qquad = \frac{79 \, \frac{4}{5} \, (5)}{\frac{27}{5}} = 59$$

Stratification results in an enormous savings in sample size over simple random sampling. However, care must be taken in using it. For we must know two things: first, the relative sizes of the strata, and, secondly, the standard deviations of the values within the strata. Misjudgment of either of these two factors will introduce bias into our estimates. Minor misjudgment will have little effect but substantial misjudgment can severely affect the estimates. For the bias remains no matter how large a sample we take from each of the stratum.

Chapter 2

Sampling Theory for Proportions

Proportions

Often, it is not an average value that interests us, but rather, a proportion.
We want to know the proportion of units in a population that possess a certain
characteristic. The characteristic of interest might be defective items in a
manufacturing process, incorrect entries in a set of books, voter preference,
and so forth.

A unit that possesses the characteristic of interest is called a target unit.
The proportion of target units is the ratio of the number of targets to the number
of units of all kinds, both targets and otherwise.

Thus, the proportion of target units in the population P, is

P = number of targets in the population
     number of units altogether in the population

The sample proportion of target units p', is

p' = number of targets in the sample
      number of units altogether in the sample

The discussion of proportions is parallel to the discussion of means.
Just as the sample mean $\bar{x}$ is used as an estimator of the population mean μ, the
sample proportion p' is used as an estimator of the population proportion P.
The precision and the degree of certainty of the estimator p', follows the same
line as that for the sample mean.

Just as the standard error of the sample mean $\sigma_{\bar{x}}$ measures the expected
variation in sample means, the standard error of the sample proportion measures
the expected variation in sample proportions. The standard error formula
for proportions is exactly analagous to that for means, and indeed, one follows from
the other. All it takes to derive the formula for $\sigma_{p'}$ from the formula for $\sigma_{\bar{x}}$
is an elementary transformation.

To each x value in the population assign the value 1 if it is a target value,
0 if not. In effect, we map every x value onto a value, say, y such that y = 1
if x is a target value and y = 0, if not.

61

Thus $P = \dfrac{\overset{N}{\underset{}{\Sigma}}\, y_i}{N}$ $= \mu_y$, where μ_y denotes the population

and $p' = \dfrac{\overset{n}{\underset{}{\Sigma}} y_i}{n}$ $= \bar{y}$ means of y values

We now need an expression for the population variance of the y values, i.e., σ^2_y

By definition of variance

$$\sigma^2_y = \frac{\overset{N}{\underset{}{\Sigma}} (y_i - \mu_y)^2}{N} = \frac{\overset{N}{\underset{}{\Sigma}} (y_i - P)^2}{N}$$

In the population of y values only 1 and 0 can occur. The proportion of 1's in the population, i.e., the proportion of target units is P. Hence, the number of times that y assumes the value 1 is NP. By subtraction, the number of times that y assumes the value 0 is N-NP or N $(1-P)$ = NQ where Q = 1-P.

Thus,

$$\sigma_y^2 = \frac{(0-P)^2 + (0-P)^2 + (1-P)^2 + \ldots (1-P)^2}{N}$$

$$= \frac{+\, NQ\,(0-P)^2 + NP\,(1-P)^2}{N}$$

$$= \frac{NQP^2 + NPQ^2}{N}$$

$$= \frac{NQP\,(P + Q)}{N}$$

But P + Q = 1, hence

$$\sigma_y^2 = PQ$$

Standard Error of Sample Proportions

Earlier we saw that for simple random samples the variance of the sample mean, omitting the finite multiplier, is

$$\sigma_{\bar{x}}^2 = \frac{\sigma^2}{n} \qquad \text{where } \sigma^2 \text{ is the population variance}$$

But, the variance of the sample proportions can be written

$$\sigma_{p'}^2 = \sigma_{\bar{y}}^2 \quad \text{since } p' = \bar{y}.$$

But $\sigma_{\bar{y}}^2 = \dfrac{\sigma_y^2}{n} = \dfrac{PQ}{n}$ 62

Taking roots, we get

$$\sigma_{p'} = \sqrt{\frac{PQ}{n}}$$

When the population has a fixed size the finite multiplier must be inserted as a factor.

Thus, for simple random samples the standard error of the sample proportion is given by

$$\sigma_{p'} = \begin{cases} \sqrt{\dfrac{PQ}{n}} & \text{when the population is infinite} \\ \sqrt{\dfrac{PQ}{n}} \ \sqrt{\dfrac{N-n}{N-1}} & \text{when the population is finite} \end{cases}$$

In order to compute $\sigma_{p'}$ we need to know the population proportion P. Rarely would this be known. Except for hypotheses testing or in situations dealing with "after the fact" analysis, it is the population proportion P that we are trying to estimate. Still we need a value for it to insert in the standard error formula. Therefore, we assume one, purely for the purpose of calculating $\sigma_{p'}$; any one of the following values will do.

1. A value of P obtained in a similar study made previously.

2. An estimate of P based on a preliminary sample.

3. In the absence of an estimate of P from a previous study or from a preliminary sample, assume P = .5. An assumed P of .5 gives the widest possible confidence interval for any sample size.

To get confidence limits for our estimate of P we appeal to the Central Limit Theorem when the sample size is large. The Central Limit Theorem applies to proportions since proportions are simply another form of means. Thus, we can construct confidence intervals for proportions just as we did for means.

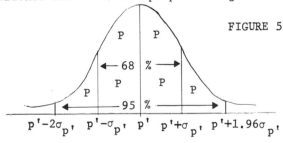

FIGURE 5

When the sample size is small use the Student-t distribution.

<u>Auditing</u>

<u>Example</u>: A set of books contains 100,000 entries. We want to estimate the percentage of incorrect entries by taking a sample and using the sample proportion of errors as an estimate of the overall proportion of errors. How large a random sample should we take in order to be 95% certain that our estimate is in error by no more than 2%.

Assuming normality a 95% confidence interval for the sample proportion corresponds to 1.96 standard errors of the sample proportion. Again for illustrative purposes and to simplify the arithmetic, we use 2 standard errors.

Thus, the sample size n must be such that

$$2\sigma_{p'} = .02$$

or

$$\sigma_{p'} = .01$$

Using the finite form of the standard error formula, we have

$$\sqrt{\frac{N-n}{N-1}} \ \sqrt{\frac{PQ}{n}} = .01$$

In order to find n we must have some value to use for P. Suppose from past audits it has been found that errors run from 1% up to 10%. Assume P to be the maximum of these values since this will call for the largest possible sample size, and will protect us against errors of underestimation.

If P = .1 then Q = 1-P = .9 and N = 100,000. Substituting accordingly we get

$$\sqrt{\frac{100,000 - n}{99,999}} \ \sqrt{\frac{(.1)\ (.9)}{n}} = .01$$

$$\frac{(100,000 - n)\ (.09)}{99,999n} = .0001$$

which gives

$$n = 892$$

<u>Example</u>: Rather than taking a sample of 892 entries, we take instead, a

sample of 400 entries and find 8 errors. What is a 95% confidence interval

for our estimate of the overall proportion of errors?

$$p' = \frac{8}{400} = .02$$

$$\sigma_{p'} = \sqrt{\frac{N-n}{N-1}} \sqrt{\frac{PQ}{n}}$$

For P use the sample proportion .02. Thus

$$\sigma_{p'} = \sqrt{\frac{100,000 - 400}{99,999}} \sqrt{\frac{(.02)(.98)}{400}} = .007$$

Therefore, we are 95% certain that the overall proportions of errors

is within the interval

$$p' \pm 2\sigma_{p'} = .02 \pm 2(.007) = .02 \pm .014$$

Note that this error margin is smaller than the one we had assumed for

a sample of 892. The reason for the narrower bands is the estimate of P

that was used in the calculation of $\sigma_{p'}$. Initially, we had assumed P = .10.

On the basis of the results of 400 sample accounts we see that this initial

estimate was much too high. Hence, a sample of 400 is more than sufficient

to achieve the desired confidence and precision.

Example: Referring to the previous illustration, what can we say with

95% certainty about the maximum proportions of errors in books? Here, we are

concerned only with the high boundary of our estimate. Therefore, a 95% confi-

dence band will not involve the middle 95% of the area under a normal curve, but

a cumulative area of 95%. The shaded area of the following illustration repre-

sents the desired confidence level.

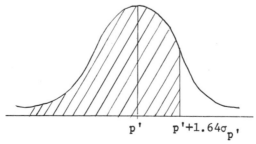

$$p' \qquad p'+1.64\sigma_{p'}$$

FIGURE 6

Hence, we are 95% certain that the proportion of errors overall is at most

$$p' + 1.64 \ \sigma_{p'}$$

or

$$.02 + 1.64 \ (.007) = .03169 \approx 3.17\%$$

"After the Fact" Analysis

Refer to the book audit illustration. Suppose a complete check is made and it is found that 4% of the entries are incorrect. How likely is it that the sampling was random?

Our sample proportion was $p' = .02$ based on a sample of 400 entries. The correct P is .04.

Let z = the number of standard errors that p' is from P

$$z = \frac{p' - P}{\sigma_{p'}}$$

$$\text{where } \sigma_{p'} = \sqrt{\frac{N-n}{N-1}} \ \sqrt{\frac{PQ}{n}}$$

In this situation we know the actual value of P. Thus

$$\sigma_{p'} = \sqrt{\frac{100,000 - 400}{99,999}} \ \sqrt{\frac{(.04) \ (.96)}{400}} = .0098$$

$$\text{and } z = \frac{.02 - .04}{.0098} = \frac{-.02}{.0098} = -2.04$$

The probability that a random sample of 400 accounts would turn up a $p' = .02$ or less when in fact P = .04

$$= \text{prob} \ [\ z \leq -2.04 \ ] = .0207$$

In other words, about two times in 100 would a random sample of 400 entries turn up such a serious underestimation as happened here.

Election Forecasting

Example: We want to estimate the percentage of the vote that the Republican Candidate for governor will get in the next gubernatorial election. Assume two candidates are running for office. How many registered voters should we randomly sample in order to be 95% certain that our estimate of that percentage will be in error by no more than 1%?

66

Choose n so that

$$2\sigma_{p'} = .01$$

or

$$\sigma_{p'} = .005$$

Since the number of registered voters is in the millions, assume an infinite population. Using the infinite form for $\sigma_{p'}$, we get

$$\sqrt{\frac{PQ}{N}} = .005$$

When we have no idea of what P might be, assume it to be .5. This assumed value for P yields the largest of all possible sample sizes and will guarantee the desired level of accuracy regardless of what P might be.

$$\sqrt{\frac{(.5)\ (.5)}{n}} = .005$$

or

$$\frac{.25}{n} = .000025$$

which gives n = 10,000.

Suppose 5142 of the sample registered voters indicate they will vote for the Republican candidate. Assuming that the sampling took place on the last day of the campaign and that the voters do not change their minds, then we are 95% certain that the Republican candidate will win the election. For a 95% confidence interval for our estimate is

$$p' \pm 2\ \sigma_{p'} = .5142 \pm .01$$
$$= .5042 \text{ to } .5242, \text{ inclusive.}$$

But anything better than 50% of the votes will give the candidate the election.

Stratified Sampling

In stratified random sampling, whether proportional or optimum allocation is used, the estimate of the population proportion is

$$p' = \sum_{h}^{S} W_h\ P_h$$

67

where s is the number of strata, W_h the relative size of the hth stratum and P_h the population proportion of the hth stratum.

Proportional Allocation

In proportional allocation the sample is allocated by the formula

$$n_h = W_h\, n, \text{ where } n = \text{overall sample size}$$

The standard error of the sample proportion is given by

$$\sigma_{p'} = \begin{cases} \sqrt{\dfrac{\Sigma\; W_h P_h Q_h}{n}} & \text{for infinite populations} \\[2em] \text{or} \\[1em] \sqrt{\dfrac{\Sigma\; W_h P_h Q_h}{n}} \; \sqrt{\dfrac{N-n}{N-1}} & \text{for finite populations} \end{cases}$$

Optimum Allocation

In optimum allocation the sample is allocated by the formula

$$n_h = \frac{nW_h\; P_h Q_h}{\Sigma\; W_h \sqrt{P_h Q_h}}$$

The standard error of the sample proportions is given by

$$\sigma_{p'} = \begin{cases} \sqrt{\dfrac{(\Sigma W_h \sqrt{P_h Q_h})^2}{n} - \Sigma\; \dfrac{W_h P_h Q_h}{N}} & \text{for finite populations} \\[2em] \text{or} \\[1em] \sqrt{\dfrac{(\Sigma\; W_h \sqrt{P_h Q_h})^2}{n}} & \text{for infinite populations} \end{cases}$$

Example: Refer to the election forecast illustration. It was seen that using simple random sampling a sample of 10,000 registered voters would be sufficient to forecast, with 95% certainty, the percentage of the vote that the Republican Candidate will get with an error margin of 1%. Suppose we stratify the population of registered voters by sex, and that 60% of the registered voters are male and 40% are female. Does stratification offer an appreciable reduction in sample size over simple random sampling?

If proportional allocation is used we choose n so that

68

$$\sigma_{p'} \quad = \quad .005$$

$$\sqrt{\frac{\overset{2}{\Sigma}\ W_h P_h Q_h}{n}} \quad = \quad .005$$

where w_1 = proportion of male voters and w_2 = proportion of female voters.

In order to solve for n we must have some estimate of voter preference by sex. Suppose we take a preliminary sample of 200 registered male voters and 200 registered female voters and find 120 males and 60 females intend to vote for the Republican candidate.

Thus, preliminary estimates for P_1 and P_2 are

P_1 = .60 = Estimate of the proportion of registered male voters who will vote for the Republican candidate

P_2 = .30 = Estimate of the proportion of registered female voters who will vote for the Republican candidate

Thus, we choose n so that

$$\sqrt{\frac{.6\ (.6)\ (.4)\ +\ .4\ (.3)\ (.7)}{n}} \quad = \quad .005$$

$$\frac{.228}{n} \quad = \quad .000025$$

$$n \quad = \quad 9120$$

or a reduction of 880 over simple random sampling.

Sixty percent of the sample size of 9,120 voters to be interviewed, or 5,472, will be male registered voters. Forty percent, or 3,648, will be registered female voters.

If optimum allocation is used we choose n so that

$$\sqrt{\frac{(\Sigma W_h \quad \overline{P_h Q_h})^2}{n}} \quad = \quad .005$$

$$\sqrt{\frac{(.6\ \ \sqrt{(.6)\ (.4)}\ +\ .4\ \sqrt{(.3)\ (.7)}\ )^2}{n}} \quad = \quad .005$$

$$\frac{(.4772)^2}{n} = .000025$$

or

$$n = 9108$$

A reduction of 892 over simple random sampling. The allocation of the sample by sex of the registered voter is:

Male registered voters:

$$n_1 = \frac{n \; W_1 \sqrt{P_1 Q_1}}{\Sigma \; W_h \sqrt{P_h Q_h}}$$

$$= \frac{9108 \; (.6) \; (.4899)}{.4772}$$

$$= 5610$$

female registered voters:

$$M_2 = M - n_1, = 9108 - 5610 = 3498$$

Cluster Sampling

In cluster sampling the population is partitioned according to some characteristic. The subdivisions are called clusters. The units within the clusters are then sampled in order to estimate the parameter of interest: a mean, perhaps, or a proportion, or even a total. With respect to the partitioning of the population, cluster sampling is similar to stratified sampling. The only difference is that in stratified sampling, sampling takes place in all stratas; whereas in cluster sampling, sampling is done only in a randomly selected number of clusters. The remaining clusters are ignored.

Cluster sampling is often more convenient and less costly than stratified sampling, though it generally involves a greater error in estimation. For there is the variance "within" the units of the clusters to be considered, as well as the variance "between" the clusters.

Formulas are available to measure these two sources of variation. However, the calculations depend upon the sample results. What is needed, especially in activity analysis, is a general formula for the maximum magnitude of these two variances in advance of the sampling itself.

70

For this reason it is worthwhile to develop an expression for the maximal magnitude of these two variances: the variance "within" the cluster units and the variance "between" the clusters themselves. Then put the two together to estimate the maximum variance of the sample estimate in cluster sampling. In activity analysis the statistics of interest are proportions and often the number of clusters are infinite. It is this kind of situation that is treated here.

Maximum Magnitude of Sampling Error
In Cluster Sampling Where the Clusters Are Infinite

Take a hypothetical population, partition it into an infinite number of clusters, such that all clusters contain an arbitrarily large number of units. Choose M number of clusters at random. In each of the M clusters randomly select k number of units and calculate the proportion of target units among those k units, and at the same time, compute the variances of these sample proportions.

We get the following:

Sample Cluster	Sample Proportion	Variance of Sample Proportion
1	P_1	$\sigma^2_{p'_1} = \dfrac{P_1 Q_1}{k}$
2	P_2	$\sigma^2_{p'_2} = \dfrac{P_2 Q_2}{k}$
.	.	.
.	.	.
.	.	.
M	P_m	

Note: P_i is the population proportion of target units in the ith cluster, for $i = 1, 2, \ldots, M$, and $Q_i = 1-P_i$.

The estimate of the population proportion is the sample average proportion

$$\bar{p} = \frac{\sum\limits^{M} P'_i}{M}$$

The variance of the sample average proportion

71

$$\sigma_{\bar{p}}^2 = \text{Var } (\bar{p}) = \text{Var} \left(\frac{\sum\limits^{M} P_i'}{M} \right)$$

The symbol Var $(\bar{p})$ is synonymous with the symbol $\sigma_{\bar{p}}^2$. The notation is introduced here because it simplifies the algebra.

From the theory of variance, the variance of a constant times a variable is the constant squared times the variance of the variable. Thus

$$\sigma_{\bar{p}}^2 = \frac{1}{M^2} \text{Var} \left(\frac{\sum\limits^{M} P_i'}{M} \right)$$

If we now assume that the sample proportions are independent variables, then the variance of the sum is equal to the sum of the variances, i.e.,

$$\text{Var} \left(\sum\limits^{M} P_i' \right) = \sum\limits^{M} \text{Var } (P_i')$$

Hence,

$$\sigma_{\bar{p}}^2 = \frac{1}{M^2} \sum\limits^{M} \text{Var } (P_i') = \frac{1}{M^2} \sum\limits^{M} \sigma_{P_i'}^2$$

$$= \frac{1}{M^2} \frac{\sum\limits^{M} P_i Q_i}{k} = \frac{1}{M^2 k} \sum\limits^{M} P_i Q_i$$

The expression $\sigma_{\bar{p}}^2$ treats only the variance "within" the units of the clusters. To get an expression for the variance "between" the clusters, compute the sample variance of the M sample proportions; that is,

$$\delta_{p'}^2 = \frac{\sum\limits^{M} (p_i' - \bar{p})^2}{M - 1}$$

Take the expected value of $\delta_{p'}^2$; i.e., the long run average value of $\delta_{p'}^2$. This expected value is

$$\sigma_{p'}^2 = \frac{PQ}{M} \text{ , where P is the population proportion of target}$$
$$\text{units and } Q = 1 - P$$

Use this expectancy as an estimate for the variance between clusters.

Now certainly, the total variance of the sample proportion in cluster sampling V is no more than the sum of the Variances "within" clusters and "between" clusters.

That is,

$$V \leq \sigma_{\bar{p}}^2 + \text{Expected value of } \sigma_{p'}^2$$

$$= \frac{\overset{M}{\Sigma} P_i Q_i}{M^2 k} + \frac{PQ}{M}$$

The values of the expressions on the righthand side of the above equations are maximized when all P's equal .5. Hence the maximum variance of the sample proportion in cluster sampling is given by

$$\text{Max } V = \overset{M}{\Sigma} \frac{(.5)\,(.5)}{M^2 k} + \frac{(.5)\,(.5)}{M}$$

$$= \frac{M\,(.25)}{M^2 k} + \frac{.25}{M}$$

or

$$\text{Max } V = \frac{.25}{M} \left(\frac{1}{k} + 1 \right)$$

where M = number of clusters selected at random.

k = number of units in each cluster that are to be sampled.

Note: In stratified sampling where M = the number of strata and k = number of units sampled in each stratum, the maximum variance of P would be simply $\frac{.25}{Mk}$.

Sampling Activity of Librarians

A college librarian wants to determine the proportion of the time he devotes to face-to-face conversations. In order to estimate this proportion he instructs his secretary to check his activity at 100 randomly selected times over a four-month period. If at 30 of those times he is engaged in face-to-face conversations, then an estimate of the proportion of the time he devotes to face-to-face conversations is

$$p' = .30$$

with variance $\sigma_{p'}^2 = \frac{P\,(1-P)}{n} = \frac{(.3)\,(.7)}{100} = .0021$

and standard error $\sigma_{p'} = \sqrt{.0021} = .046$

73

Now suppose we want to estimate the proportion of the time that all college librarians in the country devote to face-to-face conversations. If we choose 150 librarians at random and sample each one 4 times, the estimate of that proportion would have at least the same precision as the estimate for one librarian.

For each librarian is a cluster, and the number of clusters is arbitrarily large. Further, the number of instants of time in a 4-month period can be considered arbitrarily large. Thus, if we randomly choose 150 librarians, and sample each one k times, the maximum variance of our estimate of P is

$$\text{Max V} = \frac{.25}{150}\left(\frac{1}{k} + 1\right)$$

If we want the same precision for our estimate as we had for one librarian, we must choose k so that

$$\text{Max V} = .0021$$

or

$$\frac{.25}{150}\left(\frac{1}{k} + 1\right) = .0021$$

Solving for k we get

$$k = 4.$$

Conclusions

In our discussion of stratified sampling the cost of sampling has not been considered explicitly, though optimum allocation assumes implicitly that the cost of sampling is a linear function of the sample size. For any other kind of cost function the stratified formulas can be modified, appropriately.

Also, we have limited our discussion of sampling to sampling for means and sampling for proportions. Other forms of sampling such as sampling for hypothesis testing, sampling for testing paired characteristics for independence, sampling for differences, and sampling for regression will be discussed as they arise in the course of the analysis.

74

PART II

RESEARCH PROJECT ON
IN-LIBRARY BOOK USE

Introduction to Part II

Part II consists of three chapters which describe the research
project on the sampling of in-library readership of books at a college
library. Chapter 3 outlines the initial plan for the statistical
sampling and analysis. Chapter 4 explains how the data collection was
organized and what procedures were followed by the interviewers. Chapter
5 arrays the results of the research.

The significance of this research project is that it demonstrates
conclusively the feasibility of determining by empirical and precise
means just who is reading what books inside of a library. For the first
time, the field of library administration has such an instrument as this.
It is now possible to fill in a major gap in information about library use.

Chapter 3

Origin and Plan of the Study

Origin of Study[1]

The origin of the study of in-library book use, by sampling, lies in an effort
to measure and evaluate student use of library books at a school of Business
Administration. Statistical sampling techniques were developed for that purpose.

Some features of the organizational setting are described in order to show the
context for the recognition of the need for statistical methods, and their application. The Library Committee, a faculty committee, of the School of Business Administration at Rider College had been given the responsibility for evaluating the
library collection in the fields of Accounting, Business Law, Economics, Finance,
Insurance, Management, Marketing, Real Estate, and Secretarial Science. The
Library Committee had to proceed with caution. It had to avoid infringing on the
prerogatives of individual professors and academic departments, not to mention
those of the Librarian.

The Library Committee found that it could play a role in giving orientation
and offering recommendations to the academic departments on how each department
could conduct an audit of academic uses of the library. Each academic department
of the School had a representative on the Library Committee. It was legitimate
for professors to be interested in academic uses.

---

1. Much of the discussion in Chapter 3 is derived from two
   published articles. See Robert J. Daiute and Kenneth A.
   Gorman, "Sampling and Analyzing Library Book Readership,"
   New Jersey Libraries, Fall 1969, pp. 38-41. Also see
   Robert J. Daiute and Kenneth A. Gorman, "Library Use by
   Business Students," Improving College and University
   Teaching, Spring 1970, pp. 135 and 136.

Comprehensiveness Desired

Striving for comprehensiveness, the Committee identified seven sources of information for such an audit. It was hoped that appropriate statistical methods would be applied to data from the following seven sources:

>Faculty opinion on library uses and needs
>
>Student opinion on library uses and needs
>
>Student activity and faculty activity in the use of library resources
>
>Library uses and needs of major academic programs of study, as well as individual courses
>
>Authoritative library use standards that relate the library resources to academic uses
>
>Authoritative bibliographies
>
>Services of a consultant on audit design and use

The academic and library administration encouraged the Committee to give attention to identifying and using bibliographies to evaluate the library collection of business books. A list of such bibliographies would be included in the following: Theodore Besterman, _A World Bibliography of Bibliographies_ (4th ed,; Lausanne: Societas Bibliographica, 1965); Marga Franck, ed., _Bibliographic Index_, 1967 (New York: H. W. Wilson, 1968); _Subject Guide to Books in Print_, 1967 (New York: R. R. Bowker, 1967); _Paperbound Books in Print_ (New York: R. R. Bowker, Feb. 1968); footnote references in textbooks and other books; reading lists of courses, and so forth.

It was concluded that once the useful bibliography had been identified, appropriate statistical techniques could be adopted to check on the extent that a library has the items listed in the bibliography. It is wasteful of professional and clerical time to check each and every item. In a pilot study, selected Subject Guide to Books in Print categories were used. They were: "Management," "Factory Management," "Industrial Management," and "Personnel Management." There were 696 books found in these categories in Subject Guide to Books in Print.

Team Formed

The Chairman of the Library Committee next formed a team consisting of the Chairman, a professional statistician, and a student assistant.[2] This team formulated the questions to be answered by the statistical methods, and applied the statistical methods in practice. The techniques used by the team are described below.

After the useful bibliography had been selected, a random numbers table was used to assure the randomness of the sample of 100 items out of the bibliography of 696 items.[3] The purpose of the sample, of course, is to save time and money in using the bibliography and evaluating the book collection, and at the same time getting an accurate picture within measurable degrees of error. A number was assigned to each item from number 001 to 696. The first 100 numbers in the random numbers table between 001 and 696 identified the items to be included in the sample of 100 books.

---

2. The team members are Messrs. Daiute and Gorman and Miss Virginia Moody.
3. See William H. Beyer, ed., Handbook of Tables for Probability and Statistics (Cleveland, Ohio: Chemical Rubber Co., 1966).

Next, the library card catalog was used to see how many of these 100 books were actually in the library collection available for academic use. Forty-two out of the 100 were found in the catalog. Thus we could say that the library had 42% of the books in print in the management field, with 95% certainty that our error was no more than $\pm$ 9%. If one wishes to reduce the error, one can simply increase the sample size. If the 42% is regarded as too low a percentage for the library collection, the bibliography can be used as a library acquisition list.

Circulation Record Analyzed

Moving beyond the use of the results as indicated in the above paragraphs, the sample was found to have other important uses. A random sample of 10 books was selected from the 42 books found to be in the library collection. Again, a random numbers table was used to identify the 10 in the random sample. The borrowing record was copied for each book of the 10. It is standard library practice to maintain a running record of the name of borrower and the date of borrowing which is printed on a slip of paper or card at the back of the book. The names of 85 borrowers were obtained, along with the dates of borrowing, for all 10 books combined.

On the average, each of the 10 books had been borrowed 8 times, that is, the arithmetic mean is 8 for the number of times each book had been borrowed. Furthermore, the standard deviation of such borrowing was 10. This indicates wide differences in demand for borrowing different books. A preliminary survey showed that the books that have been borrowed 20 to 30 times are books that contain required reading assignments. The median, a measure of central tendency that eliminates the influence of extreme values, was 3 for the 10 books. It should be noted that there tends to be an understatement of the number of times a book has been borrowed, when that book has been borrowed a large number of times. It is standard practice for the library to discard the form for recording names and dates when the form is filled up. A new form is inserted in the place of the old, used-up form.

The names of students can be identified from among the total list of borrowers. The mean and standard deviation of borrowing for students only can be computed.

Furthermore, annual rates of borrowing for each book can be computed. Probably, a pattern will be found in the rates of borrowing that will permit fitting a curve to the annual rates. It could be hypothesized that in the earlier years after its acquisition, the annual rate of borrowing of a book will rise; then, in later years, the rate will decline and tail off, until finally the book no longer appears in the master bibliography of books in print.

Multivariate analysis can be applied to explain variance in borrowing practices among students. Data are usually available at a registrar's office or college computer center on each student's place of residence, sex, major field of study, academic average, and so forth. These data can be used in the variance analysis. Thus, it might occur that 20% of the variance in borrowing among students is due to the place of residence, students living off of the campus perhaps being more likely to borrow than those living on campus, it was thought at the time.

In addition to tracing the use of books by borrowers, a method was devised for sampling the use of books within the library building itself. It was necessary to find a random sample of the times to conduct the survey of what the students are reading. Once this random sample of times was found, then a random sample of students could be taken according to a sample of study and reading locations in the building. About 1,100 students need to be included in the total sample in order for there to be 95% certainty that the sampling error is $\pm$ 2%. Such a procedure also could measure what proportion of the books being used are Business books and permit the analysis of the Business books into significant subject matter categories.

At this point in the planning it was seen that the statistical techniques described thus far are available for sampling master bibliographies and sampling the behavior of library users for the purpose of describing and evaluating the academic uses of the library collections. Also, important implications for academic policies and programs could be derived from the evaluations. It was appreciated that sampling would permit the analysis of demand for book use and foster a desirable and proper organizational response to a demand that arises inside the organization.

Further, it was seen that these statistical techniques are economical to use. The academic organizational setting for formulating and applying the statistical procedures appeared favorable for the use of the sampling methods.

The methods described could be applied on behalf of each academic department to furnish comparisons. Also, the sampling methods can give significant comparisons in the usage of books among the different libraries, it was pointed out.

Sampling Book Readership
Inside the Library

Subsequently, the planning for developing information on academic uses of the library was limited in scope to the topic of how to sample in-library book use of the Rider College library. The team of the professor of Management and the professor of Quantitative Methods was continued. Intensive professional work was required at this stage. A committee, as a committee, could not do the job. However, the results of the professional staff work on sampling methods were reported back to the Library Committee for its consideration.

The purpose of the professional staff work then came to be that of determining statistical sampling methods for finding what books are being read by students inside the library. The professional statistician carried the main responsibility for identifying and applying the relevant sampling theory. Once the sample data were collected, the data could provide useful information for planning effective student use of needed books.

Statistical sampling was considered ideal under the circumstances of the situation. Statistical sampling has the twin attributes of being economical and unobtrusive; at the same time, sampling provides a <u>comprehensive</u> picture of the activities being surveyed. And it was recognized that similar sampling methods also can be applied to the related topic of who is borrowing which books and reading the books outside of the library.

Simple random sampling was used. A random sample can be used to assure that the characteristics of readership population will be found in the sample within a measurable sampling error.

A sample size of 600 items appeared to be the best size, at this juncture. It was felt that a sample size of less than 600 would produce too much distortion in the estimated error of the smaller percentages common to some categories of students and books. And a sample size of more than 600 could lead to a large increase in the survey time and cost, but only a small decrease in the estimated error.

It was recognized that the sample randomness here has the two dimensions of random time and random place. Time and place of the sampled activity are simple aspects yet fundamental. The use of random numbers tables assured randomness of sample times and places. In the first approximation of the steps in selecting random times for the sample the following tentative plan was adopted. Taking the official calendar and schedule of hours of the library for a semester, or a school year, assign a 4-digit number to each hour, beginning with 0001 to be assigned to the first hour of the first day, 0002 to the second hour, and so on.

Then, select 4-digit random numbers from a random numbers table until 600 library hours have been identified for the sample. Once the 600 hours in the sample had been identified, it was provided in the initial plan that a random numbers table would be used to find at random the specific minute of each sample hour when the survey interview should be conducted. The final plan, actually used, modified this step.

The procedure was similar for the random selection of the reading locations where the interviews should be held. The floor plan of the library would be examined first. Next, a multiple-digit number could be assigned to reading locations: each chair at a table; each study carrel; each chair in a lounge, and so forth. For each random time in the sample, a random location would be identified as the random place of the interview. A random numbers table would furnish random numbers that would identify the sample locations which have the corresponding numbers. Thus, the two dimensions of the random sample--random time and random location--can be achieved.

Data Collection

In collecting the data, if an interviewer finds a sample location is unoccupied, he should have in hand a list of a sequence of reading locations, all having been selected at random, so that he can proceed to find a student-occupied location following the prescribed sequence. If no reading locations at all are found to be occupied, the interviewer should resume interviewing at the next randomly selected time.

Once the sample student is identified and approached, the interviewer should obtain from the student the student's name and the full bibliographical description of the book that the student is reading. Other pertinent data, such as type of book, field of study, cumulative average, place of residence of reader, and so forth, are available from official records of the school. Such records should be open for examination for legitimate research and administrative purposes. Even when all of the necessary data have been collected, a big question still presents itself: What are the inferences that can be drawn from the data? This question, in part, can be resolved into the technical question of how best to array and analyze the data.

Arraying and Analyzing Data

A fruitful way to proceed is to array data in matrix format and then apply the Chi-Square test, it was recognized. Below is a simplified matrix which has 9 cells of hypothetical data that will serve an illustrative purpose.

Students Classified by School of Major	Books Classified by Subject Matter			
	Education	Liberal Arts	Business	
Education	(15) 10	(75) 80	(60) 60	150
Liberal Arts	(20) 30	(100) 120	(80) 50	200
Business	(25) 20	(125) 100	(100) 130	250
	60	300	240	600

The numbers not in parentheses are assumed figures. They, the numbers, were chosen to illustrate the data that would be collected during the sampling data collection.

One attribute of student readers is illustrated in the matrix, namely the Major Field of Study. For example, the number 10 in the upper lefthand corner, or cell, is illustrative of the actual number of students in the sample majoring in Education who were reading Education books.

The numbers in the parentheses are estimated numbers derived from the null hypotheses that the student's Major Field of Study has no influence on the type of book that the student will read in the library. The numbers (15), (20), and (25) in the "Education" column are in the same proportion (10 percent, that is, 60/600) to the subtotals of students by major field that are listed along the righthand side of the matrix. Similarly, the numbers (75), (100), and (125) are 50 percent of 150, 200, and 250 respectively; (60), (80), and (100) are 40 percent of 150, 200, 250 respectively.

Next, we might ask: Are the differences between actual and estimated numbers statistically significant? The Chi-Square test can be applied to find whether there is statistical significance at certain desired levels of significance. In the illustration at hand, the Chi-Square test gives the result of 37.19. Testing at the 5 percent level, this result is highly significant in light of the table value of 9.488 for 4 degrees of freedom. In other words, less than 5 percent of the time would the sample differences of this order be found, if Major Field of Study had no influence. Thus, it can be concluded that the null hypotheses should be rejected; that is, one should infer that Major Field of Study does influence what books a student reads in the library. This inference obtains when we consider the influence of all three illustrative majors.

Further Analysis

The original matrix can be subdivided into derived matrices in which all readings of any two majors can be tested for significant differences. When Education and Business majors are compared, for example, the submatrix of estimated vs. actual observations would be:

Students Classified by School of Major	Books Classified by Subject Matter			
	Education	Liberal Arts	Business	
Education	(11) 10	(68) 80	(71) 60	150
Business	(19) 20	(113) 100	(119) 130	250
	30	180	190	400

The Chi-Square test of 6.48 proved to be greater than the table value of 5.99. Thus, there is found a significant difference between the two groups, at the 5 percent level of significance for 2 degrees of freedom.

Also, the reading in a single field of any two majors can be tested for significant differences. Looking at, say, students majoring in Business and students majoring in Education, there is the question of whether there is a significant difference in their reading of, say, Liberal Arts books. Given the hypothetical figures, there is less than a 1 percent probability that differences of the magnitude indicated would occur if there is no influence of Major Field of Study. The foregoing assumes the normality of the differences between sample proportions.

The same type of analysis can be used for other individual attributes of students, such as sex, ethnic origin, place of residence, cumulative average, and so forth. Reader attributes can be used in combination too; for instance, Female-Education majors, Female-Liberal Arts majors, and Female-Business majors. Broad categories of books being read can be analyzed. For example, Education books include guidance, curriculum, administration, testing, and so on. These last two types of analysis mentioned above were not adopted in the final plan.

The Plan Summarized

The plan for the research project came to consist of the plan for the three parts of: (1) the statistical sample design; (2) the organization for interviewing and data collection; and (3) the analysis of the compiled data. The plan, in broad outline, calls for a random sample of book readership inside the library to be obtained. The sample size needed is 600 to assure the desired sampling error. The use of random numbers tables provides randomness of the two dimensions of time and place of the book reading. The brief manual for data collection tells how interviewers should proceed in conducting interviews in the library so as to assure that the statistical design of the sample is applied in practice. The hypothetical matrices discussed in earlier paragraphs show how the collected data will be analyzed according to the Chi-Square test and other statistical tests. Such analyses permit the drawing of valid statistical inferences about relationships between reader characteristics and book attributes of those books being read in the library.

Chapter   4

Organization and Procedures for Data Collection

Student Interviewers

Two student organizations were used in the interviewing and the validation
of the interviewing program. The two are Alpha Phi Omega fraternity and Phi Chi
Theta fraternity, respectively. The former is a service fraternity of men which
has a chapter on the Rider campus. The latter is a professional business women's
fraternity also on the Rider campus.

The attributes of Alpha Phi Omega can be described in the following terms:
The purpose of this fraternity shall be to assemble college men in the fellowship
of the Scout Oath and Law, to develop leadership, to promote friendship, to provide service to humanity, and to further the freedom that is our national, educational and intellectual heritage. The cardinal principles center around leadership, friendship, and service. It is the policy of Alpha Phi Omega to include in
its membership men of social fraternities and nonmembers, men of all departments
of the college, upon being so elected by the respective chapters and upon fulfill-
ing the membership preparation prescribed by the national fraternity and by the
chapters. The major fields of service include service to the student body, faculty,
members of the fraternity, youth of the community, and the nation as participating
citizens.

The relevant characteristics of the Phi Chi Theta fraternity can be described
briefly. The purpose of Phi Chi Theta is to promote the cause of higher Business
Education and training for all women; to foster high ideals for women in Business

careers; and to the attainment of such ends. Only women with satisfactory scholastic status in the fields of Business Administration, Economics, Marketing, Secretarial Science, and Business Education are asked to become members of the fraternity.

Special note should be taken of the fact that undergraduate students did serve both as interviewers and validators. It was an important part of this research project to determine whether it is feasible to use students in such roles. Happily, both student organizations did perform effectively.

Organizational Context
For Institutional Research

There is another organization which must be taken into account in discussing a research project of this kind. It is not the data collection and validating organization of the two fraternities, but it is the organizational context of the college within which the research is conducted. It is within this context that resources are obtained, interviews conducted, and data processed at the computer center. And it is this organizational context which can be resistant to the efficient conduct of the research. Largely, it can be a matter of the affected units of this organization being willing to assume only the barest minimum of responsibility for seeing the project through to a successful conclusion.

In one episode, for example, a subordinate administrator would not permit several chairs to be put in place at reading carrels in the library. It was essential to the research design that each carrel have a chair. There had to be an equal opportunity for readers to be seated at each reading location in order for the sample to be truly random and representative of the readership population being sampled. Only after the president intervened were the chairs installed.

From an organizational point of view, the problem would be that of the research project requiring essential horizontal relationships of cooperation between the research project's principal investigators and the school's administrative personnel. The needed horizontal relationships might not be forthcoming, or they might be present only to a minimal degree. The basic pattern of organization relationships at the school can be vertical relationships radiating downward on the vertical plane from the president of the institution. The orientation of subordinates often is to their relationship to their boss and the chief executive, and not so much to horizontal and diagonal communication and co-ordination.

Perhaps the best that can be done when this kind of situation develops, as it sometimes does, is: (1) establish in advance a detailed schedule of steps to be taken by the institution's administrators in connection with the research project; and (2) have the chief executive officer inform his subordinates of his interest in seeing that the schedule is observed by them in practice. When unanticipated problems arise, as they do inevitably, again it is essential that the chief executive affirm his interest in seeing that the research project be carried to a successful completion. Thus, the vertical relationships can be used to assure the needed horizontal relationships in the organizational context.

Procedures for Data Collection

This section will describe the several steps that were taken in translating the general plan into specific procedures to be followed by members of the two student fraternities in conducting interviews and validating the interviews.

It was necessary to select times and places of interviews at random. In the final plan, it was decided to conduct interviews in the library during a 60-day period from September 11, 1969 (the first day of classes) to November 9, 1969 inclusive. In the selection of the random times, a 4-digit number was assigned to each one of the approximately 8,900 5-minute intervals the library was open during that 60-day period. It should be noted that the adoption of the 5-minute interval is a refinement of the earlier statement of the plan. Four-digit random numbers were obtained from E. S. Pearson, editor, _Tracts for Computers_ (Cambridge: Cambridge University Press, 1960) until 700 random times had been identified. Appendix A gives an illustrative listing of the sample times for the first two days of interviews. A total of 700 sample times had been selected in an effort to achieve the desired number of interviews. Again, the initial plan called for 600, not 700, sample times.

In the selection of the random places or carrels, a count was made of the library carrels and other reading places to be included in the scope of the study. In general, they are the carrels that are to be found in the immediate vicinity of the open stacks of books on the first floor and second floor of the Rider Library. Appendix B which contains a sample of the interview questionnaire form, shows the layout and the total number (397) of the reading places. A 3-digit number was assigned to each carrel as shown in the diagram of the layout.

Next, 3-digit random numbers were selected from random numbers tables so that for each random time there would be listed a sequence of 5 randomly selected carrel numbers. Appendix A presents these sequences for two illustrative days for each random time listed.

Before the beginning of the Fall semester, a group meeting was held of the members of Alpha Phi Omega who would serve as interviewers. The procedures to be followed were explained and discussed in detail. Questions that occurred to the interviewers were answered.

This phase of the project can be especially interesting and rewarding to researchers. It is a real exercise in translating abstract concepts into operational behavior. For example, the question arose about what to do if a student-reader is found on an interview occasion to be seated at a carrel that has several books open on it. What answer did we give? The answer followed this line: It can be assumed that a reader can be reading only one book at one time. The interviewer might be able to infer from direct observation which one of the books is being read. If he cannot, then he can ask the reader which one is being read at that moment. If the interviewer still cannot determine which one is being read, then he counts the occasion as one in which he could not find a reader of a book at that location, and the interviewer moves on to the next interview location in the sequence of 5 alternative carrel locations. The general proposition is that the interview procedure must implement faithfully the sample design that includes the sample time and the sequence of 5 sample locations to be visited in sequence until a book reader is found. If no book reader is found at any of the 5 carrels, then this fact is noted by the interviewer at the conclusion of his attempt to conduct an interview.

The story is similar when it comes to assuring that the sample design random times are observed in practice. Library clocks and student wrist watches might not be accurate. The question raises the issue of finding an authoritative source of accurate time. It was decided that an interviewer should synchronize his own watch with a master clock at the telephone switchboard at Rider, about 10 minutes before the scheduled start of a sample 5-minute interval. Thus, the randomness of sample time would be observed in practice, it being critical that the sample times be implemented exactly according to plan.

With respect to the validating of interviews, this procedure is standard practice in sampling. A sample of 50 sample times was selected at random from the total of 700 sample times. The women students of Phi Chi Theta fraternity did follow the standard interview procedure on these 50 occasions. The results of the validators' interviews can be compared to the results of the regular interviewers' interviews being validated to see if there are any discrepancies, and to see if any corrective action needs to be taken. See Appendix F for a more complete discussion of validation of interview procedure.

Coding the Data

When the interview forms are completed and returned, it becomes necessary to translate the information collected into terms that are suitable for processing by the Rider IBM 1130 computer at the computer center. Appendix C is a sample of a work sheet used to show how to translate interview information about the book being read (if any) into the computer program code number. Once the code number is assigned, the information can be punched into the IBM cards by the keypunch operator at the computer center.

Appendix D contains a sample of the code sheet for the computer center data bank on undergraduate daytime students at Rider. A coded tabulation of student characteristics has been furnished by the computer center. The project secretary entered the pertinent information on student characteristics into the interview forms.

Appendix E presents the coding system that was used by the research project. The project secretary entered the proper code numbers in the appropriate columns of the IBM Fortran Coding Form which is used for that purpose. After this step is completed, the data are in a form to be keypunched into IBM cards.

Chapter 5

Research Results Including Simulation

The results of this research project can be discussed in terms of the topics of:

1. General results

2. Reading of library and nonlibrary books by type of book

3. Characteristics of book readers

4. Matrix analysis

5. T test analysis

6. Profile of the student reader

7. Use of library carrels by time of day and day of week.

Each one of the topics listed above will be discussed in turn.

General Results

It had been intended that overall results would be derived from a total of 700 attempted interviews of book readers inside the library. The actual number of interview attempts proved to be 661. The 661 interview attempts succeeded in obtaining interviews of 64 library book readers and interviews of 204 book readers who were reading books not taken from the library collection in the stacks. Of the 393 interview attempts that were made but did not result in interviews, 353 found carrels unoccupied and 40 found a carrel occupied by a reader of something other than a book. There was obtained a print-out of internal validation of data and random check and print-out of data.

It is evident that the goal of 600 completed interviews has not been realized. In one sense, this failure is a procedural problem. It indicates that a much larger number of interview attempts must be made, or a larger number of carrels sampled on each interview attempt, if 600 interviews are to be achieved. From another angle, however, the small number of readers of library books interviewed when over 600 interview attempts were made, can be regarded as one of the most significant substantive findings of this research project--that is, there is low utilization of the library for the purpose of reading library books inside the library.

It was found that, of the total number of readers in the sample, 20 percent are readers of library books; 66 per cent, nonlibrary books; and 12.9 percent, other reading matter. The standard error of the estimate for the percentage of library book readers is 2.3 percent, which means that a 95 percent confidence interval for the estimate is $\pm$ 4.5 percent.

Types of Books

Types of library books being read have been determined and can be summarized as follows: The relative frequency of reading Social Science books is significantly higher than for any other type of library book. More specifically, the percentage of (Dewey Decimal System) Social Science books in the sample is 50 percent. The standard error is 6.2 percent. This result means that a 95 percent confidence interval for the percentage is 12.3 percent. The second highest percentage is 17.1 percent, well outside the confidence interval for the Social Science library books.

The lowest three percentages of reading are in Pure Science, Technology, and the category of Geography and History, running between 3 and 6 percent. All the latter percentages were well outside the 95 percent confidence intervals for the two immediately higher percentages.

The foregoing percentages of relative frequency of reading are a measure of demand for the library books and can be discussed as an inventory problem. Library administration can balance the availability of books and the demand for books; books can be stocked in proportion to demand. There should be a larger supply on hand of those types of books that are more frequently used. Of course, low-demand books must be stocked, at times to a disproportionately large degree. The desire to make available such books can be met, in part, by the procedure of stocking such books at a central library or depository, and shipping to the place of need at the time of need. This practice would reduce duplication of low-demand books at the local libraries. When trade-offs among categories of books are undertaken, the trade-offs can be accomplished more effectively by reference to economic criteria, and not just to the criteria to be found in ecology, sociology, aesthetics, and so forth.

The distribution of textbook reading in the library can be described at this point. One hundred and one textbooks being read were required textbooks in Liberal Arts courses; 66, Business Administration; and 7, Education. The percentages are 58 percent, 38 percent, and 4 percent, respectively. The analysis of textbook reading in the library can be conducted in a fashion parallel to library book reading.

The listing below is the textbook reading tally:

Total number of textbooks   174

Liberal Arts   101

Art	3	Math	9	Psych	9	
Bio	7	Phil	6	Russi	2	
Engl	31	Phys	1	Soc	6	
French	1	PolSci	7	Span	5	
Hist	14					

Business Administration 66

Acc	11	Mgt	10
BLaw	7	Mkt	9
Econ	6	QMeth	9
Fin	12	Sec	2

Education   7

Major Field of Study

One section of the print-out lists relative frequency of book readership by Major Field of Study of the reader. The relative frequency of use by Business Administration majors at .496 is significantly higher than relative frequency for any other field of study. The second highest is Liberal Arts majors at .300 relative frequency, which is well below a 95 percent confidence interval of .061 for Business Administration majors. Also, the relative frequency of use for Liberal Arts majors is significantly higher than the .204 relative frequency for Education majors, the latter being below a 95 percent confidence interval of .056 for Liberal Arts majors.

For the Education Master and Business Master categories, it was found that both would have lower relative frequencies than the lowest measured relative frequency in the listing, and both would have 95 percent confidence intervals lower than the lowest listed interval. Seven Evening School students, exclusive of master's students, also were found in the sample.

The percentages of reading by Major Field of Study can be compared to the corresponding percentages for the daytime undergraduate population. In that population, 46.9 percent of the students are Business Administration majors; 27.7 percent, Liberal Arts majors; and 25.4 percent, Education majors. There is no significant difference between Business Administration readers and their proportionate representation in the population. The same holds for Liberal Arts majors. Education majors, however, read significantly less than their proportionate share in the population. The test for significance is based on the normal curve of error at 5 percent level of significance using a one-tail test.

Cumulative Average

If there is any idea that students who have poor academic records are reading books in the library to a relatively large degree, it is not borne out by the results of this study at Rider. The arithmetic mean of the cumulative averages of book readers in the sample is 2.52 with a standard error of .03 and a 95 percent confidence interval of $\pm$ .07. The mean of the cumulative averages for the daytime undergraduate student population as a whole is 2.40, well below the 95 percent confidence interval of the sample mean of the library readers.

Thus, it can be said with better than 95 percent certainty that the mean cumulative average of the library readers is significantly higher than that of the daytime undergraduate population.

Any study that attempts to determine academic achievement of library book readers should make use of empirical methods similar to those used in the immediate study in order to identify precisely who actually is using the library books. Furthermore, it should be noted that this study draws no conclusions about the validity of the cumulative average as a measure of academic achievement, but simply points out that the library readers' mean cumulative average is higher than for the undergraduate population. It can be argued that the cumulative average is not a good measure of academic achievement because of variations among instructors, courses, and schools in the scales used in awarding grades.

Place of Residence

The sample of student readers contains 55.5 percent who reside in dormitories on the campus, 33.8 percent who are commuters, and 10.6 percent who reside in fraternities or sororities on campus. The daytime undergraduate student population has 57.0 percent who live in dormitories, 27.5 percent commuters, and 15.5 percent residing in fraternities or sororities.

Dormitory students read in proportion to their share in the population. Commuters read more than their proportionate share. Sorority and fraternity students read books in the library less than their proportionate share. Again, the one-tail normal curve of error test, with 5 percent level of significance, was used in testing for significant differences.

Class Year

In the sample of student readers, there are 31.1 percent Freshmen, 35.4 per-cent Sophomores, 17.3 percent Juniors, and 14.5 percent Seniors. In the day-time undergraduate population there are 38.9 percent Freshmen, 26.0 percent Sophomores, 17.8 per cent Juniors, and 16.8 percent Seniors.

Freshmen read books in the library significantly less than their propor-tionate share of the student population. Sophomores read significantly more than their proportionate share. Both Juniors and Seniors read the same as their respective proportionate shares.

Mean Class Year

The sample's mean class year for men and women students combined is 2.15; men alone, 2.29; and women, 1.89. The daytime undergraduate population's mean class year for men and women students combined is 2.12; men alone, 2.23; and women, 1.97.

No significant difference exists between the sample's mean class year and the population's mean class year for men and women together, men alone, or women alone.

Sex

Men students make up 65.2 percent of the students in the sample. Women students constitute 34.8 percent of the students in the sample. Men students comprise 58.8 percent of the daytime undergraduate population; women students, 41.2 percent.

Men students read books in the library significantly more frequently than their proportionate share of the population. Women students read less than their proportionate share.

Summary of Matrix Analysis

In order to determine whether relationships exist between various characteristics of the readers of books in the library, the Chi-Square (χ^2) test has been applied. A 5 percent level of significance has been used. The tables below summarize the results. In some cases, the matrices were regrouped in order to apply the χ^2 test. Even after such regrouping, certain characteristics could not be tested.

Table 1

Null Hypotheses:

There is no relationship between library book or
not and the several characteristics of the reader

Characteristics of the Reader	Critical Value for Test	χ^2 Value	Acceptance or Rejection of Null Hypotheses
Sex	3.84	2.07	Accept
Time of Week (Weekday or Weekend)	3.84	0.23	Accept
Time of Day	5.99	4.49	Accept
Class Year	7.82	0.98	Accept
Student or Nonstudent	3.84	8.99	Reject
Cumulative Average	No χ^2 test possible without regrouping		

Table 1 indicates that the only relationship between reading of library book or
not and the several characteristics of the reader is in connection with student
or nonstudent readers. When the χ^2 value is greater than the critical value, the
null hypotheses is rejected.

Table 2

Null Hypotheses:

There is no relationship between the kind of library
book read and the several characteristics of the reader

Characteristics of the Reader	Critical Value for Test	χ^2 Value	Acceptance or Rejection of Null Hypotheses
Sex	3.84	1.60	Accept
Time of Day	5.99	0.31	Accept
Class Year	5.99	2.86	Accept
Cumulative Average	No χ^2 test possible without regrouping		
Major Field	5.99	0.41	Accept
Place of Residence	3.84	1.58	Accept
Student or Not	No χ^2 test possible without regrouping		

No relationships exist between kind of library book, on the one hand, and any other characteristics of the reader, on the other hand, in the instances where the χ^2 test was possible.

Table 3

Null Hypotheses:

There is no relationship between the major field
of study and the several characteristics of the
reader

Characteristics of the Reader	Critical Value for Test	χ^2 Value	Acceptance or Rejection of Null Hypotheses
Sex	5.99	80.89	Reject
Class Year	12.59	6.63	Accept
Cumulative Average	No χ^2 test possible without regrouping		
Place of Residence	No χ^2 test possible without regrouping		
Library Book or Not	5.99	3.34	Accept

The only relationship identified between Major Field of Study and other characteristics of the reader is the relationship to Sex of reader. The χ^2 value for Sex is greater than the critical value; thus, the null hypotheses is rejected.

Table 4

Null Hypotheses:

There is no relationship between residence of a
reader and the several characteristics of a reader

Characteristics of the Reader	Critical Value for Test	χ^2 Value	Acceptance or Rejection of Null Hypotheses
Sex	3.84	8.71	Reject
Time of Week (Weekday or Weekend)	3.84	21.02	Reject
Time of Day	5.99	40.66	Reject
Class Year	7.82	23.10	Reject
Cumulative Average	3.84	0.17	Accept
Library Book or Not	3.84	0.21	Accept
Major Field	5.99	4.54	Accept

Sex and Class Year of the reader, as well as Time of Week and Time of Day of reading, are related to the residence of the reader, as shown in Table 4. No other relationships exist. In the case of Sex, Class Year, Time of Week, and Time of Day, the χ^2 values are greater than their respective critical values.

Table 5

Null Hypotheses:

There is no relationship between the weekday reading
and the several characteristics of the reader

Characteristics of the Reader	Critical Value for Test	χ^2 Value	Acceptance or Rejection of Null Hypotheses
Sex	9.49	7.86	Accept
Time of Day	15.51	13.29	Accept
Class Year	No χ^2 test possible without regrouping		
Cumulative Average	No χ^2 test possible without regrouping		
Major Field	15.51	10.34	Acccpt
Place of Residence	No χ^2 test possible without regrouping		
Student or Not	No χ^2 test possible without regrouping		
Library Book or Not	9.49	5.11	Accept

No relationships exist between weekday reading and any other characteristics of the reader, in the instances where the χ^2 test was possible.

The χ^2 test is a broad test that treats a matrix as a whole. The χ^2 test combines the individual cell differences in a certain way to give a single test result for the whole matrix. The χ^2 value is the basis for acceptance or rejection of the null hypotheses. Even where the null hypotheses is accepted by the χ^2 test, there still might be significant differences between cells within the matrix. The T test can be used to test for the significance of these individual cell differences.

Summary of T Test[1]

The individual cells will be tested using a one-tail T test at a 5 percent level of significance. The reason for the one-tail test, instead of the two-tail test, is that the one-tail test determines more readily whether one percentage is greater than another, first with respect to rows and second, columns. The results of the tests are summarized in the paragraphs below. It should be understood that all differences cited in the following discussion are statistically significant at a one-tail 5 percent level of significance.

Library Book or Nonlibrary Book by Sex of Reader

No significant difference is found between men
and women in reading nonlibrary and library books
And no significant difference is found on the part
of either men or women in the reading of nonlibrary
and library books.

Library Book or Nonlibrary Book by Weekday -- Weekend

Nonlibrary books are read with greater relative frequency on weekends than on weekdays. The reverse holds
for library books.

Library Book or Nonlibrary Book by Class Year

No significant differences are found among class
years of readers in the reading of library and
nonlibrary books.

Library Book or Nonlibrary Book by Cumulative Average

Students who have the highest cumulative averages
read nonlibrary books with greater relative frequency than do those who have middle and lowest
cumulative averages. However, the students who

---

1. The phrase T test refers to the Student-t-Test.

have the highest cumulative averages read
library books relatively less frequently.

Students who have middle cumulative averages
read library books more frequently than nonlibrary books. The reverse holds for the
students who have the highest cumulative
averages. For the lowest students, there
is no significant difference.

Library Book or Nonlibrary Book by Time of Day

In the afternoon, nonlibrary books are read
with a greater relative frequency than in
the morning or evening, while library books
are read with a greater relative frequency
in the afternoon than in the morning or
evening.

In the afternoon, library books are read more
frequently than nonlibrary books.

Library Book by Sex of Reader

Men and women displayed no significant difference
in relative frequency of book reading by type
of library book.

Men readers read Social Science books more
frequently than Literature or Other library
books.

Women readers read Literature and Other library
books more frequently than Social Science library
books.

Library Book by Student and Nonstudent

No significant difference was found in the relative frequency of reading of different categories of library books by student and nonstudent readers.

For Rider students, there is more frequent reading of Pure Science than Other library books; the reverse is the case for nonstudent readers.

Type of Library Book by Residence of Student

Dormitory students read more Literature books than do commuters. No significant difference is found in the reading of other categories of library books.

Dormitory students read more Literature books than Social Science, Pure Science, and Other library books.

Commuters read less Literature books than Social Science, Pure Science, and Other library books.

No significant difference is found in the reading of library books by Fraternity and Sorority students.

Library Book by Class of Rider Reader

Freshmen read less frequently Technology library books than do Sophomores or Juniors. Sophomores read more frequently Literature library books than do Juniors or Seniors.

114

Sophomores read Literature books more
frequently than either Social Science or
other books.

Juniors read Pure Science and Technology
books more frequently than Social Science,
Literature, or Other.

For Seniors, there is no significant
difference in any of the categories of
library books.

Library Book by Major Field

Education majors read Other library books more
frequently than do Business majors.

Business majors read Technology books more
frequently than either Literature or Other
library books.

Library Book by Cumulative Average

The student with the lowest cumulative average
reads Other library books more frequently than
Pure Science. Cumulative average has virtually
no significance in the student reading of types
of library books, except that the students with
the lowest cumulative average read Other library
books more frequently than those with the middle
cumulative average. The former also read Other
library books more often than Social Science
books.

Library Book by Time of Day

Technology books are most fequently read in
the morning and evening.

There is no significant difference in the
reading of any other category of books by
time of day.

In the afternoon, Social Science, Literature
and Other library books are read more frequently
than Technology library books.

Library Book (Using Two Categories of Library Books--Social Science and All Other)

With one exception, no significant differences
were found in relationships between the type
of library book (Social Science and Non-Social
Science library book) being read in the
library and the characteristics of the reader.
The characteristics include: sex, Rider student
or not, residence of the student, class year,
major field of study, cumulative average, and time
of day of reading. The one exception to the finding
of no significant differences is in the relationship
between the type of library book and the class year
of the Rider reader.

Sophomores read all other library books relatively
more frequently than they read Social Sicence
library books.

Major by Library and Nonlibrary Book

Library books are used more frequently by Education

majors than nonlibrary books. No significant difference is found for any other pairing.

,Nonlibrary books are read more frequently by
Liberal Arts majors than by Education majors.
There are no significant differences for any
other pairing.

Library books are read more frequently by Education
majors than by Liberal Arts majors. There are
no significant differences for any other pairing.

Major by Residence

For Liberal Arts majors, those in fraternities
and sororities read less than those in dormitories
or commuters. For Education majors, those in
fraternities and sororities read books in the
library significantly greater than do those
who are commuters. Business Administration
majors who are dormitory students read less
than those who are in fraternities and sororities or commuters.

Among dormitory students, Liberal Arts students
read significantly more frequently than do
Business Administration students. For fraternity and sorority students, Liberal Arts students
read significantly less frequently than do
Education and Business Administration students.

Major by Class Year

Liberal Arts Freshmen read significantly more frequently than do Liberal Arts Juniors. Business
Administration Freshmen read significantly less
frequently than Business Administration Sophomores
and Juniors.

For Freshmen students, both Liberal Arts and Education
majors read more frequently than do Business Administration
majors. No other pairing of majors displayed any significant difference.

Major by Cumulative Average of Rider Reader

No significant difference in cumulative averages was
found in relative frequency of book reading among
Liberal Arts, Education and Business Administration
majors. Nor was there any significant difference
found in pairing students according to cumulative
average, major-by-major.

Major by Sex of Reader

In Liberal Arts and Education, women read significantly more frequently than men; the reverse
holds for Business Administration.

For men, Business Administration majors read
more frequently than do Liberal Arts or Education
majors. For women, Business Administration majors
read significantly less than either Liberal Arts
or Education; furthermore, Education majors read
significantly more frequently than do Liberal
Arts majors.

Major by Time of Day

No significant difference was found in the time
of day--morning, afternoon, or evening--in which
Liberal Arts, Education and Business Administration
majors are most likely to read books in the
library. Nor was there any significant difference
found in relative frequency of book use by time
of day, major-by-major.

Residence by Sex of Reader

Of dormitory students found reading books in
the library, women read significantly more
frequently than do men book readers. Of commuter
students, men read significantly more frequently
than do women. Of fraternity and sorority
students, there is no significant difference
in reading between men and women.
Among men, commuters read books in the library
more frequently than do dormitory men; while,
among women, dormitory women read books in
the library more frequently than do commuter
women.

Residence by Library Book or Not

Fraternity and sorority students read library
books more frequently than nonlibrary books
in the library. For both dormitory and commuter
students there is no significant difference in
the reading of the two types of books.

Fraternity and sorority students more frequently
read library books in the library than do
dormitory or commuter students. Dormitory and
commuter students each read more frequently
nonlibrary books than do fraternity and sorority
students.

Residence of Reader by Class Year

Of dormitory readers: Freshmen read books in
the library relatively more frequently than
do Sophomores, Juniors, or Seniors; Sophomores,
than Juniors or Seniors; and Juniors, than
Seniors.

Of commuter readers, both Juniors and Seniors
read relatively more frequently than Freshmen.
Also, among commuter readers, Seniors read
relatively more frequently than Sophomores.

Of Freshmen, dormitory students read more
frequently than do commuter, or fraternity
and sorority students.

Of fraternity and sorority readers, Juniors and Seniors
read relatively more frequently than do Freshmen,
and Seniors read relatively more frequently than
Sophomores.

Of Juniors, commuters read significantly more
frequently than do dormitory students.

Of seniors, commuters, as well as fraternity and
sorority students, read more frequently than do
dormitory students.

Residence of Reader by Major

Of dormitory readers, Liberal Arts students read
more frequently than do Business Administration students.
Of fraternity and sorority students, both Education
majors and Business Administration majors read more
frequently than do Liberal Arts majors.
Of commuter readers, Business Administration majors
read more frequently than do Education majors.

Residence by Cumulative Average of Rider Reader

No significant differences were found in cumulative
averages of Rider student readers as among dormitory,
commuter, and fraternity and sorority readers.

Residence by Time of Day of Rider Reader

Dormitory students read relatively less frequently
in the morning (8:00 a.m. to 12:59 p.m.) than in
the afternoon (1:00 p.m. to 5:59 p.m.) or evening
(6:00 p.m. to 10:30 p.m.) and relatively more
frequently in the evening than the afternoon.
Commuter students read relatively more frequently
in the morning than the afternoon or evening, and
relatively more frequently in the afternoon than
the evening.
Fraternity and sorority students read relatively
more frequently in the evening than in the morning
or afternoon.
In the morning, commuter readers read more
frequently than either dormitory readers or

fraternity and sorority readers.

In the evening, dormitory readers, as well as
fraternity and sorority readers, read more
frequently than do commuter readers.

Day by Residence of Student

On Tuesday, commuters read relatively more
frequently than dormitory students. On Sunday,
fraternity and sorority students read relatively
more frequently than do either dormitory or commuter students, and dormitory students relatively
more frequently than commuters.

Dormitory students read relatively more frequently
on Monday than Tuesday, and on Monday than Friday.
And dormitory students read relatively more frequently on Saturday and Sunday than on Tuesday.
Dormitory students read relatively more frequently on Saturday and Sunday than on Friday.
Commuter students read relatively less frequently
on Sunday than they do on any other day of the
week.

Fraternity and sorority students read relatively
more frequently on Sunday than on Monday, Tuesday,
Wednesday, or Thursday.

Day by Class Year of Student

Both Juniors and Seniors read with greater relative
frequency on Monday than do Freshmen students.
Seniors read with greater relative frequency than

do Sophomores and Juniors on Tuesday. Juniors read with greater relative frequency than do Freshmen, Sophomores or Seniors on Wednesday.

Freshmen read with greater relative frequency than Seniors on Thursday. Also, on Thursday, Sophomores read with greater relative frequency than do Seniors; other readers, than Juniors; and other readers, than Seniors. On Sunday, Freshmen read with greater relative frequency than either Sophomores or Juniors. Freshmen are most likely to read on a Sunday and least likely to read on a Monday. Freshmen read relatively less on Monday than they do on Tuesday, Thursday, or Sunday, and relatively more on Sunday than on Wednesday or Friday.

Day and Sex

It was found that the relative frequency of reading by women students is significantly higher on Monday than for men students, while the reverse holds on Friday. On the other five days, there was no significant difference between relative percentages of men and women readers.

The analysis reveals, furthermore, that men students read relatively more frequently on Tuesday and Friday than they do on Monday; the reverse holds for women. For all other pairs of days, for each sex, there is no significant difference in book readership in the library.

Day by Nonlibrary Book Versus Library Book Use

In comparing nonlibrary book use and library book use according to the day of the week, there is no significant difference between the relative proportion of the two types of books except on Thursday when nonlibrary book reading is relatively greater than library. There is no significant difference between readership of library and nonlibrary books on the other 6 days of the week.

With respect to nonlibrary books alone, they are read relatively more frequently on Thursday than on Friday, while library books are read with more frequency on Friday than Thursday. For any other pairing of days there is no significant difference for either library or nonlibrary books.

Day by Student Versus Nonstudent

Nonstudents were found to be reading books in the library relatively more frequently on Friday than do the Rider students. Student readers read relatively more frequently than nonstudent readers on Thursday. On the other five days of the week, there is no significant difference in relative use by student readers versus nonstudent readers. Nonstudent readers do read relatively more frequently on Monday than do student readers on Thursday; and the former read more frequently on Friday than on Tuesday, Wednesday, or Thursday. Nonstudent readers also read more frequently

on Saturday than do nonstudent readers on Thursday.
Student readers read relatively less frequently
on Friday than they do on Tuesday, Wednesday, or
Thursday.

Day by Major of Rider Reader

Liberal Arts majors are most likely[2] to be
found reading on a Monday and least likely
on a Saturday. An Education major is the same.
A Business Administration major is most likely
to be found on a Tuesday and least likely to be
found on a Saturday.

Both Liberal Arts and Education majors read relatively more frequently on Monday than do Business
Administration majors. Liberal Arts majors read
relatively more frequently on Wednesday than do
Education majors. For all other pairings, there
is no significant difference in relative frequency
of book reading by day of the week.

For Liberal Arts majors there is a relatively
greater frequency of reading on Monday than
Friday or Sunday. Also, for Liberal Arts majors
there is relatively greater frequency of reading
on Wednesday than on Friday or Sunday.

For Education majors, there is relatively greater
frequency of reading on Monday than Wednesday.

---

2. The phrase "most likely" means largest of all
   but not necessarily significantly larger than any
   other.

For Business Administration majors, there is relatively less frequent reading on Monday than on Tuesday, Friday or Sunday.

For all other pairings of days there were no significant differences according to type of major of the student readers.

Day by Cumulative Average of Rider Reader

The top student is most likely to be found reading on a Friday and least likely on a Saturday. A student with a cumulative average between 2.00 and 2.99 is most likely to be found reading on a Monday and least likely on a Saturday.

A student with a cumulative average between 0.00 and 1.99 is most likely to be found reading on a Wednesday, and least likely on a Tuesday or Sunday.

There is a significant difference on Wednesday in relative frequency of book reading by students who have the lowest cumulative average (in the range of 0.00--1.99) and students who have a middle cumulative average (in the range of 2.00--2.99).

There is no other pairing of readers by cumulative average that displays any significant difference according to day of the week.

Those with the lowest cumulative average read relatively more frequently on Wednesday and Saturday than on a Tuesday or a Sunday.

Those with the middle cumulative read relatively

more frequently on a Tuesday than on a Wednesday, Friday or Saturday.

For the highest academic student there are no significant differences between one day and another. There are no other pairings that display significant differences.

Day by Time of Day of Reading

It has been pointed out that the day is divided into three parts--morning (8:00 a.m. to 12:59 p.m.), afternoon (1:00 p.m. to 5:59 p.m.), and evening (6:00 p.m. to 10:30 p.m.). On a Wednesday, the relative frequency of reading in the afternoon is greater than the evening. On Friday, the relative frequency of reading is greater in the morning than either the afternoon or evening. There is greater relative frequency of reading on a Friday morning than any other morning of the week. In the afternoon, Friday and Tuesday afternoon have less frequency of reading.

Sunday evening has greater relative frequency of reading than Wednesday and Friday evening only. Tuesday evening has greater relative frequency of reading than Friday.

Profile of the Typical Man Student
and Woman Student Library Reader

The data on library reading can be summed up graphically in terms of the characteristics of a typical man and a typical woman student reader. The typical man student library reader is a first-semester Sophomore who has a cumulative average of 2.48. Most likely he lives in a dormitory; least likely, a fraternity. Most likely his major field is Business Administration; least likely, Education. He prefers nonlibrary books to library books. However, when he does read a library book he generally chooses a Social Science book. He is most likely to be found in the library on a Tuesday; least likely, on a Saturday. He would rather read in the afternoon or morning than in the evening.

The typical woman student library reader is a second semester Freshman with a cumulative average of 2.55. Most likely she lives in a dormitory; least likely, a sorority. Most likely her major field is Liberal Arts; least likely, Business Administration. She prefers nonlibrary books to library books. But when she reads a library book, it tends to be one in an area other than Social Science. She is most likely to be found in the library on a Monday and least likely, there on a Saturday. She is more inclined to read in the evening or afternoon than in the morning.

In short, men and women student library readers tend to be alike in their place of residence, preference for nonlibrary books, and disdain for Saturday reading. They differ in their class year, cumulative average, major field, time and day of reading, and choice of library books.

Simulation of Carrel Utilization

According to the sampling plan, an interview attempt was concluded when an occupant was found in one of five randomly chosen carrels or when five carrels had been sampled, whichever came first. An interview was completed only when

the occupant of a carrel was reading a book. If he was reading something else,

note was made of it, but he was not interviewed; nor were any other carrels

sampled in that attempt.

In coding the sample results into punched cards we indicated the times of

the interview attempts only for those that were actually completed. But this

is all that is needed to simulate the rate of occupancy of the carrels (book

readers as well as nonbook readers).

The rate of occupancy is simulated by hour and by day. The discussion

below will be confined to the simulation by hour, that by day is analogous.

Simulation by Hour of the Day.

The theoretical distribution of the interview attempts by hour of the day

is rectangular because their times were randomly chosen.

However, because of the schedule of library hours, some qualification is

necessary. The library hours are as follows:

> Monday through Friday: 8:00 a.m. to 10:30 p.m.
>
> Saturday: 10:00 a.m. to 5:00 p.m.
>
> Sunday: 2:00 p.m. to 10:30 p.m.

The hours between 2:00 p.m. and 5:00 p.m. are full library hours and occur

daily; the others are either partial or do not occur every day. Account must

be made of this disproportion in allocating the interview attempts.

Interpret a library hour to begin with an integer clock hour and end just

before the next integer clock hour. For instance, the first library hour begins

at 8:00 a.m. and ends just before 9:00 a.m. Giving full library hours a weight

of 1 and the half hour from 10:00 p.m. to closing a weight of 1/2, the weighted

frequency distribution of library hours is shown in Table 6 that follows.

Table 6
Weighted Frequency Distribution of Library Hours

Library Hours	Number of Days Library Open	Weighted Value
8:00 a.m. -- 9:00 a.m.	5	5
9:00 a.m. -- 10:00 a.m.	5	5
10:00 a.m. --11:00 a.m.	6	6
11:00 a.m. --12:00 p.m.	6	6
12:00 p.m. --1:00 p.m.	6	6
1:00 p.m. -- 2:00 p.m.	6	6
2:00 p.m. -- 3:00 p.m.	7	7
3:00 p.m. -- 4:00 p.m.	7	7
4:00 p.m. -- 5:00 p.m.	7	7
5:00 p.m. -- 6:00 p.m.	6	6
6:00 p.m. -- 7:00 p.m.	6	6
7:00 p.m. -- 8:00 p.m.	6	6
8:00 p.m. -- 9:00 p.m.	6	6
9:00 p.m. -- 10:00 p.m.	6	6
10:00 p.m. --10:30 p.m.	6	3
		88

The interview attempts by hour of the day are allocated on the basis of the relative weighted values.

Five eighty-eighths (5/88) of the interviews are allocated to each of the hours between 8:00 a.m. and 10:00 a.m., 6/88 to each of the hours between 10:00 a.m. and 2:00 p.m. and between 5:00 p.m.; and 10:00 p.m.; 7/88 to those between 2:00 p.m. and 5:00 p.m.; and 3/88 to the closing half hour.

For the first hour of the library day the expected number of interviews attempts is:

5I/88 where I = total number of interview attempts.

130

The actual number of interviews completed during the first hour is tabulated by T_1, and the number of times a nonbook reader was found is estimated to be:

5N/88 where N = total number of nonbook readers found.

Hence, the expected relative frequency of finding a carrel occupied by a reader is given by:

$$\text{PROB} = \frac{T_1 + \frac{5N}{88}}{5I/88} \qquad (1.1)$$

But in each interview attempt five carrels are checked for a reader. Thus, PROB can be interpreted to be the probability of finding at least one carrel occupied in five attempts.

We have then
$$\begin{aligned}\text{PROB} &= p \text{ (at least 1 of 5 carrels occupied)} \\ &= 1-p \text{ (all 5 carrels empty)}\end{aligned} \qquad (1.2)$$

The question is: What is the percent of carrel occupancy if PROB is the probability of finding at least one of five randomly chosen carrels occupied?

Let P_1 be the average percentage of occupancy during the first hour. Approximating this probability using the binomial theorem, and substituting into (1.2), we have: $\text{PROB} = 1- P_1^0 (1-P_1)^5$, or, (1.3) upon substituting (1.1) into (1.3) and simplifying

Solving (1.4) for P_1, we get:

$$P_1 = 1 - \sqrt[5]{1 - \frac{T_1 + \frac{5}{88}N}{\frac{5}{88}I}}$$

which is the simulated percentage of occupancy during the first library hour

The standard error of this estimate is given by: $\text{ERROR} = \sqrt{\dfrac{P_1(1 - P_1)}{\frac{5}{88}I}}$

Multiplying ERROR by 1.96 we get a 95 percent confidnece interval for P_1.

Similarly, the percent of carrel occupancy is simulated for the rest of the library hours.

For example, the simulated percent of occupancy for the seventh hour in the library day, i.e., between 2:00 p.m. and 3:00 p.m. is:

$$P_7 = 1 - \sqrt[5]{1 - \frac{T_7 + \frac{7}{88}N}{\frac{7}{88}I}}$$

the standard error,
$$\sqrt{\frac{P_7(1-P_7)}{\frac{7}{88}I}} \quad , \quad \text{and a 95}$$

percent confidence interval for P_7, 1.96 times the standard error.

Summary of Simulation Results

According to the simulation the highest percent of hourly carrel occupancy is between 8:00 p.m. and 9:00 p.m. with an average occupancy of 27 percent and a 95 percent confidence interval of 12.9 percent; the lowest percent of hourly carrel occupancy is between 8:00 a.m. and 9:00 a.m. with an average occupancy of 3.5 percent and a 95 percent confidence interval of 5.9 percent.

The highest percent of daily occupancy is Sunday with an average occupancy of 19.9 percent and a 95 percent confidence interval of 9.8 percent; the lowest percent of daily occupancy is Saturday with an average occupancy of 5.6 percent and a 95 percent confidence interval of 6.2 percent.

The overall average percent of occupancy is 12.2 percent with a 95 percent confidence interval of 3.1 percent.

Summary and Conclusions of Research Study

The research plan called for a sample size of 600 with the reading locations and reading times selected at random using random numbers tables. Two student organizations--Alpha Phi Omega fraternity and Phi Chi Theta fraternity--were used to conduct interviews and validate interviews, respectively. In the organizational context of the project, a problem can present itself in enlisting ccoperation of various subunits in the institutional organization. To overcome these obstacles, the interest and support of the chief executive officer are needed.

Moving on to the details of the sampling plan, 700 5-minute intervals were selected at random from the approximately 8,900 5-minute intervals when the library would be open during the period from September 11, 1969 to November 9. For each time thus selected, five carrel locations were selected at random. The interviewers were instructed to obtain the name of a book reader and bibliographical information about the book being read at a designated carrel which the interviewer would go to at the designated time. Validation procedure made use of a sample of 50 times selected at random from the original sample of 700 times.

Next, the data were coded drawing upon the interview results and a data bank maintained at the computer center.

The results of the statistical analysis can be summarized under the following seven headings:

1. General results

2. Reading of library and nonlibrary book by type of book

3. Characteristics of book readers

4. Matrix analysis

5. T Test analysis

6. Profile of the student reader

7. Use of library carrels by time of day and day of week

Out of the 661 actual interview attempts, only 64 resulted in an interview of a library book reader. About three times as many book readers were reading nonlibrary books as were reading library books. Fifty percent of the library books being read in the library are classified as Social Science books. The categories read least are Pure Science, Technology, and Geography and History running between 3 and 6 percent of library books being read in the library. Of the 174 textbooks (nonlibrary book category) being read at time of interview, 101 are Liberal Arts textbooks; 66, Business Administration textbooks; and 7, Education textbooks.

With respect to characteristics of readers, Business Administration majors read relatively more frequently than either Liberal Arts or Education majors. However, only Education majors read less than in proportion to their number in the undergraduate population.

The mean cumulative average of library readers is higher than that of the daytime undergraduate population.

Interestingly, commuting students read books more frequently than in proportion to their share of the student population, while fraternity and sorority students read less. Together Freshmen and Sophomores make up two-thirds of the book readers. However, Freshmen read less and Sophomores more than their proportionate share of the student population.

Men students read about twice as frequently as women, and men read more frequently than their proportionate share, while women do not read as much as their proportionate share.

The χ^2 test has been applied to the matrix analysis. The rejection of the null hypotheses by the χ^2 test permitted the following relationships to be identified:

relationship between reading library book or not

and whether one is a student or nonstudent reader

relationship between Major Field of Study of the

reader and the Sex of the reader

relationship between residence of a reader and these

characteristics of a reader: Sex; Time of Week;

Time of Day; Class Year.

No other relationships exist.

When individual cells were tested using the T test, relationships were
found that were not revealed by the χ^2 test. The detail of the interrelationships is shown in the body of this report. The richness of the detail is
illustrated in the statement below on the relationship between whether a
reader is reading a library book or nonlibrary book and the cumulative
average of the student reader:

Students who have the highest cumulative averages

read nonlibrary books with greater relative frequency

than do those who have middle and lowest cumulative

averages.

However, the students who have the highest cumulative

averages read library books relatively less frequently.

Students who have middle cumulative averages read

library books more frequently than nonlibrary books.

The reverse holds for the students who have the

highest cumulative averages. For the lowest students,

there is no significant difference.

The student profile of readers at the library shows that men and women student readers are alike in their place of residence, preference of non-library books, and disdain for Saturday reading. They differ in their Class Year, cumulative average, Major Field, Time of Day, and choice of library book.

The simulation of carrel utilization displayed a pattern of high use of 27 percent between 8:00 p.m. and 9:00 p.m., low use of 3.5 percent between 8:00 a.m. and 9:00 a.m. Sunday is the day of greatest use at a rate of 17.5 percent average occupancy, while Saturday is lowest at 5.6 percent.

The following conclusions can be derived from the study:

The project demonstrated the feasibility of sampling book readership inside a library.

The project demonstrated the feasibility of using students as interviewers in data collection.

The project demonstrated the feasibility of analyzing the collected data, with the use of an IBM 1130 computer.

Finally, the project demonstrated the feasibility of deriving valid statistical inferences about book readership. The statistical inferences can serve as premises or assumptions in library planning in such matters as library location and construction, book acquisitions, budgeting, staffing, library hours of operation, and so forth.

PART III

RATIONALE OF COMPUTER METHODS

Introduction to Part III

Part III of <u>Library Operations Research</u> explains the computer methods used in the Rider research. The underlying logic of the methods is described. The logic is outlined at a level of generalization that makes it applicable to any type of computer, whatever the requisite computer language. The specific computer programs of the Rider research, written in FORTRAN IV language, are included in Appendix I.

The computer methods of Part III are four in number. They are:

Explanation of Program for Print-Out of Data, Internal Validation of Data and Random Check

Descriptive Statistics and Simulation

Testing a Matrix of Sample Results for Independence Between Row Elements and Column Elements (Chi-Square test)

Testing Pairs of Matrix Elements for Significant Differences Using the Student-t test

The first of the four explanations listed above consists of the explanation of the types of checks for errors, the pertinent flow chart used, and a portion of the print-out.

The second explanation provides a description of the counts on interviews attempted and interviews completed. It also outlines the measurement of relative frequency of reading by selected categories. The simulation of library use is explained. The flow chart is included, along with the print-out of descriptive statistics and simulation.

The third explanation explains and illustrates testing for independence between row elements and column elements. This method enables one to answer a question of this type: Does a relationship exist between the day a person is reading and his sex? The Chi-Square test is explained, the flow chart is presented, and the print-out of results is given.

The fourth method explained can overcome limitations of the Chi-Square test. This last method tests pairs of matrix elements for significant differences, using the Student-t test. An extended illustration is given in the explanation.

Chapter 6

Explanation of Program for
Print-Out of Data, Internal Validation
of Data and Random Check

This program identifies transcription errors and duplication errors. Also, it determines whether data have internal consistency.

The program gives a print-out of the coded data under appropriate headings. A number of cards are chosen randomly. They are cross-checked against the original interview forms to verify proper transcription. The number of cards selected in the random check is printed-out. A probability statement is made in reference to the certainty that the maximal percent of transcription errors is 5 percent overall if the random check is error-free.

The cards are compared to see if there are duplicate cards. When a duplicate is found it is identified by line number. A notation is recorded for each card that contains uncertain information or interviewing errors. For example, Evening School students with no matriculation code are flagged. Also, cards are identified which indicate an interview took place when in fact the interview validator found that no interview did occur.

In determining whether the data possess internal consistency, the following tests are applied:

1. Do code numbers in each category assume valid values? If not, an error message is prepared which indicates an invalid code and prints-out immediately below the print-out of the data from the card.

2. If no interview took place according to the entry in the Interview Column, then all columns should be zero, except for the Interview Attempt Column. If this pattern does not exist, an error message indicates the inconsistency.

3. Does a matriculated student have a cumulative average recorded? If not, an error
   message prints that the "cumulative average is missing." (Note: A qualfication
   needs to be added. In some cases the lack
   of a cumulative average is not an error;
   for example, first semester Freshmen do
   not have a cumulative average.)

4. Inconsistencies among column entries are
   noted. For example, if an interview took
   place, then non-zero entries must appear
   in the Sex, Day and Time Columns. If such
   entries are not recorded, inconsistencies
   occur. If the interviewee is recorded as
   reading a library book, then a non-zero
   entry should appear in the Kind of Library
   Book Column. If an interviewee is a Rider
   student then non-zero entries should appear
   in the Major and Year Columns. Any inconsistencies in relation to such entries are
   noted and printed-out below the data print-
   out.

Finally, the program gives a print-out of the number of cards read and

the number of errors detected. A portion of the print-out follows the flow

chart which is presented on the following pages.

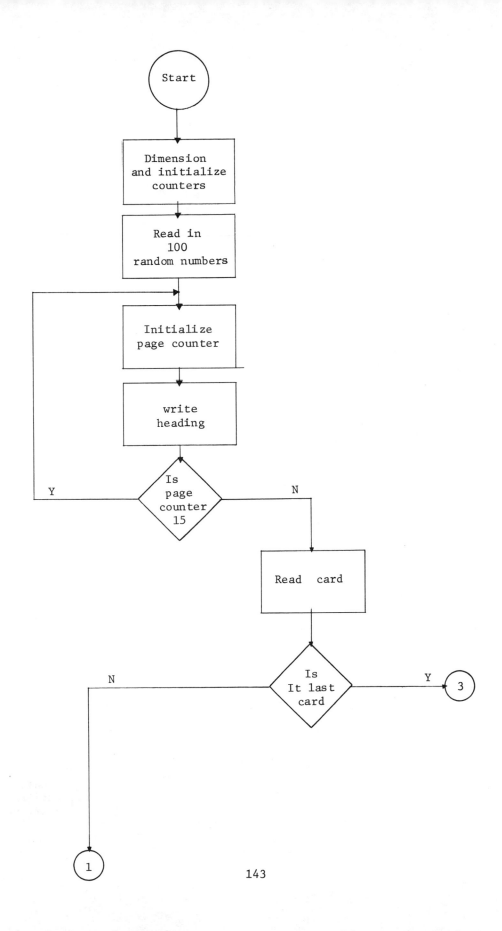

143

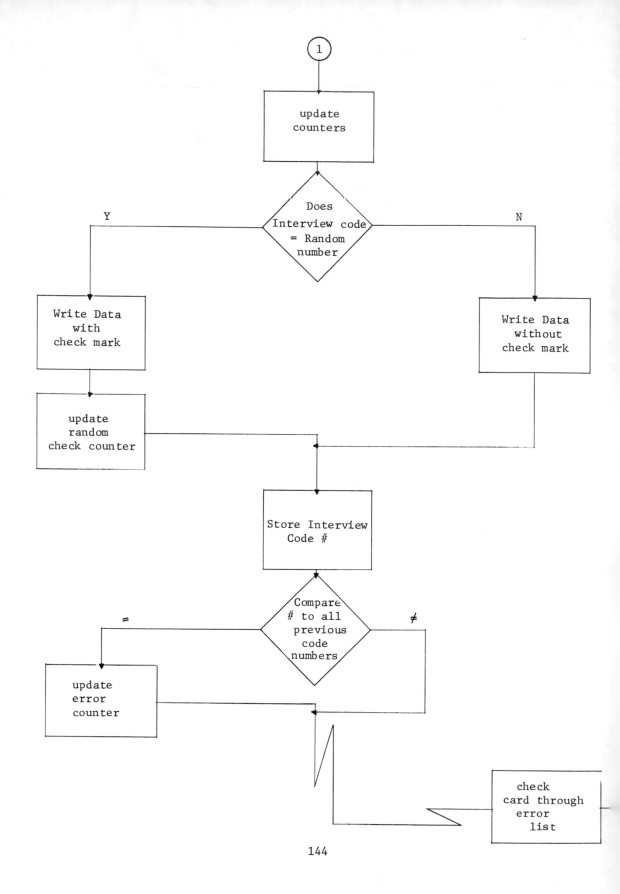

144

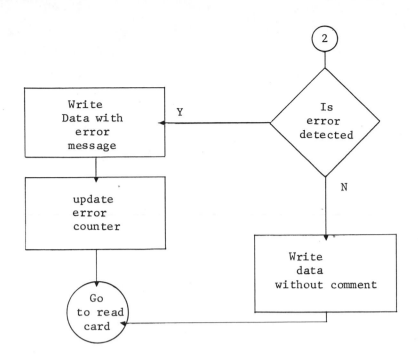

Write
Data with
error
message

Y

Is
error
detected

N

update
error
counter

Write
data
without comment

Go
to read
card

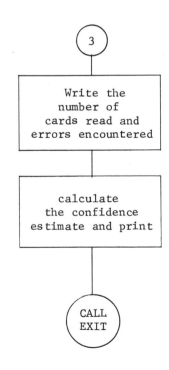

3

Write the
number of
cards read and
errors encountered

calculate
the confidence
estimate and print

CALL
EXIT

note: first page of print-out

LINE NO.	INTW. TRY	INTW.	SEX	DAY	TIME	LBRY BK. OR NOT	RIDER STDNT	KIND OF LIB.BK.	CLASS YEAR	MAJOR	RES.	CUM. AVG.
1	1	0	0	0	0	0	0	0	0	0	0	0.00
2	2	0	0	0	0	0	0	0	0	0	0	0.00
3	3	0	0	0	0	0	0	0	0	0	0	0.00
4	4	0	0	0	0	0	0	0	0	0	0	0.00
5	6	0	0	0	0	0	0	0	0	0	0	0.00
6	7	1	0	0	0	0	0	0	0	0	0	0.00
7	8	2	1	4	8	0	1	0	2	1	1	2.30
8	9	0	0	0	0	0	0	0	0	0	0	0.00
9	10	2	1	4	8	0	1	0	1	3	1	0.00
10	11	0	0	0	0	0	0	0	0	0	0	0.00
11	12	0	0	0	0	0	0	0	0	0	0	0.00
12	13	2	2	4	13	0	1	0	1	1	1	0.00
13	14	0	0	0	0	0	0	0	0	0	0	0.00
14	15	2	2	4	14	0	1	0	2	1	1	2.25
15	16	2	2	4	14	0	1	0	1	1	1	0.00

CHE

146

LINE NO.	INTW. TRY	INTW.	SEX	DAY	TIME	LBRY BK. OR NOT	RIDER STDNT	KIND OF LIB.BK.	CLASS YEAR	MAJOR	RES.	CUM. AVG.	
301	320	2	1	2	8	0	1	0	1	3	1	0.00	
302	321	0	0	0	0	0	0	0	0	0	0	0.00	
303	322	2	1	2	11	1	1	1	1	3	2	2.24	
304	323	2	2	2	12	0	1	0	2	1	1	0.00	

CUM. AVERAGE MISSING.

LINE NO.	INTW. TRY	INTW.	SEX	DAY	TIME	LBRY BK. OR NOT	RIDER STDNT	KIND OF LIB.BK.	CLASS YEAR	MAJOR	RES.	CUM. AVG.	
305	324	2	1	2	13	0	1	0	1	3	1	0.00	
306	325	2	1	2	14	0	1	0	4	1	2	2.01	
307	326	2	1	2	14	0	1	0	2	3	3	2.35	
308	327	0	0	0	0	0	0	0	0	0	0	0.00	
309	328	0	0	0	0	0	0	0	0	0	0	0.00	CHECK
310	329	2	1	3	5	0	1	0	3	1	2	2.67	
311	330	2	1	3	6	0	1	0	3	3	1	2.70	CHECK
312	331	0	0	0	0	0	0	0	0	0	0	0.00	
313	332	0	0	0	0	0	0	0	0	0	0	0.00	
314	333	2	1	3	7	0	1	0	2	3	1	1.78	CHECK
315	334	2	1	3	9	1	1	5	2	3	1	2.42	

note: last page of print-out

LINE NO.	INTW. TRY	INTW.	SEX	DAY	TIME	LBRY BK. OR NOT	RIDER STDNT	KIND OF LIB.BK.	CLASS YEAR	MAJOR	RES.	CUM. AVG.	
661	677	0	0	0	0	0	0	0	0	0	0	0.00	CHECK

INTERNAL VALIDATION OF THE 661 DATA CARDS COMPLETED.

25ERRORS HAVE BEEN FOUND,AND SO INDICATED.

62 OF THE 661 DATA CARDS HAVE BEEN RANDOMLY CHOSEN FOR CODING ERROR CHECKS.

IF THE RANDOMLY SAMPLED CARDS ARE OK,THEN IT IS   96.79300 PERCENT CERTAIN

THAT AT MOST 5 PERCENT OF THE CARDS HAVE ERRORS.

Chapter 7

Descriptive Statistics and Simulation

Data cards are read, tabulated and analyzed to yield two sets of output:

1. descriptive statistics
2. simulation of library use.

The descriptive statistics include:

1. Counts on interviews attempted and interviews completed. Interviews completed are decomposed into non-book readers, library book readers and other book readers.
2. Relative frequency of reading
   (1) library books
   (2) types of library books
   (3) other than library books.
3. Relative frequency of reading by
   (1) time of day
   (2) day of the week
   (3) class year
   (4) residence
   (5) major field
   (6) male readers
   (7) cumulative average.

Along with relative frequencies, standard errors and 95 percent confidence intervals are given for all categories except reading by time of day and day of the week.

4. Average reader by
   (1) cumulative average
   (2) class year
   (3) sex.

These statistics too include standard errors and 95 percent confidence intervals.

The simulation of library use is an hour by hour, day by day simulation of in-library reading.

Below are presented the flow chart for descriptive statistics and the print-out of both the descriptive statistics and the simulation.

FLOW CHART

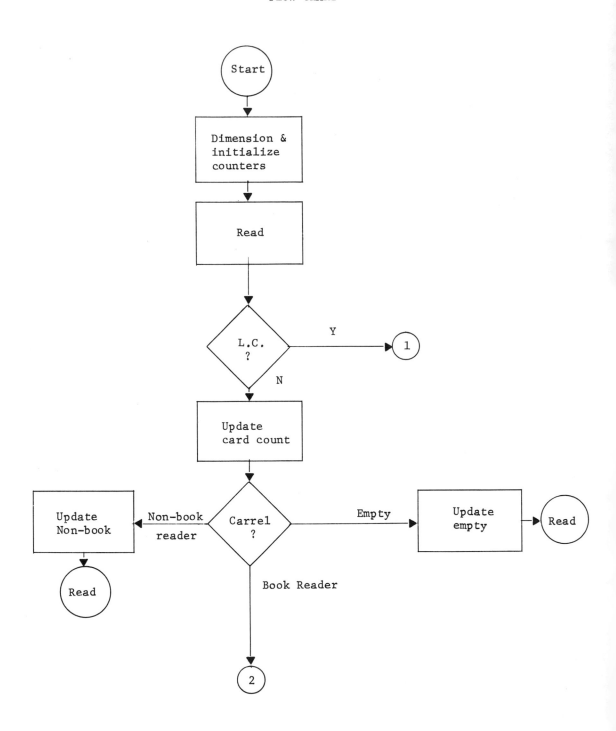

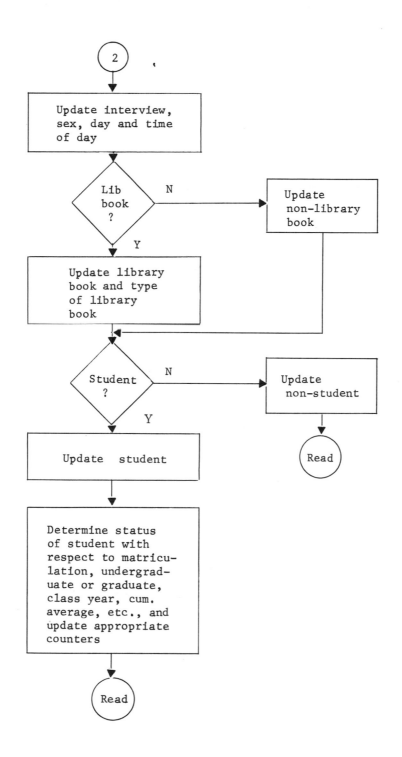

151

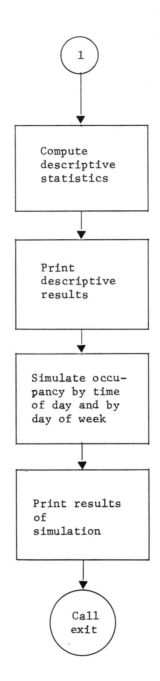

1

Compute
descriptive
statistics

Print
descriptive
results

Simulate occu-
pancy by time
of day and by
day of week

Print results
of
simulation

Call
exit

DESCRIPTIVE STATISTICS

Counts

Interview Attempts	661
Interviews Completed	268
Non-book Readers	41
Library Book Readers	64
Other Book Readers	204

Note: Non-book readers are not included in interviews completed.
They were not interviewed.

Library Book Reading

Library book codes as follows

1 - Social Science
2 - Pure Science
3 - Tech. or Applied Sci.
4 - Literature
5 - Geog. or Hist.
6 - Other

Code	Relative Frequency of Use	Standard Error	95 Percent Confidence Interval (Plus-minus)
1	0.500	0.062	0.123
2	0.031	0.021	0.043
3	0.062	0.030	0.059
4	0.171	0.047	0.093
5	0.062	0.030	0.059
6	0.171	0.047	0.093

Reading by Day of the Week

Day of the week codes as follows

Monday - 1, Tuesday -2, etc.

Day in Week	Rel. Frequency Reader Found
1	0.186
2	0.167
3	0.156
4	0.171
5	0.134
6	0.037
7	0.145

Note: There are actual relative frequencies not simulated ones.

Reading by Time of Day

Time of day codes as follows

1 - 8:00 A.M. to 8:59 A.M.
2 - 9:00 A.M. to 9:59 A.M.
etc.

Time of Day	Rel. Frequency of Readers
1	0.014
2	0.037
3	0.063
4	0.055
5	0.063
6	0.070
7	0.078
8	0.115
9	0.044
10	0.048
11	0.063
12	0.108
13	0.123
14	0.093
15	0.018

Note: These relative frequencies are actual ones not simulated ones

Readers by Class Year

Class year codes as follows

1 - Freshman
2 - Sophomore
3 - Junior
4 - Senior
5 - Graduate
6 - Other

Code	Relative Frequency of Use	Standard Error	95 Percent Confidence Interval (Plus-minus)
1	0.311	0.029	0.056
2	0.354	0.030	0.058
3	0.173	0.023	0.046
4	0.145	0.022	0.043
5	0.000	0.000	0.000
6	0.015	0.007	0.015

Readers by Cumulative Average

Cum. Average	Relative Frequency	Standard Error	95 Percent Confidence Interval
0.00 to 0.49	0.000	0.000	0.000
0.50 to 0.99	0.000	0.000	0.000
1.00 to 1.49	0.000	0.000	0.000
1.50 to 1.99	0.073	0.021	0.041
2.00 to 2.49	0.446	0.040	0.079
2.50 to 2.99	0.340	0.038	0.075
3.00 to 3.49	0.100	0.024	0.048
3.50 to 3.99	0.040	0.015	0.031

Other Results Codes As Follows

1 - Readers who are rider students
2 - Sample carrels unoccupied
3 - Male readers
4 - Reading that is library books
5 - Reading that is other than books

Code	Relative Frequency of Use	Standard Error	95 Percent Confidence Interval (Plus-minus)
1	0.947	0.013	0.026
2	0.532	0.019	0.038
3	0.652	0.029	0.056
4	0.207	0.023	0.045
5	0.132	0.019	0.037

Readers by Residence

Percent of Rider Readers by Residence

Place of Residence Codes as follows

1 - Dormitory
2 - Commuter
3 - Sorority or Fraternity

Code	Relative Frequency of Use	Standard Error	95 Percent Confidence Interval (Plus-minus)
1	0.555	0.031	0.061
2	0.338	0.029	0.058
3	0.106	0.019	0.037

Readers by Major Field

Percent of Rider Readers by Major

Major Field Codes as Follows

1 - Liberal Arts
2 - Education
3 - Buoincoo
4 - Education Master
5 - Business Master

Code	Relative Frequency of Use	Standard Error	95 Percent Confidence Interval (Plus-minus)
1	0.300	0.028	0.056
2	0.204	0.025	0.049
3	0.496	0.031	0.061
4	0.000	0.000	0.000
5	0.000	0.000	0.000

Average Reader

The following Statistics Relate to Cumulative Average and Class Year.

	Sample Mean	Standard Deviation	Standard	95 Percent Confidence

Average Reader

The following Statistics Relate to Cumulative Average and Class Year.

	Sample Mean	Standard Deviation	Standard Error of Sample Mean	95 Percent Confidence Interval of Sample Mean
Cum. Avg.	2.51	0.43	0.03	0.07
Class Year	2.15	1.03	0.06	0.12
Cum.Avg.Male	2.48	0.42	0.04	0.08
Cum.Avg. Female	2.55	0.47	0.06	0.12
Class Year Male	2.29	1.05	0.08	0.16
Class Year Female	1.89	0.92	0.09	0.19

Simulation of Carrel Occupancy by Time of Day

Time of Day	Percent of Occupancy	Standard Error	95 Percent Confidence Interval
1	0.036	0.030	0.059
2	0.076	0.043	0.085
3	0.109	0.046	0.091
4	0.095	0.043	0.085
5	0.109	0.046	0.091
6	0.123	0.049	0.096
7	0.116	0.044	0.086
8	0.190	0.054	0.106
9	0.066	0.034	0.067
10	0.082	0.041	0.080
11	0.109	0.046	0.091
12	0.216	0.061	0.120
13	0.271	0.066	0.129
14	0.174	0.056	0.110
15	0.064	0.051	0.101

Simulation of Carrel Occupancy by Day of the Week

Day of Week	Percent of Occupancy	Standard Error	95 Percent Confidence Interval
1	0.136	0.032	0.064
2	0.120	0.031	0.061
3	0.111	0.030	0.059
4	0.124	0.031	0.061
5	0.094	0.028	0.055
6	0.056	0.031	0.062
7	0.200	0.050	0.098

Average Percentage of Occupancy 0.122
Standard Deviation of Occupancy 0.061
95 Percent Confidence Interval for Occupancy 0.031

Chapter 8

Testing a Matrix of Sample
Results for Independence Between
Row Elements and Column Elements

Characteristics of Readers

Certain characteristics of the sampled readers are examined to see
whether the results indicate a relationship between these characteristics
in the population of all library readers at the library studied. Illustrative
of the kinds of questions to be answered are: Do the sample results indicate
a relationship between the day a person reads in the library and his sex?
between the day a person reads in the library and his major field? between
the day a person reads in the library and his residence status? Does a
student's grade point average influence his reading? Is there a relationship
between a reader's major and his class year?

Matrix Representation

These questions are the same essentially. That is, in each case the
aim of the question is to determine whether or not a relationship exists
between paired characteristics of the reader. A matrix is a convenient
device for arraying paired characteristics. An m by n matrix is a rectangular
array of elements in m rows and n columns and is a convenient device for
arraying paired characteristics of a reader. An example of a matrix is
discussed below.

The example is based on the fact that in the sampling of in-library
book reading we found 250 matriculated students reading a book. Grouping
into a matrix by major and by sex the indicated distribution of frequencies
was obtained.

158

	Liberal Arts	Education	Business	
Male	34	15	114	163
Female	41	36	10	87
	75	51	124	250

The entries are called cell frequencies and, for convenience, are represented by a subscripted variable a_{ij}, where a denotes the actual sample frequencies. The first subscript i indicates the cell row and the second subscript j, the cell column.

Thus

	Liberal Arts	Education	Business	
Male	$a_{11} = 34$	$a_{12} = 15$	$a_{13} = 114$	163
Female	$a_{21} = 41$	$a_{22} = 36$	$a_{23} = 10$	87
	75	51	124	250

Once the data have been arrayed in matrix form, statistical testing can be carried out. Basic to such testing is the concept of the null hypotheses.

Null Hypotheses (H_o)

The null hypotheses (H_o) is a statement that in the population a certain type of relationship holds. In connection with the illustration at hand, the null hypotheses (H_o) is: the major field of study of a reader is independent of the reader's sex. H_o also could be stated, thusly: there is no relationship between the major field of a reader and the reader's sex. This hypothesis will then be tested, on the basis of sample results, and either accepted or rejected at some stated level of significance.

159

The level of significance is the probability of rejecting H_0 when in fact H_0 is true. A 5% level of significance, for example, means that in rejecting H_0 we run a 5% risk of being wrong.

In testing H_0, we must construct an expected matrix. In order to obtain the expected matrix in the first place, we assume H_0 is true.

Expected Matrix Assuming H_0 Is True

If it is true that the major field of study of a reader is independent of his sex, then in a sample of 250 readers the likely number of female Education majors would be 250 times the product of the probabilities that a reader is a female and is an Education major. Using the relative frequencies from the sample to approximate these probabilities we get:

$$\text{Expected number of readers who are female Education Majors} = 250 \frac{(87)}{(250)} \frac{(51)}{(250)}$$

$$= 17.74$$

Denoting the expected number of readers who are female Education majors by e_{22}, we can write

$$e_{22} = n \frac{R_2}{n} \frac{C_2}{n} \quad \text{or} \quad \frac{R_2 C_2}{n}, \text{ where}$$

n = sample size

R_2 = total frequencies in row 2

C_2 = total frequencies in column 2

The expected number of readers who are male Business majors (e_{13}) is:

$$e_{13} = \frac{R_1 C_3}{n} = \frac{(163) (124)}{250} = 80.84$$

Continuing in this way we calculate the expected cell frequencies for all cells and array them in an expected matrix as follows:

160

Expected Matrix If H_o Is True

	Liberal Arts	Education	Business
Male	48.90	33.25	80.84
Female	26.10	17.74	43.15

Or symbolically

	Liberal Arts	Education	Business
Male	$e_{11} = 48.90$	$e_{12} = 33.25$	$e_{13} = 80.84$
Female	$e_{21} = 26.10$	$e_{22} = 17.74$	$e_{23} = 43.15$

Chi-Square (χ^2) Statistic

Next, we compare the differences between the actual cell frequencies and the expected cell frequencies. If the magnitude of these differences is such that they cannot be explained by random sampling variation, we reject H_o. In order to determine what kind of differences are acceptable, and what are not, we need a measure and a standard to which the measure can be compared. The measure we use is the χ^2 statistic and the standard is the Chi-Square distribution.

The χ^2 statistic is computed as follows: in each cell subtract the expected frequencies from the actual ones, square the difference, divide by the expected frequencies, and sum the overall cells.

For the Major by Sex Matrix the χ^2 statistic is

$$\chi^2 = \frac{(34 - 48.90)^2}{48.90} + \frac{(15 - 33.25)^2}{33.25} + \frac{(114 - 80.84)^2}{80.84}$$
$$+ \frac{(41 - 26.10)^2}{26.10} + \frac{(36 - 17.74)^2}{17.74} + \frac{(10 - 43.15)^2}{43.15}$$

$$= 80.89$$

161

Chi-Square Distribution

The Chi-Square distribution is the theoretical sampling distribution of the χ^2 statistic. It is a family of curves dependent solely upon the number of independent observations in the sample array, called degrees of freedom, or d.f. for short.

When sample results are arrayed in a matrix of m rows by n columns the degrees of freedom are the product of one less than the number of rows (m - 1) times one less than the number of columns (n - 1).

The Chi-Square distribution is tabulated for various degrees of freedom and for various levels of significance. The tabulated values are the maximum values of the χ^2 statistic to be expected when in fact H_o is true. These expected maximum values are called the critical values of the χ^2 test. Here, a most important qualification must be added. The Chi-Square distribution of critical values is based on the assumption that each cell of the matrix has at least 5 frequencies. If the assumption is not met the Chi-Square distribution is not applicable without regrouping the sample results.

Chi-Square (χ^2) Test

In testing a matrix for independence at the 5% level of significance, we accept H_o if the χ^2 statistic is $\leq$ critical value of the test, and reject H_o if $\chi^2 >$ critical value. The rationale of the test is that if H_o is true, 95% of the time the sample statistic χ^2 will fall below the critical value of the test and only 5% of the time would it fall above.

For the Major by Sex Matrix

$$\chi^2 = 80.89$$

$$d.f. = (2)\ (1) = 2$$

At the 5% level of significance for 2 degrees of freedom the critical value of the test is 5.99.

Since 80.89 > 5.99, we reject the hypothesis that there is no relationship between the major field and the sex of the reader, and assert that one is dependent on the other. In making this assertion we run a 5% risk of being wrong.

<u>Summary</u>

The following is a summary of the Chi-Square testing procedure. The procedure for testing a matrix of sample results for independence between rows and columns can be summarized as follows:

1. Write the matrix of actual sample results.

2. State the null hypotheses H_o; namely independence between rows and columns.

3. State the level of significance of the test. (In our tests the 5% level is used.)

4. Check the cells for at least 5 frequencies. If the matrix fails to meet the requirement, the χ^2 test cannot be run without regrouping.

5. If the minimal cell count requirement is met, compute the expected frequencies under the assumption that H_o is true. The expected frequencies of the cell in the ith row and jth column (e_{ij}) is given by

$$e_{ij} = \frac{C_j\ R_i}{n}$$

where C_j = total frequencies of jth column

R_i = total frequencies of ith row

n = sample size.

163

6. Write the expected matrix.

7. Compute the χ^2 statistic.

$$\chi^2 = \frac{(a_{ij} - e_{ij})^2}{e_{ij}}$$

8. Calculate the degrees of freedom of the sample.

   d.f. = (m - 1)(n - 1), where

   m = number of rows in the matrix
   n = number of columns in the matrix

9. Compare the χ^2 statistic to the critical value of the test as given by the Chi-Square distribution at the 5% level of significance in the appropriate degrees of freedom.

10. If $\chi^2 \leq$ critical value, accept H_o, otherwise reject it.

Need for Computer

Characteristics of the readers are classified by column and by row. There are four major groups of matrices. They are: Major Field of Study Group; Day of Week Group; Kind of Library Book Group; and Residence of Reader Group. Each group is identified by its column description. For example, the Major Field Group consists of five matrices. They are: (1) Major Field by Sex Matrix; (2) Major Field by Library Book or Not Matrix; (3) Major Field by Residence Matrix; (4) Major Field by Class Year Matrix; and (5) Major Field by Cumulative Average Matrix. For each one of these five matrices, the Major Field is the column heading; the other five characteristics, as listed immediately above, are the respective row titles. The format of each of the five matrices can be depicted, thusly:

MAJOR FIELD

	Business	Education	Liberal Arts
Male			
Female			

164

MAJOR FIELD

	Business	Education	Liberal Arts
Library Book or Not — Yes			
No			

MAJOR FIELD

	Business	Education	Liberal Arts
Commuter			
Residence — Dormitory			
Fraternity or Sorority			

MAJOR FIELD

	Business	Education	Liberal Arts
Freshman			
Sophomore			
Class Year — Junior			
Senior			

MAJOR FIELD

	Business	Education	Liberal Arts
Cumulative Average — 0 to 2.49			
2.50 to 4.00			

Similar treatment has been given to the other three groups of matrices. The complete list of matrices used is presented below, by groups:

Major Field Group

>Sex
>Library Book or Not
>Residence
>Class Year
>Cumulative Average

Day of Week of Reading Group

>Sex
>Library Book or Not
>Rider Student or Not
>Residence
>Class Year
>Major Field
>Cumulative Average
>Time of Day

Kind of Library Book

>Sex
>Rider Student or Not
>Residence
>Class Year
>Major Field
>Cumulative Average
>Time of Day

Residence Status of Reader Group

>Sex
>Library Book or Not
>Time of reading, i.e., Weekday or Weekend
>Class Year
>Major Field
>Cumulative Average
>Time of Day

Each matrix is tested for independence between column and row characteristics at the 5% level of significance using Chi-Square. A very large number of calculations is required here. These calculations are repetitive and ideally suited for a computer.

166

General Description of Program

Four computer programs were written, one for each matrix group. There is a program for the Major Field Group, a program for the Day of Week of Reading Group, a program for Kind of Library Book Group, and a program for the Residence Status of Reader Group. Each program groups the readers into the above listed matrices. Next, the matrices are printed, one at a time, and tested by means of the Chi-Square test subprogram. Just one subprogram handles the testing for all groups.

The subprogram comprises the following routine:

1. Check on matrices for proper tabulation; that is, a check is made to determine if the grand total of rows is equal to the grand total of columns.

2. Each cell of a matrix is tested for 5 or more frequencies. If a matrix cell contains less than 5 frequencies, a message is printed that the Chi-Square test can be run only if there is regrouping.

3. Assuming the null hypotheses to be true the expected matrix is computed according to the assumption.

4. The sample size is printed.

5. The χ^2 statistic is computed and the degrees of freedom calculated.

6. The χ^2 statistic is compared to the critical value of the Chi-Square distribution at the 5% level for the specified degrees of freedom. The results are printed.

Computer Logic for Chi-Square Testing of Major Field of Study Matrix Group

In this section there are (1) the program symbols, (2) the flow chart, and (3) the computer print-out of the results for the Chi-Square testing of the Major Field Group of matrices.

Program Symbols:

Major by several characteristics of the reader matrices.

ASMX (6,7) =   Major by sex.

167

ALMX (6,7) = Major by library or nonlibrary book.

,ARMX (6,7) = Major by residence of student reader.

ARMX (6,7) = Major by class year of the student reader.

EMX (6,7) = Matrix for calculating expected cell frequencies.

TROW (6) = Counter for calculating row totals of matrices.

TCOL (7) = Counter for calculating column totals of matrices.

P (7) = Counter for calculating the ratio of the frequencies in each column of the matrix to the total frequencies.

CHI (30) = Critical values of Chi-Square distribution at the 5% level for degrees of freedom from 1 to 30 inclusive.

AMX (6,7) = Dummy matrix. Each of the major group matrices are transformed to the AMX matrix preparatory to going through the χ^2 subcounters.

NOTE: All matrices are dimensioned 6 by 7, the size of the largest matrices. The matrices AYMX, AAMX and ATMX were not used. Nor were the counters INTW, RIDER, MATR and RECC.

FLOW CHART

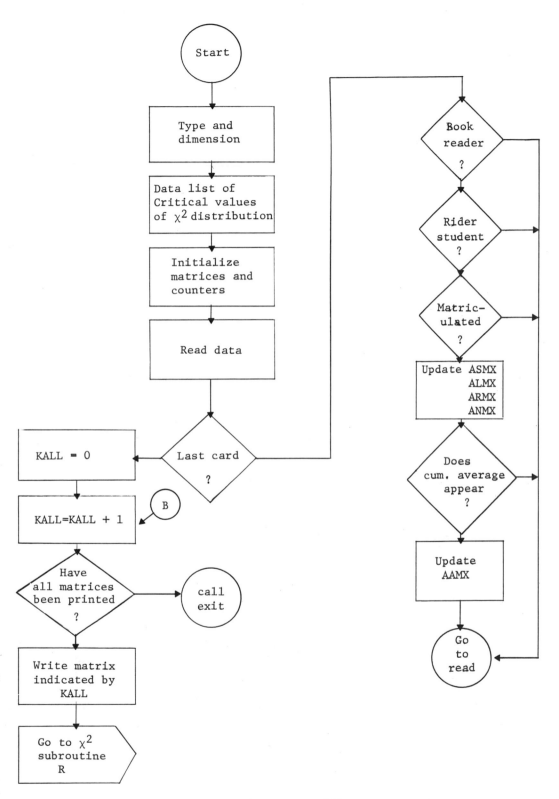

χ^2 Sub-Routine R

R

Cell frequencies > 5 ? —— N —— Write No test possible —— B

Y

Matrix tabulation OK —— N —— Write Error message —— B

Y

Calculate expected cell frequencies

Write expected Matrix and sample size

Calculate d.f. and write d.f. and critical value of test

Write Null Hypotheses

Compute χ^2 statistic

Write χ^2 statistic

Write: accept Null —— Y —— is $\chi^2 <$ critical value —— N —— Write: reject Null

B

MAJOR BY SEX OF READER MATRIX

	Liberal Arts	Education	Business
Male	34.00	15.00	114.00
Female	41.00	36.00	10.00

Null Hypothesis

There is no relationship between the Major Field and the sex of the library reader.

Expected Matrix if Null Hyp. True

	Liberal Arts	Education	Business
Male	48.90	33.25	80.84
Female	26.10	17.74	43.15

Sample size is 250.

Test hypothesis using Chi-Square at a 5 percent level of significance. The number of degrees of freedom is 2, and the critical value for the test is 5.99

Chi-Square value = 80.89

Significant difference at 5 percent level between actual results and expected results. Reject the Null Hypothesis.

MAJOR BY KIND OF BOOK MATRIX

	Liberal Arts	Education	Business
Non-library	61.00	35.00	99.00
Library	14.00	16.00	25.00

Null Hypothesis

There is no relationship between the Major Field and
the kind of books read in the library, that is library
book or non-library book.

Expected Matrix if Null Hyp. True

	Liberal Arts	Education	Business
Non-library	58.50	39.78	96.72
Library	16.50	11.22	27.28

Sample size is 250.

Test hypothesis using Chi-Square at a 5 percent level of significance.
The number of degrees of freedom is 2, and the critical value for the
test is 5.99

Chi-Square value = 3.34

No significant difference at 5 percent level between actual
results and expected results. Accept the Null Hypotheses.

MAJOR BY RESIDENCE OF STUDENT MATRIX

	Liberal Arts	Education	Business
Dormitory	52.00	29.00	60.00
Commuter	22.00	13.00	47.00
Frat or Sor	1.00	9.00	17.00

Null Hypothesis
There is no relationship between the Major Field and
the residence of the student.

No Chi-Square test possible without regrouping.

MAJOR BY CLASS YEAR OF STUDENT MATRIX

	Liberal Arts	Education	Business
Freshman	28.00	20.00	31.00
Sophomore	28.00	15.00	47.00
Junior	9.00	9.00	26.00
Senior	10.00	7.00	20.00

Null Hypothesis
There is no relationship between the Major Field and
the class year of the reader.

Expected Matrix if Null Hyp. True

	Liberal Arts	Education	Business
Freshman	23.70	16.11	39.18
Sophomore	27.00	18.36	44.64
Junior	13.20	8.97	21.82
Senior	11.10	7.54	18.35

Sample size is 250.

Test hypothesis using Chi-Square at a 5 percent level of significance.
The number of degrees of freedom is 6, and the critical value for the
test is 12.59

Chi-Square value = 6.63

No significant difference at 5 percent level between actual
results and expected results. Accept the Null Hypotheses.

MAJOR BY CUM. AVG. OF RIDER READER MATRIX

	Liberal Arts	Education	Business
0 to 1.59	2.00	2.00	7.00
2 to 2.59	35.00	21.00	60.00
3 to 4.00	5.00	6.00	10.00

No Chi-Square test possible without regrouping.

Chapter 9

Testing Pairs of Matrix Elements
For Significant Differences
Using Student-t Test

Introduction

When a matrix is tested for independence between column and row entries by the Chi-Square (χ^2) test the differences between expected and observed results are pooled and compared to some standard critical value. What matters are the overall differences. Significant differences between pairs of cells are not detected by the χ^2 test. For this, a more precise test is needed. The Student-t statistic provides the means for testing pairs of cells for significant differences.

Testing Procedure

The four major groups of matrices that were earlier tested for independence by χ^2 are now analyzed by the computer, cell by cell, to see where significant differences exist. The Major Field of Study matrix will be used to illustrate the analysis. Readers are grouped into these matrices:

      (1) major field by sex
      (2) major field by library book or not
      (3) major field by residence
      (4) major field by class year
      (5) major field by cumulative average
          (for those who have a cumulative average)
      (6) major field by day of week
      (7) major field by time of day.

The Chi-Square tests of the last two matrices were not included in the print-out of χ^2 results because the tests could not be run without regrouping. In each matrix the data are analyzed first by row, then by column.

Analysis By Row

In each matrix transform the row entries to relative frequencies using the row totals as bases; that is, every row adds up to 1. The entries in a row are fractional parts of 1. To illustrate, take the Major Field by Residence matrix:

Major Field

		Liberal Arts	Education	Business	Totals
	Dormitory	52	29	60	141
Residence	Commuter	22	13	47	82
	Fraternity or Sorority	1	9	17	27
	Totals	75	51	124	250

Transforming this numerical matrix to a matrix by percentages with respect to rows we get:

Major Field

	Liberal Arts	Education	Business	Totals
Dormitory	0.368	0.205	0.425	1
Commuter	0.268	0.158	0.573	1
Fraternity or Sorority	0.037	0.333	0.629	1

Note: the row totals differ slightly from 1 because of rounding.

By writing the matrix in this form we can treat any combination of two cell proportions in a given column as though they were sample proportions from two populations. These sample proportions can be tested then for significant differences using the Student-t Test.

In each column, compute the Student-t statistic for the differences between two proportions, for every combination of proportions, two at a time. That is, in each column row 1 is compared to row 2, row 1 is compared to row 3 and row 2 is compared to row 3. The Student-t statistic for the difference between two sample proportions is

$$t = \frac{p_2' - p_2'}{\sigma p_2' - p_2'}$$

where p_1' and p_2' are the two sample proportions and where $\sigma p_1' - p_2'$ is the standard error of the difference between these two sample proportions.

$$\sigma p_1 - p_2 = \sqrt{P(1-P)\left(\frac{1}{n_1} + \frac{1}{n_2}\right)} \quad \text{where } P = \frac{n_1 p_1' + n_2 p_2'}{n_1 + n_2} \quad \text{and}$$

are the sample sizes on which the sample proportions p_1' and p_2' are based.

To illustrate the computation of the Student-t statistic for the difference between these sample proportions, take the entries in row 1 and row 2 in column 1.

First, calculate P,

$$P = \frac{141\ (.368) + 82\ (.268)}{223} = .331$$

then $\sigma p_1 - p_2$,

$$\sigma p_1 - p_2 = \sqrt{(.331)(.669)\left(\frac{1}{141} + \frac{1}{82}\right)} = .065$$

then t,

$$t = \frac{.368 - .268}{.065} = 1.53$$

Next, compute the degrees of freedom d.f. $= n_1 + n_2 - 2 = 221$.

Then, compare the Student-t statistic to the critical value of the
Student-t distribution at the 5 percent level (one tail) for the appropriate degrees of freedom. That critical value is 1.64. Since the sample
t-statistic is less in absolute value than the critical value, the difference between the sample proportions in row 1 and row 2 of column 1 is not significant.

The computer print-out of the results of the testing of all combinations of row proportions, two at a time, for each column are given below:

Major by Residence of Student Matrix

Matrix by Percentages With Respect to Rows

	Liberal Arts	Education	Business
Dormitory	0.368	0.205	0.425
Commuter	0.268	0.158	0.573
Fraternity or Sorority	0.037	0.333	0.629

Test for signifcant difference between row elements in all
columns two at a time using t-test, one tail, 5 percent
level of significance.

Column	Row	Row	T-Value	Crit. Val.	D.F.	Significant
1	1	2	1.53	1.64	221	No
1	1	3	3.39	1.64	166	Yes. Row 1 percentage greater than row 3
1	2	3	2.55	1.66	107	Yes. Row 2 percentage greater than row 3
2	1	2	0.86	1.64	221	No
2	1	3	-1.45	1.64	166	No
2	2	3	-1.96	1.66	107	Yes. Row 3 percentage greater than row 2
3	1	2	-2.12	1.64	221	Yes. Row 2 percentage greater than row 1
3	1	3	-1.94	1.64	166	Yes. Row 3 percentage greater than row 1
3	2	3	-0.51	1.66	107	No

In the first line the entries in row 1 and row 2 of column 1 are tested to see if one of the two entries is significantly greater than the other. The value of the Student-t statistic is printed under the column heading "T-Value." The critical value of the test as given by the Student-t distribution table is indicated under the column heading "Critical Value." The degrees of freedom of the test are indicated under the column heading "D.F." If one of the two row entries is significantly greater thant the other the direction of that difference is entered under the column heading "Significant." If the T-Value, in absolute value, is less than or equal to the critical value, there is no significant difference, and the word "no" is printed under the column heading "Significant." If the absolute value of the T-Value is greater than the critical value the difference is significant. The sign of the T-Value indicates the direction of the significance. A positive sign (i.e., no sign) indicates the first entry in the comparison is greater than the second entry; a negative sign indicates the second entry is the greater one.

Analysis By Column

The rationale of the analysis by columns is much the same as that by rows. In each matrix transform the column entries to relative frequencies using the column totals as bases; that is, every column adds up to 1.

The Major by Residence matrix expressed in percentages with respect to columns would look as follows:

Major Field

	Liberal Arts	Education	Business
Dormitory	0.693	0.568	0.483
Commuter	0.293	0.254	0.379
Fraternity or Sorority	0.013	0.176	0.137
	1	1	1

180

Again as with the row totals because of rounding the column totals will differ slightly from 1.

In each row all combinations of proportions, two at a time, are tested for significant differences; that is, in row 1, column 1 is compared to column 2, column 1 is compared to column 3, and column 2 is compared to column 3. The same is done for all other rows.

The computer print-out of the results of the testing of all combinations of column totals, two at a time, for each row are given below.

Matrix By Percentages With Respect to Columns

	Liberal Arts	Education	Business
Dormitory	0.693	0.568	0.483
Commuter	0.293	0.254	0.379
Fraternity or Sorority	0.013	0.176	0.137

Test for significant differences between row elements in all rows, two at a time using t-test, one tail, 5 percent level of significance.

Row	Col	Col	T-Value	Crit. Val.	D.F.	Significant
1	1	2	1.43	1.64	124	No
1	1	3	2.88	1.64	197	Yes. Col. 1 percentage greater than Col. 3
1	2	3	1.01	1.64	173	No
2	1	2	0.47	1.64	124	No
2	1	3	-1.23	1.64	197	No
2	2	3	-1.57	1.64	173	No
3	1	2	-3.32	1.64	124	Yes. Col. 2 percentage greater than Col. 1
3	2	3	0.66	1.64	173	No

The number of computations involved in running these tests is considerable. To perform them by hand would be unthinkable. The analysis of the Major by Residence matrix alone involves 18 different compares. The analysis of the Major Field Group as a whole involves 156 compares, and the Major Field Group is just one of four matrix groups tested.

There is presented below a portion of the print-out of results of the T Test showing relationship between type of Library book being read and several characteristics of the reader.

Library Book by Residence of Student Matrix

Soc. Sci.   Other

Matrix by Percentages with Respect to Rows.

0.400	0.600
0.578	0.421
1.000	0.000

Test for significant difference between ELTS. in column two at a time using T-Test-one Tail-5 per. level.

Column	Row	Row	T-Value	Crit. Value	D.F.	Significant
1	1	2	-1.25	1.67	52	No
1	1	3	-1.66	1.68	35	No
1	2	3	-1.16	1.73	19	No
2	1	2	1.25	1.67	52	No
2	1	3	1.66	1.68	35	No
2	2	3	1.16	1.73	19	No

Matrix by Percentages with Respect to Columns.

0.518	0.724
0.407	0.275
0.074	0.000

Test for significant differences between ELTS in rows two at a time using T-Test-one Tail-5 per. level.

Row	Column	Column	T-Value	Crit. Value	D.F.	Significan
1	1	2	-1.58	1.67	54	No
2	1	2	1.03	1.67	54	No
3	1	2	1.49	1.67	54	No

LIBRARY BOOK BY CLASS OF RIDER READER MATRIX

Soc. Sci.   Other

Matrix by Percentages with Respect to Rows.

0.555	0.444
0.315	0.684
0.500	0.500
0.600	0.400

Test for signifcant difference between ELTS. in column
two at a time using T-Test-one Tail-5 per. level.

Column	Row	Row	T-Value	Crit. Val.	D.F.	Significant
1	1	2	1.47	1.68	35	No
1	1	3	0.26	1.71	24	No
1	1	4	-0.22	1.70	26	No
1	2	3	-0.90	1.71	25	No
1	2	4	-1.47	1.70	27	No
1	3	4	-0.42	1.74	16	No
2	1	2	-1.47	1.68	35	No
2	1	3	-0.26	1.71	24	No
2	1	4	0.22	1.70	26	No
2	2	3	0.90	1.71	25	No
2	2	4	1.47	1.70	27	No
2	3	4	0.42	1.74	16	No

Matrix by Percentages with Respect to Columns.

0.384	0.275
0.230	0.448
0.153	0.137
0.230	0.137

Test for significant differences between ELTS in rows
two at a time using T-Test-one Tail-5 per. level.

Row	Col	Col	T-Value	Crit. Val.	D.F.	Significant
1	1	2	0.85	1.67	53	No
2	1	2	-1.69	1.67	53	Yes. Col 2 percentage greater than Col 1
3	1	2	0.16	1.67	53	No
4	1	2	0.89	1.67	53	No

PART IV

SELECTED PROBLEM AREAS
OF LIBRARY OPERATIONS

Introduction to Part IV

Part IV includes five chapters that illustrate how sampling
can be applied to selected problem areas of library operations.
Chapter 10, for instance, treats the use of sampling in timing the
activities of library staff personnel. Chapter 11 develops the
sampling methods for auditing the loss of books from the library's
collection. Chapter 12 reviews studies which have been made of the
relationship between academic curriculum and library use. It is found
that the methods and results of sampling in-library book readership
fit neatly into the pattern of usage revealed by the studies which
have been reviewed. Chapter 13 discusses the methods and benefits
of sampling a system of libraries. Finally, Chapter 14 examines
the value of sampling in-library book readership to provide an objective basis for quantitative standards of the library.

Chapter 10

Sampling Time Use of Library Staff Personnel

Some background discussion is in order before we turn to an outline of how to sample the behavior of library staff personnel. When Scientific Management was in its heyday during the first couple of decades of this century, one of the techniques associated with it was time study. Frederick W. Taylor and his associates discussed how the standardized work of the operative worker, conducted in uniform working conditions, could be analyzed into elements of the worker's cycle of work. A time-study man, with stop-watch in hand, then could proceed to make repeated timings of the time actually taken for each element. The average time for each element could be computed next. The sum of these average times would give the average time for the complete cycle of all elements.

Adjustments and allowances would have to be made in the average actual cycle time thus calculated. For example, the actual average time would be adjusted in accordance with the rating of the tempo or speed of work of the subject worker. If he worked faster than average, for instance, the actual time would be adjusted upward accordingly, to obtain a standard time. If unavoidable delays occurred, an estimated allowance for that factor would have to be provided for in the standard time, too.

Time-Delay Sampling

Subsequently it became recognized that statistical sampling could be used to estimate allowances like the time-delay allowances which are referred to in the preceding sentence. Ralph N. Barnes explains:

> The basis of a wage incentive system is to pay
> the worker in proportion to his productivity.
> One of the factors influencing his productivity
> is the occurrence of interruptions or delays.

> As a result, daily productive output is seldom
> the result of the total time per day divided by
> the normal time per piece found by time study.
>
> Since many of these delays occur through no
> fault of the worker, he should not be penalized
> for them. Therefore, an allowance must be made
> for time lost because of unavoidable interrup-
> tions, variations, or delays.[1]

Work sampling can be used to determine such allowances. Barnes has

described the studies that demonstrate the reliability, validity, and econ-

omy of work sampling. It was found that work sampling, when repeated, would

give the same results. Thus, work sampling is reliable in measuring time-

delay ratios, for example. Also, Barnes showed that the same proportion of

productive time lost due to delays will be found whether sampling is used or

time study is conducted on all operations. That is, the sampling is valid,

as proven by empirical results. As a matter of fact, work sampling has such

desirable attributes of economy and of being capable of being interrupted at

any time, which render it superior to regular time study in many respects.[2]

(See Appendix G for the extended excerpt from Barnes' Work Sampling.)

Given the uses and advantages of time study and of sampling in relation

to time study, one might have expected that the sampling of supervisory and

administrative work would have become popular long ago. Such is not the case,

however. Some writers on the subject contend that managerial work is intan-

gible and nonrepetitive and that it is difficult to measure the output of man-

agerial work. Therefore, they conclude, management should not be subjected to

time study, whether by the common type of observation or by sampling. Develop-

ments in industrial engineering never have led to full-scale time study of

executives.

---

1. Ralph N. Barnes, Work Sampling (2nd ed.; New York: Wiley, 1957),
   pp. 185 and 186.

2. Ibid. pp. 187-191.

Sampling Clerical Force

However, other types of work, indirect labor and clerical, for instance, have been considered suitable subjects of time study and work sampling. Bertrand L. Hansen describes a study of clerical activities.[3] He describes how the method of sampling he first used was stratified sampling; then random sampling was adopted. Randomly-selected five minute intervals provided the office manager's schedule for conducting the survey. At these times, he noted the type of work being performed by the clerks and whether they were subject to interruptions. It proved to be entirely possible to identify types of unproductive activity to which too much time was being devoted. (See Appendix H for excerpt from Hansen's Work Sampling for Modern Management.)

Sampling Executive Behavior

While the time-study techniques of the industrial engineer were evolving to incorporate sampling of manual and clerical workers, notable developments were taking place in management theory. Chester Barnard's book, The Functions of the Executive, was first published in 1938. One chapter in that book dealt with bases of specialization.[4]

Barnard recognized this critical importance of the basis of specialization. He devised an operational classification of executive activities. His classes being operational, help researchers make empirical studies of executive performance. Instead of planning, organizing, directing and controlling, Barnard chose the following scheme of classification:

> Place where work is done
> Time at which work is done
> Persons with whom work is done

---

3. Bertrand L. Hansen, Work Sampling for Modern Management (Englewood Cliffs: Prentice-Hall, 1960), pp. 128-130.

4. Chester Barnard, The Functions of the Executive (Cambridge: Harvard, 1951), Ch. 10.

Things upon which work is done
Method or process by which work is done.[5]

Place and time are such familiar bases of specialization one can overlook their great influence, Barnard noted. More recently, in 1951, Sune Carlson conducted a time study of executive behavior, adapting Barnard's scheme of classification listed above.[6] Emphasizing communication and decision-making Carlson measured and analyzed time of the executive according to:

> Place of work
> Contact with persons and institutions
> Technique of communication.

Carlson also tried to describe:

> Nature of question handled
> Kind of action taken.

He did not use statistical sampling; but, instead, he did try to account for every minute of an executive's activities for what Carlson hoped would be a representative period of a month or two.

Even though Carlson's findings were derived from experience in Sweden, it is of interest to list the leading conclusions of his study:

> Executives work too many hours in total
> They're constantly in face-to-face contact
>   with people
> They're subject to frequent telephone
>   interruptions
> Their attendance at committee meetings
>   often wastes time.

---

5. Ibid., pp. 127 ff.

6. Sune Carlson, Executive Behavior (Stockholm: Strombergs, 1951), pp. 31 ff.

However, Carlson's empirical methods did not prove altogether satisfactory in describing the substance of the decision made nor the effectiveness of the action decided upon. Furthermore, Carlson's methods did not resolve adequately the two issues of (1) how to assure the representativeness of the data on executive conduct and (2) how to prevent executive behavior from being influenced by the very carrying out of the survey itself.

In spite of these limitations, Carlson's approach has been popularized in Peter Drucker's well-received book The Effective Executive. In that book, Drucker writes:

> "The first step toward executive effectiveness is therefore to record actual time-use. The specific method in which the record is put together need not concern us here. There are executives who keep such time logs themselves. Others, such as the company chairman just mentioned, have their separate secretaries do it for them. The important thing is that it gets done, and that the record is made in 'real' time, that is at the time of the event itself, rather than later on from memory."[7]

Hansen reproduces the results of a work sampling study of top plant and operating managers, which uses a more detailed scheme of classification of executive activities. The table below

---

7. Peter Drucker, The Effective Executive (New York: Harper & Row, 1967), p. 35.

Table 7

How Managers Spend Their Time in the Plant

	Top Plant Management*		Operating Managers**	
	Percent of time	Hours per month	Percent of time	Hours per month
Talking (Oral Communication):				
Consultation	10.5	14.2	3.6	4.8
Deciding on course of action	9.4	12.6	6.3	8.5
Discussion	6.2	8.3	4.0	5.3
Interviewing visitors	3.0	4.0	3.5	4.7
Telephone:				
Alone	} 8.8	} 11.8	{ 7.1	{ 9.6
Others waiting			{ 1.1	{ 1.5
Dictating:				
To secretary	} 3.7	} 5.0	{ 0.3	{ 0.4
To dictating machine			{ 1.6	{ 2.2
Meetings:				
Regularly scheduled	1.4	1.9	4.0	5.4
Special	8.0	10.8	6.0	8.1
Luncheon Discussions	14.3	19.4	11.0	15.0
Visiting other offices	14.7	20.0	36.1	48.9
TOTAL TALKING	80.0	108.0	84.6	114.4
Writing:				
Letters	1.4	1.9	1.8	2.4
Notes	2.7	3.7	2.0	2.6
Reading:				
Published material	) 13.2	) 17.7	(2.6	(3.5
Correspondence			{ 5.8	{ 7.8
From data			(0.8	(1.1
Miscellaneous:				
Clerical work	0.7	1.0	1.2	1.6
Thinking	2.0	2.7	1.2	1.6
Total	100.0	135.0	100.0	135.0

* General Manager, Plant Manager, Director of Industrial and Public
  Relations, etc.

** Managers of Operations, Quality Control, Industrial Engineering,
  etc.

Source: Bertrand L. Hansen, Work Sampling for Modern Management (Englewood Cliffs:
    Prentice-Hall, 1960), p. 13, reprinted from C. L. Brisley, "Tips to Help
    You Save Time," Factory Management and Maintenance, December 1958, p. 60.

shows the recapitulation of results derived from 5,250 observations taken over a
15-week period of time. Hansen's conclusions are similar to Carlson's; namely,
"By doing a better job of communicating, more time can be spent on the creative
thinking process."

Enough has been said about time study, work sampling, and sampling of executive behavior in general, to demonstrate the reasonableness of sampling and timing
the behavior of library adminstrators and other staff personnel at a library.

Communication Activity of Chief Librarian

Let us consider now, specifically how the sampling would be undertaken of
the personnel at a college library. What is the number and status of personnel
employed at a college library? For illustrative purposes, let us assume a full-
time library staff of a college libary that consists of 28 persons. One would be
the chief (or college) librarian and nine would be subordinate administrators who
also would have professional technical duties. The balance of 18 would be com-
prised of both nonadministrative professionals and clerical employees. Such a
library might well employ an additional 40 students as student assistants during
the school year.

Statistical sampling can be used, in an extension of the Carlson methods,
to get a representative picture, unobtrusively, of how the chief librarian spends
his time. For example, sampling can show the frequency of resort to different
forms of communication by the chief librarian. It can describe, too, how this
executive spends his time in each form of communication.

If a study is desired of how just one chief librarian engages in communication, as a step in his decision-making, one may select a random sample of 600
occasions when the administrator has engaged in such communication during the
year. Four types of communication form a comprehensive list: telephone conversations; informal face-to-face contact; attendance at conferences and committee

194

meetings; and reading of reports and books. Random numbers tables can be used to select the random times of communication for the random sample. The chief librarian himself, his secretary, or an interviewer can maintain a record of type of communication at sample time. Suppose the results of the sampling are as follows:

		Frequency	
Type of Communication	Number	% of Total	Standard Error (%)
Telephone conversation	250	42	2.0
Informal face-to-face contact	200	33	2.0
Reading of reports and books	100	17	1.5
Attendance at conferences and committee meetings	50	8	1.0
Total of Sample	600	100	

Given these hypothetical results, it can be said that 42%, with standard error of 2%, of the executive's total number of communications are telephone conversations; 33%, with standard error of 2%, informal face-to-face contact; 17%, with standard error of 1.5%, reading of reports and books; 8%, with standard error of 1% attendance at conferences and committee meetings.

It is justifiable to translate frequency of sample observations of an activity into the proportion of the time spent at that activity. Although an executive spends more time at one activity than another, the random checking process will pick him up more frequently at that one activity than at the other. If there are 10 units of time during which he engages in one activity, and 5 units of time during which he engages in the other activity, then sampling will pick up the former activity twice as frequently as the latter activity. See the Ralph Barnes' excerpt in Appendix G for additional support for this statement.

All Administrators at One Library

If a study were made of communication activities for the 10 administrators combined of a library, just 208 sample communication occasions would be
needed for each executive, at most. A 2080-item sample, at the most, would
show the overall communication practices of all the administrators, within the
standard error of 1%. The low standard error for all categories reflects the
relatively large 2080 sample size.

All Library Administrators in U.S.

If a study were made of communications for all library administrators in
the United States, first 3000 executives from that population would be selected
at random. Then each library administrator in the sample would have his communication behavior sampled 2 times during the year, in order for the standard
error to be the 1%. Or 4000 administrators could be sampled one time each, with
the same 1% standard error. The economy and power of sampling should be evident
in this illustration.

An additional time dimension of communication behavior also can be treated
by means of sampling methods. In the case of sampling the one chief librarian,
for example, a record could be made of the time during which the executive was
engaged without interruption in the sample type of communication. A critical
statistical question is: How large a sample must be taken to be 95% certain that
the estimate of average time in, say, face-to-face contact is within ± 2 minutes?
If the sample standard deviation is 12 minutes, the sample size needs to be 144
(that is, $1.96 \frac{12}{\sqrt{n}} = 2$). If the standard deviation is as low as 1, the required
sample size is only 1.

Sampling Subordinate Administrators

Sampling methods, of appropriate sample size and sampling error, can be
devised to determine th portion of time subordinate library administrators are
devoting to their administrative duties in comparison to their technical duties

196

in acquisitions, cataloguing, circulation, or what have you. Furthermore, the proportion of time devoted to subprofessional clerical activities can be found. The results of this phase of sampling staff behavior would be revealing about the extent to which authority is being delegated, technical activities are encroaching on administrative responsibilities, and clerical work is detracting from professional performance.

Sampling Clerical Personnel

Finally, sampling methods can be devised to measure the time devoted to nonproductive activity versus productive activity on the part of clerical personnel, students, and others who make up the nonmanagerial personnel of the staff. Such a measurement would serve to indicate whether corrective action is needed by library administrators. For, make no mistake of it, wages and salaries of personnel make up the largest portion of library costs. And hourly labor costs of productive labor can be twice as large as nominal hourly rates of pay.[8]

8. See Richard Dougherty and Fred Heinritz, Scientific Management of Library Operations (New York: Scarecrow Press, 1966), Ch. 10.

Chapter 11

Auditing the Collection

Introduction

The auditing of accounts is standard practice in the field of accounting. It has as its purposes the confirmation of the accuracy of the accounting entries and records, and also, the determination of the honesty of those persons who maintain the accounting records. The use of statistical sampling in conjunction with auditing procedures is widely adopted in the accounting profession among auditors these days.

Refer to the chapters on sampling theory for several detailed illustrations of sampling as it is used in auditing by accountants. In those examples it was shown that by choosing a random sample of accounts one can determine, with any desired degree of confidence, the average dollar value of an account, the total dollar value of all accounts, the percentage of incorrect entries, all within any pre-assigned margin of error.

In a manner parallel to business auditing, sampling can be used to audit the book collection of a library. That is, sampling can be employed in determining the loss of books from the collection. Such loss of books, or inability to account for the whereabouts of missing books, can be due to thefts by library users or other causes. It should be noted that book "loss" here does not refer to mutilation of books or the destruction of mutilated books at the initiative of the library. However, the sampling technique described here could be adapted readily to pinpoint the incidence of mutilation.

In the procedure for conducting the library audit, it is necessary to make use of a master list of books. That master list of books has the form of the master shelf list. The shelf list indicates the books that should be found in the library's collection, either on the shelves or in circulation.

Sampling by Computer

For computer processing, the master list (shelf list) should be recorded on tape or some other form of storage, such as punched cards or discs. In the process of storing, a number is assigned to each book. It should be noted that each book, not each book title, is assigned a number; the distinction is important because some titles have multiple volumes.

The computer can be programmed to enable it to generate random samples. Using those random numbers, the computer can select any predetermined random sample of books to be checked.

Once the random selections have been made, the computer can analyze the sample and print the results according to the format below:

Code	Book	Call Number	Year of Acquisition		
Number	Title, Vol., Author	Number	Date		
(1) Date Borrowed	(2) Date Returned	In Circulation Now	Lost Because Overdue	On Shelf	
If never borrowed	-- --	Yes (No) No if (1) blank Yes if (2) blank or Yes if (1)>(2)	Yes (No)	Yes (No)	
If borrowed date					

The purpose of the code number is to assure that duplicate books are distinguished from one another. The book identification is in standard bibliographical terms. The purpose of the call number is for use in classification and subsequent statistical analysis. If a book has never been circulated, the Date Borrowed column will have no entry and the Date Returned column will have no entry. If a book has been circulated the Date Borrowed column will have an entry and the Date Returned column might or might not have an entry. For the In Circulation Now column, the entry is yes if the date borrowed is greater than the date returned. Otherwise, no is the entry in the In Circulation Now column.

A book is considered lost when it is overdue for an excessively long time. The question of when a book is overdue so long that it is likely never to be returned depends on the library's experience. For purposes of our illustration we are using six months as an operational definition of excessive overdue. That is, it is assumed that if a book is overdue for six months or longer it will never be returned. Let us say that less than 5 percent of those books that are in circulation six months or longer after due date are returned. On this basis the six-month definition was adopted to identify an overdue book as lost.

The On Shelf column has a yes entry if the In Circulation Now column entry is no, and vice versa.

The computer serves as the source of great savings of labor cost in sampling. It is important to stress this point. The computer itself has checked all books lost because of overdue. The actual handwork in the sampling is limited to the checking of sample books which should be on the shelves.

Checking the Checkers

We explain now how to check the checkers who have checked by hand the sample books that should be on the shelves. When it comes to controlling the checking of books which should be on the shelves, a random sample of 100 books can be selected. Here a decision rule is needed. A convenient rule is: if one or more errors by checkers turn up in the sample of 100, do a complete re-check of all the books that were supposed to be on the shelves in the main sample.

If no error appears in the sample of 100, accept the results of the first check by the checkers. In accepting these results we are 95 percent certain that the overall error due to the checker is no more than 1.53 percent. This degree of confidence follows from the fact that we are 95 percent certain that the true proportion of defectives is at most

$$1.64\sigma_{p'} = \sqrt{\frac{P(1-P)}{n}}\sqrt{\frac{N-n}{N-1}}$$

Assuming n − .10N

Then $\frac{N-n}{N-1}$ = $\frac{N-.10N}{N-1}$ = $.90\frac{N}{N-1}$

$\approx$ .90 if N is large since in that case

$$\frac{N}{N-1} \approx 1$$

and therefore

$$\sqrt{\frac{N-n}{N-1}} = \sqrt{.90}$$

Our estimate of P is the sample proportion p' which in this case is zero (0). That's fine so far as estimating the population proportion is concerned. But in computing the standard error of our estimate, we must have a non-zero approximation for P.

To get a non-zero approximation for P assume that one more check would give an error. Hence, a non-zero estimate of P and a high one at that, would be $p' = \frac{1}{101}$. The sample size is now 101.

Thus, we are 95 percent certain that checker errors at most

$$= 1.64 \sqrt{\dfrac{\dfrac{1}{101} \cdot \dfrac{100}{101}}{101}} \sqrt{.90}$$

$$= .0153 \text{ or } 1.53\%$$

When the master file is stored on tape, a check on errors in the source
documents can be made, using exactly the same procedure as indicated here. That
is, one can take a random sample of 100 source documents. If one or more errors
turn up, do a complete check. If no errors turn up, accept the source documents, with the same degree of confidence that we have in accepting a checker's
results.

Let us proceed with the discussion of auditing the book collection. Familiar technical issues must be resolved. One is the question of the proper
size of the sample. In order to determine sample size, assumptions are made
about the number of books in the library and the desired level of precision
for our estimate of "lost" books. Let us assume that the library has 200,000
books according to the master list; that is, N = 200,000. Next, let us say
that we want 95 percent certainty that our estimate is in error by no more than
1 percent.

These assumptions indicate that we must choose the sample size n so that

$$1.96\sigma_{p'} = .01$$

$$\sigma_{p'} = \dfrac{.01}{1.96} = \dfrac{1}{196} \quad \text{or} \quad \sqrt{\dfrac{N-n}{N-1}} \sqrt{\dfrac{P(1-P)}{n}} = \dfrac{1}{196}$$

If we take P to be 5 percent, then we get

$$\sqrt{\frac{200,000 - n}{199,999 \, n}} \qquad \sqrt{(.05)\,(.95)} \quad = \quad \frac{1}{196} \qquad \text{or}$$

$$n = 1809$$

The figure of 5 percent was chosen for P because it seems reasonable in light of a study of lost books by Braden at the libraries of Ohio Sate University.[1] She used systematic sampling to find that 4.37 percent of the books in a sample of 5642 were missing.

Stratification

A sample size of 1809 is required in order to estimate the proportion of lost books with the desired level of precision and certainty, if simple random sampling is used. Stratification, however, does not decrease the sample size appreciably. This point will be illustrated. Suppose we group the books into 6 strata and assume a breakdown as follows:

Strata	% of Total Books	Prior Estimate of % of Loss
1. Social Science	40	3%
2. Pure Science	5	6%
3. Technology or Applied Science	25	6%
4. Literature	15	10%
5. Geography or History	10	4%
6. Other	5	5%
	100	

1. See Irene A. Braden, American Library Association Bulletin, October 1968, p. 1129

Proportional Allocation

If we use proportional stratification, a 95 percent confidence interval with an error margin of 1 percent would require that we choose n so that

$$\sigma_{p'} = \frac{1}{196}$$

Now for proportional allocation

$$\sigma_{p'} = \sqrt{\frac{N-n}{(N-1)n}} \sqrt{\Sigma\, W_h P_h Q_h}$$

$$= \sqrt{\frac{200,000-n}{199,999n}} \sqrt{\begin{array}{l} .4(.03)(.97)+.05(.06)(.94)+.25(.06)(.94) + \\ .15(.1)(.9)+.1(.04)(.96)+.05(.005)(.995) \end{array}}$$

$$= \sqrt{\frac{200,000-n}{199,999n}} \sqrt{.04615}$$

Hence choose n so that

$$\sqrt{\frac{200,000-n}{199,999n}} \sqrt{.04615} = \frac{1}{196} \qquad \text{which}$$

Gives n = 1757, a reduction over simple random sampling of only 52

Optimum Allocation

For optimum allocation

$$\sigma_{p'} = \sqrt{\frac{N-n}{(N-1)n}} \sqrt{(\Sigma W_h P_h Q_h)^2}$$

$$= \sqrt{\frac{200,000-n}{199,999n}} \sqrt{(2164)^2}$$

Using Optimum allocation and choosing n so that

$$\sigma_{p'} = \frac{1}{196}$$

We get

n = 1741, which is 68 less than that called for by simple random

sampling

The savings in sample size afforded by stratification is hardly worth the

risk of bias we run by stratifying.

Sample Information

Important information can be obtained from the sample.

1. An estimate of the percentage of lost books
   can be made.

2. An estimate of the average annual loss rate
   can be calculated.

3. A model can be developed to project the annual
   dollar loss for future years.

4. The results can be used to formulate options
   for dealing with the loss.

5. The results can be used to evaluate the
   feasibility of installing an electronic
   detection system or closing in the stacks.

6. The sufficiency of the sample makes it un-
   necessary to engage in a complete check of
   all books in the collection.

Percentage of Lost Books

The percentage of lost books is simply the number of books lost in the sample

divided by the number of books in the sample.

If the sample proportion p' is $\leq$ the assumed population proportion (i.e., .05)

then the initial 95 percent confidence interval holds. That is, we are 95 percent

certain that the loss rate overall is within 1 percent of our estimate. If p' >

.05 then the confidence interval must be adjusted accordingly.

that is

$$\sigma p' = \sqrt{\frac{P(1-P)}{1809}} \sqrt{\frac{N-1809}{N-1}} \qquad \text{where for P}$$

Put in sample proportion annual loss rate.

Annual Average Loss Rate

Once the overall magnitude has been measured, the average annual rate of book loss can be estimated. A comprehensive picture of the rate of loss would require us to reconstruct the rate of loss beginning 20, 30 or more years ago.

A simplified illustration will be used here in order to explain the statistical methods involved. Thus, the average annual book loss rate will be calculated for the year 1969, 1970, 1971 and 1972.

A key consideration is the question of when the lost book was "last seen." Last seen is not the same thing as the date of loss of the book, however. Last seen is the most recent date when it became a matter of library record that the book, subsequently lost, can be confirmed as having been in the library collection. An example of a last-seen date for a book would be the most recent date on which the book had been charged out to a borrower (or, if never borrowed, the date of acquisition).

Table 8

Average Annual Book Loss Rate for 1969-1972

	(1)	(2)	(3)	(4)
Year	Number of Books in Sample	Number of Books Lost	Weighting Factor (Divisor)	Estimated Annual Loss Rate $(2)/(1)\frac{1}{3}$
1969	120	2	$3\frac{1}{2}$	.0049
1970	90	2	$2\frac{1}{2}$	.0089
1971	100	1	$1\frac{1}{2}$	.0067
1972	80	0	$\frac{1}{2}$	.000
	390			

Projection of the Annual Dollar Loss

After the above table is prepared, the data can be plotted in a Scatter Graph; that is, the annual loss rate is plotted as follows

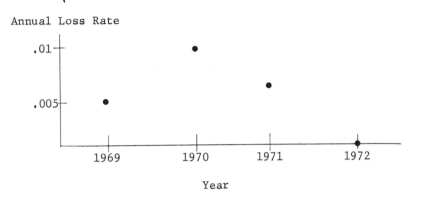

If we assume a linear relationship, between loss rate and year, a least squares line can be fitted to the scattered points. The line has the form of: $y' = a + bx$, where y' is the estimated annual rate of loss for a given year.

Annual Loss Rate

Last Seen	No. in Sample	No. Missing	Cumulative Years	Estimated Annual Loss Rate
1969	120	2	$3\frac{1}{2}$	$\frac{2}{120} \cdot \frac{1}{7/2} = .0049$
1970	90	2	$2\frac{1}{2}$	$\frac{2}{90} \cdot \frac{1}{5/2} = .0089$
1971	100	1	$1\frac{1}{2}$	$\frac{1}{100} \cdot \frac{1}{3/2} = .0067$
1972	80	0	$\frac{1}{2}$	$\frac{0}{80} \cdot \frac{1}{1/2} = .000$

Putting this information into a time series where y = estimated annual rate of loss we get

Year Last Seen	x	y
1969	-3	.0049
1970	-1	.0089
1971	1	.0067
1972	3	.000

$$b = \frac{\Sigma xy}{\Sigma x^2} = \frac{-.0169}{20} = .000845$$

$$a = y - \frac{.0205}{4} = .005125$$

$$y' = a+bx = .005115 - .000845x$$

Test to see if b is significantly different than zero. Since b is estimated from sample data, another sample might yield a different b. If 95 percent of the time these sample b's would fall in an interval that excluded zero (0) then b is significantly different than 0; if the interval includes 0 then the sample value of b = .000845 is not significantly different from zero at the 5 percent level of significance.

A 95 percent confidence interval of b is b ± 4.303 standard error of b

$$= b \pm 4.303 \; \sigma_b \text{ where } \sigma_b = \frac{\sigma}{\sqrt{\Sigma (x-\bar{x})^2}}$$

and where σ is the standard deviation of annual loss rates about the least squares line. The figure 4.303 is used to multiply σ_b rather than 1.96 because in computing σ_b we must estimate σ by the sample estimate.

$$\frac{\Sigma y^2 - a\Sigma y - b\Sigma xy}{n - 2} = .0038$$

For this reason the t - statistic must be used, the t value for 95 percent certainty with 2 degrees of freedom is 4.303.

Thus a 95 percent confidence interval for b is
$$-.000845 \pm 4.303 \; \frac{(.0038)}{\sqrt{20}}$$

$$= -.000845 \pm .0037$$

Since this interval includes 0, we conclude that b is not significantly different than zero and we can assume that the annual loss rate is a constant.

The estimate of this annual loss rate is

$$y' = a = \bar{y} = .005125;$$

and its standard error is $\sigma_{\bar{y}} = \dfrac{\sigma}{\sqrt{n}} \quad \dfrac{.0038}{\sqrt{4}} = .0019$

Thus, if the annual loss rates are normally distributed about their average lines, we can be 95 percent certain that the annual loss rate is no more than

$$\bar{y} = 2.353 \; \sigma\bar{y} = .005125 + 2.353 \, (.0019)$$

$$= .009595$$

It is to be noted that we use the value of 2.353 which is the value associated with a cumulative area of .95 for 3 degrees of freedom. We use the cumulative area because our interest is in a maximal bound for our estimate.

An annual dollar value can be computed for lost books as follows:

$$\text{Expected annual loss} = \left(\begin{array}{c}\text{Number of}\\\text{Volumes}\end{array}\right) \left(\begin{array}{c}\text{Expected Loss}\\\text{Rate}\end{array}\right) \left(\begin{array}{c}\text{Average Cost of}\\\text{Book}\end{array}\right)$$

$$V . \bar{y} . \bar{c}$$

If we assume that the sample results yield an average dollar loss of $10.00 per book, then the expected loss for 1972 is

$$(200,000) \; (.005125) \; (\$10) = \$10,250$$

Ignoring variation in the average cost of a book, we can get an upper bound for our estimate by using the figure $\bar{y} + 2.353 \; \sigma\bar{y} = .009595$ for the loss rate.

Upper bound for = (200,000) (.009595) (10) = $19,190
dollar loss

Alternatives Suggested by Sample Results

1. Accept the losses due to theft and do nothing.

2. Install an electronic detection system at an installation cost of $30,000 and an annual maintenance cost of $4000. The dectection system is expected to eliminate theft from the shelves.

3. Close the shelves. This too should eliminate theft from the shelves. To close the shelves will cost $4000 initially and will necessitate hiring extra people to service the check-out desk. Suppose the extra cost is estimated to be $7000 per year.

Evaluation of The Three Alternatives

We shall compare the three alternatives on the basis of their capitalized costs on a ten year basis. By capitalized cost of an alternative we mean the initial cost of that alternative plus the present value of the annual cost streams for the next ten years. First, the comparisons will be made assuming a constant library collection of 200,000 volumes. Then, the library collection will be allowed to vary.

Capitalized Cost When Collection Is Held Constant

If the annual loss L for the next 10 years is constant, and if money is worth 8 percent per year, then the present value of the annual stream of L for the next 10 years is

$$PV = L \left(\frac{1 - (1 + .08)^{-10}}{.08} \right)$$

Capitalized Cost of Doing Nothing (Constant Collection)

Let CC = Capitalized Cost

$$CC = PV = 10,250 \left(\frac{1 - (1.08)^{-10}}{.08} \right)$$

$$= 10,250 \ (6.71008)$$
$$= \$68,778$$

210

Capitalized Cost of Detection System (Constant Collection)

In addition to the installation cost of $30,000, the detection system includes an annual maintenance cost of $4000 and an annual loss due to non-returnables which, let's say, is one fourth the annual loss rate. Thus the annual loss becomes $2.563. Hence, the annual cost stream is

$4000 + $2,563 = $6563

Therefore, capitalized cost = $30,000 + $6563 (6.71008)
        of Detection System

$$= $74,038$$

Capitalized Cost of Closed Stacks (Constant Collection)

CC = $4000 +($7000 + $2563)(6.71008)

   = $4000 + $9563 (6.71008)

   = $68,169

Using capitalized cost as the criterion for choosing an option, we would close in the stacks, since for that alternative the capitalized cost is the least.

Capitalized Cost When Collection is Allowed to Vary

Suppose at year 1 the library collection is V volumes, we add to that collection V at an annual rate of a and the annual loss rate is $\bar{y}$. Assume additions and losses are taken at the year's end, then the total number of books in the collection is

End of Year	Books in Collection
1	V
2	$V(1 + a)$
3	$V(1 + a)^2$
k	$V(1 + a)^{k-1}$

The number of books lost each year is

End of Year	No. Lost
1	$V\bar{y}$
2	$V(1 + a)\bar{y}$
3	$V(1 + a)^2\bar{y}$
k	$V(1 + a)^{k-1}\bar{y}$

If the average cost of a book is $\bar{c}$ then the present value of the annual stream of book losses for k years at an interest rate of i per year is

$$PV = \bar{c}V\bar{y}(1 + i)^{-1} + \bar{c}V(1 + a)\bar{y}(1 + i)^{-2} + \ldots + \bar{c}V(1 + a)\bar{y}(1-i)^{-k}$$

If $a = i$, then

$$PV = \bar{c}V\bar{y}(1 + i)^{-1} + \bar{c}V\bar{y}(1 + i)^{-2} + \ldots + \bar{c}V\bar{y}(1 + i)^{k-1}(1 + i)^{-k}$$

But $L = \bar{c}V\bar{y}$ hence

$PV = Lk(1 + i)^{-1}$ Where L is the constant annual loss obtained when V is held constant.

$$PV = L (1 + i)^{-1}[1 + (1 + a)(1 + i)^{-1} + \; + (1 + a)^{k-1}(1+i)^{-(k-1)}]$$

The terms in brackets form a geometric series with ratio $(1 + a) (1 + i)^{-1}$ and from algebra its sum is

$$= \frac{1 - \left((1 + a)(1 + i)^{-1}\right)^n}{1 - (1 + a)(1 + i)^{-1}} = \frac{1 - \left(\frac{1 + a}{1 + i}\right)^n}{1 - \frac{1 + a}{1 + i}}$$

$$= \frac{1 - \left(\frac{1 + a}{1 + i}\right)^n}{\frac{i-a}{(1+i)}} = \frac{1 - \left(\frac{1 + a}{1 + i}\right)^n}{(i-a)(1 + i)^{-1}}$$

thus,

$$PV = L (1 + i)^{-1} \left(\frac{1 - \left(\frac{1 + a}{1 + i}\right)^n}{(i-a)(1 + i)^{-1}}\right)$$

$$= L\left(\frac{1 - \left(\frac{1 + a}{1 + i}\right)^n}{i - a}\right)$$

for $i \neq a$

212

Hence, the present value at a rate of i per year of an annual stream of variable book losses is given by

$$PV + \begin{cases} Lk(1+i)^{-1} & \text{if } i = a \\ L\left(\dfrac{1 - \left(\dfrac{1+a}{1+i}\right)^n}{i-a}\right) & \text{if } i \neq a \end{cases}$$

where k = prevailing worth of money

a = rate at which books are added to collection

L = first year's loss

In our illustration k = 10, i = .08, L = \$10,250 if nothing is done about theft and \$2563 if the detection system is installed or if the stacks are closed. For a assume a value of .01.

Capitalized Cost of Doing Nothing (Increasing Collection)

$$CC = PV = 10,250 \quad \frac{1 - \left(\dfrac{1.01}{1.08}\right)^{10}}{.07}$$

$$= \$71,502$$

Capitalized Cost of Detection System (Increasing Collection)

CC = 30,000 + PV of annual stream of 4000 for 10 years

= PV variable annual stream of book losses

= 30,000 + 4000 (6.71008) + 2563 (6.9757)

= 30,000 + 26,840 + 17,878

= \$74,718

Capitalized Cost of Closed Stacks (Increasing Collection)

CC = 4000 + 7000 (6.71008) + 2563 (6.9757)

= 4000 + 46,971 + 17,878

= \$68,849

213

Again, closed stacks is best, only here, where the collection is steadily increasing, the savings are more pronounced than when we assume a constant collection. It is best by ($71,502 - $68,849) or $2653, whereas under the assumption of a constant collection, the savings was $609.

Theft By Librarian

The Library Journal has reported the decision on a case in which a librarian was accused of stealing, purloining and converting federal property on loan to his library. It seems that the librarian turned books over to a book dealer without getting permission from the library trustees. The book dealer paid for the books with checks made out personally to the librarian. The librarian was found guilty and his appeal to a U.S. Circuit Court was denied.[2]

There are several ways of using sampling to detect theft by someone other than a user of the library. One method is by randomly sampling the book invoices and checking to see whether the invoiced books in the sample are in circulation or on the shelves. If the loss rate of the sample books is greater than the average loss rate beyond that attributable to chance variations, one should look for a cause other than user theft.

---

2. Library Journal, June 15, 1969, p. 2400.

Chapter 12

Curriculum and Library Use

Knox College Study

A basic study was conducted by Patricia Knapp to relate college teaching practices in courses to student use of the library at Knox College at Galesburg, Illinois.[1] She examined the library records on book withdrawals for the Spring of 1954. Also, she examined information in courses having to do with required and recommended books to read.[2] She found that over 90 percent of library book withdrawals were for use in academic courses;

Table 9

Summary of Total and Per Capita Withdrawals of 738
Students, Classified by Course Relationship

| Classification | Loans | | | Titles | | |
	No.	% of Total	Per Capita	No.	% of Total	Per Capita
Reserve	4185	58.67	5.67	1961	40.80	2.68
Bibliography	251	3.52	0.34	228	4.74	0.31
Non-Bibliogrpahy	2296	32.19	3.12	2216	46.11	2.99
Total Course	6732	94.38	9.12	4405	91.66	5.97
Non-Course withdrawals	401	5.62	0.54	401	8.34	0.54
Total	7133	100.00	9.65	4806	100.00	6.5

Source: Knapp, p. 15.

specifically, 94.38 percent of withdrawals were for course purposes, while only 5.62 percent of withdrawals were for non-course purposes.

1. Patricia B. Knapp, College Teaching and the College Library (Chicago, Illinois: American Library Association, 1959).

2. Ibid., p. 15.

In general, a few students borrowed a great many books, while many students borrowed few or no books during the study period. Statistically significant associations were found between selected characteristics of students and the pattern of book withdrawals. With respect to the Sex of the student, for instance, the average woman borrowed 4 books for every 3 books borrowed by the average man from the general collection.[3]

The top quarter of students in scholastic aptitude had greater per capita borrowing than did any other group, except for reserve books, where second group students outranked them.[4] In addition, the higher the grade point average of the student, the higher the rate of per capita borrowing by the student.[5]

Class year of student was related to borrowing practices. An increase in per capita withdrawals prevailed from class to class, running from the freshman to the senior year.[6]

Finally, Knapp found that for both Sex and Class Year of student, no statistically significant association was found with withdrawals of books for non-course purposes.[7]

Some effort was made by Knapp to determine in-library use of books. Reference is made to the use of a questionnaire to "spot-check [to determine] the use of library materials in the library, not recorded in circulation."[8] The data reported and analyzed are data on book loans. It can be assumed here that no precise statistical sampling methods were used in the internal "spot-check."

3.   Knapp, p. 25.

4.   Ibid., p. 24.

5.   Ibid., p. 25.

6.   Ibid., p. 26,27.

7.   Ibid., p. 29.

8.   Ibid., p. 3.

Knapp found that there were limiting factors operating in student use of the library. That is, smaller class size and more advanced classes were associated with greater use of books, particularly for problem-solving purposes. The small, advanced course could be regarded as library-dependent.

Knapp identified as a library-dependent course, a course for which 80 percent or more of the students borrowed books. She found 34 library-dependent courses out of a total of 116 courses.[9] Only a small number of courses appeared fairly high on all scales which ranked courses according to extent of use of library.[10] The problem-solving use of the library can be regarded as the highest and best use.[11] In addition, the attitude of faculty members toward the library and librarians might also have some influence on student use of the library.

Knapp concludes that the three-part use of the library--using books, using information resources of the library and using the library for problem-solving--can be achieved when there is a (1) conscious analysis of the total curriculum to see the relevance of library resources and (2) specific designing of courses to bring about different levels of use of the library.[12]

Selected comments can be made on the Knapp study. (1) Some differences in results are to be noted as between the Knapp study and our study of library use. Individual differences in readership are to be expected among libraries. Such differences point to the need for sampling many libraries in order to find the variation in library use. When several libraries are studied, the norm and variations around the norm can be calculated. Reference should be made to how a system meets this need.

---

9. Ibid., p. 36.

10. Ibid., p. 44.

11. Ibid., pp. 76ff and p. 92.

12. Ibid., p. 97.

(2)   The type of approach taken by Knapp, which relates curriculum to library, can serve as the basis of a model to predict library use. The course structure of the school would predict library usage and book needs. Thus, the supply of books required by the library would be greater if there is a larger porportion of small, advanced courses being offered. If more courses have large enrollment and are of an introductory, survey type, it could be anticipated that the library would serve as a study area where students would read their own books.

Again, a systems approach could be taken to find the implications for library use of differences among curriculum at different schools.

(3)   The sampling plan explained in Chapter 3 of this book is adaptable to identify course purpose of reading; for example, the interviewer could ask such a question. Furthermore, appropriate analysis could be carried out with no loss of generality.

(4)   Finally, the sampling of in-library use would fit well into the picture of determining the correlation between in-library and out-of-library use of library books.

College of the Desert Study

A study by Richard Hostrop extends to the community college level the Knapp approach of relating curriculum to library use. [13] Hostrop studied the library of the College of the Desert, a California junior college.

Hostrop used three kinds of circulation records that were kept during all or part of the final 13 weeks of the fall semester, 1965-1966. One kind was the withdrawal slips for reserve books which permitted the recording of borrower's name, author's name, title, call number. The course for which a book was borrowed was noted. And, for each book or periodical checked out during the period Janu-

13.   Richard W. Hostrop, Teaching and the Community College Library (Hamden, Conn.: The Shoe String Press, 1968).

ary 3rd to January 21st, a record was maintained of the name of the instructor for whose course each book was borrowed and for what purpose.[14]

An automated circulation system is in use at the library of the College of the Desert. Thus, a print-out was prepared for each student in the school, listing each book borrowed from the general collection (along with periodicals borrowed) during the investigation period.

A questionnaire was prepared, as part of the study, for students to fill out on the extent and nature of in-library use. The questionnaire was distributed on each one of 5 different days of the week during 5 consecutive weeks; a different day of the week was selected for each of the 5 weeks.[15]

The table below shows the results of the examination of book withdrawals by full-time students.

Table 10

Summary of Total and Per Capita Withdrawals of
413 Full-Time Students Classified by
Course Relationship

Withdrawals	No.	% of Total	Per Capita	No.	% of Total	Per Capita
Total withdrawals	3385	100.00	8.19	2538	100.00	6.06
Course Withdrawals						
Reserve	400	11.82	.97	133	5.24	.32
General	2610	77.10	6.32	2030	79.98	4.84
Total	3010	88.92	7.29	2163	85.22	5.76
Noncourse Withdrawals	375	11.08	.90	375	14.78	.90

Source: Hostrop, p. 22.

14. Hostrop, pp. 8, 9.
15. Ibid., p. 8.

219

From the table above it can be seen that 88 percent of withdrawals were course-related, for full-time students.

The experience virtually was the same for part-time students.

Table 11

Summary of Total and Per Capita Withdrawals of
304 Part-Time Students Classified by
Course Relationship

| Withdrawals | Loans | | | Title | | |
	No.	% of Total	Per Capita	No	% of Total	Per Capita
Total Withdrawals	1419	100.00	4.68	1050	100.00	3.45
Course Withdrawals						
Reserve	155	10.92	.51	133	12.66	.44
General Collection	1085	76.47	3.57	738	70.29	2.43
Total	1240	87.39	4.09	871	82.95	2.86
Noncourse Withdrawals	179	12.61	.59	179	17.05	.59

Source: Hostrop, p. 24.

Hostrop describes the results of the survey of library use which was not recorded as circulation. Some 470 questionnaires were filled out by 380 students, on the 5 different days during 5 consecutive weeks. Ninety students filled out more than one questionnaire on the same or a different sample day. The 380 students comprise one-third of the 1,004 full-time and part-time matriculated students.[16] Hostrop found that 18.6 percent of the full-time and 38 percent of the part-time students made not a single loan.[17]

---

16. Ibid., p. 27.

17. Ibid., p. 27.

Table 12

Use of College of the Desert Library As
Reported on 470 Questionnaires Filled
Out by 380 Students

Type of Use	Responses No.	Responses %	Summary No.	Summary %
Check-ins and Check-outs				
Return books	30	4.6		
Return periodicals	12	1.8	85.	12.9
Charge out books	36	5.5		
Charge out periodicals	7	1.0		
Course Work				
Assigned reading in library materials other than reserve books	24	3.6		
			150	22.9
Look up material for papers, reports, term papers, etc.	126	19.3		
Noncourse Work				
For general reading not assigned in class	64	9.8		
To study own books	298	46.2		
			415	64.2
Other reasons (look at globe, sharpen pencils, looking for someone, etc.)	53	8.2		
Totals	650	100.00	650	100.00

Source: Hostrop, p. 26.

Special attention should be directed to the fact that 46.2% of the responses indi-

cated that the purpose for going to the library "is to study own books." In other

words, about 59% of the book reading in the library consisted of students reading

their own books (3.6% + 19.3% + 9.8% + 46.2% = 78.9%; 46.2% ÷ 78.9% = 59%). However, we should qualify this conclusion by keeping in mind that some respondents gave more than one reason for going to the library.

With respect to characteristics of student users of the library, Hostrop concluded that:

> (1)　Student use of library materials at College of the Desert is largely course stimulated and somewhat comparable to the circulation figures of senior institutions, though there is a tendency toward less course use than reported in previous studies. However, in-use of the Library is markedly divergent from that reported for senior institutions. These institutions show a marked tendency toward using the library in a direct library-instructional sense. Responses to mailed questionnaires, in-library use questionnaires, and questionnaires on the use of public libraries, as well as frequent observation by the investigators in the library, indicate thatthe Library at College of the Desert and the public libraries as well are used, in the main, as a place to do homework out of textbooks." (p. 38)

> (2)　"Full-time students made much greater use of the Library both in loan circulation and in the in-use of the Library than did the party-time student..." (p. 39)

> (3)　Borrowing of periodicals and reserve books was associated with cumulative units completed (which can be taken as a type of measure of class year.) That is, the more advanced the student's standing, then the greater is resort to borrowing such items. (p. 61)

> (4)　Female students were found to be borrowing books from the general collection to a greater extent than do male students. (p. 61)

A few comments can be offered on Hostrop's findings. (1) When library books are used in the library their use is course-related. (2) The picture of library use inside the library is similar to the picture provided of library use by examination of circulation data.

Study of Three Community College Libraries

In a recent study reported by Kenneth Allen, methods he used for surveying library utilization are explained and the results summarized.[18] Libraries of community colleges studied are those at: Illinois Central College, East Peoria, Illinois; Shawnee Community College, Karnak, Illinois; and Waubonsee Community College, Sugar Grove, Illinois.

To measure utilization, a questionnaire was administered to all students and faculty members who entered the library during Monday, Wednesday, and Friday of the week beginning December 1, 1969, and Tuesday and Thursday of the week beginning with December 8, 1969. Allen explains that the alternate dates were assigned in consecutive weeks in order not to burden the students and librarians.[19]

A total of 4,657 responses was obtained to the library utilization questionnaire for the three schools combined. 1,430 persons entered the library more than once daily while 3,222 persons entered the library only one time per day.[20]

The most frequently mentioned primary reason for entering the library was "to study without using library materials."

18. Kenneth W. Allen, Use of Community College Libraries (Homewood, Illinois: Linnet Books, 1971).

19. Ibid, p. 31.

20. Ibid, p. 42.

Table 13

Full-Time and Part-Time Students Listing Their
Primary Reason for Coming to the Library

	Full-Time		Part-Time		Total	
	N	%	N	%	N	%
To study own materials	2464	63.2	376	53.9	2840	61.8
To find a friend	341	8.7	52	7.4	393	8.5
Independent study	95	2.4	26	3.7	121	2.6
Use library materials	839	21.5	178	25.5	1017	22.1
Check out materials	161	4.1	66	9.5	227	4.9
Total	3900	100.00	698	100.00	4598	100.0

$x^2 = 51.500$ df = 4   significant at .001 level

Missing observations = 59

Source: Allen, p. 121.

Almost 62 percent had that reason compared to 22.1 percent who wished to "use library materals."

A large proportion of respondents (43.6 percent of Freshman students and 43.8 persent of Sophomore students) reported that they were not using the library for a particular course. The complete tabulation is given on the following page. For Freshman students, Occupational-type courses were the most-frequently mentioned type, while Physical Education courses were least-frequently mentioned. For Sophomore students, the courses in the Humanities division were most-frequently mentioned and courses in Physical Education were least-frequently mentioned, when the student went to the library for a course-related purpose.

Table 14

Faculty and Students by Classification Responding to the Question,
"If you are using the library for a particular course,
in what division is the course located?"

	Freshman		Sophomore		Unclassified		Faculty		Total	
	N	%	N	%	N	%	N	%	N	%
Humanities	333	12.1	277	17.8	43	16.9	15	17.2	668	14.4
Social Studies	410	14.9	220	14.2	42	16.5	17	19.5	689	14.8
Mathematics & Science	365	13.2	217	14.0	22	8.7	5	5.7	609	13.1
Occupational	424	15.4	146	9.4	16	6.3	16	18.4	602	12.9
Physical Education	24	0.9	14	0.9	5	2.0	8	9.2	51	1.1
Does not apply	1203	43.6	680	43.8	126	49.6	26	29.9	2035	43.7
Total	2759	100.	1554	100.	254	100.	87	100.	4654	100.

$x^2 = 135.201$ df = 15   significant at .001 level   missing observations = 3

Source: Allen, p. 120.

Some of the more interesting findings of the Allen study on student character-istics associated with library use are:

(1) Sophomore students did not have more
favorable attitudes and utilization
pattern than Freshman students.

(2) Full-time students did depend on the
library more than did part-time students,
and the former had the more favorable
attitudes and utilization pattern. [21]

---

21 . Allen, p. 71.

(3) Day students stated that 63.3% came to
     the library to study while 21.6% came to
     use library materials. Night-students
     reported that 47.6% came to study and
     27.2% came to use library materials. [22]

What kinds of general comments can be made about the Allen study? (1) The

Allen study helps to show that a systems approach reveals differences in use among

libraries. A study of an individual library would fail to point up such varia-

tions. (2) The reading of their own books in the library is the most common use

of the library by the students studied.

In commenting on all the studies discussed in this chapter, as well as the

"feasibility" study of sampling in-library use, a pattern is found to prevail.

Most library use, which includes in-library use along with books used in circu-

lation, is directly related to course work by students. If the course design

and content allow or encourage it, the use of the library by the student will take

the form of a study hall where he reads his textbooks.

On this last point, it appears that the measurement of library use at a col-

lege can serve as a barometer or index to measure and evaluate the effectiveness

of curriculum and faculty.

---

22. Ibid., p. 45.

Chapter 13

Sampling the Library System

System Defined and Illustrated

The definition of a system is a loose-knit one which can encompass many different disciplines, such as physics, biology, economics and management. The hallmark of a system is interrelatedness of parts.

Thus, gravitational influences maintain a continuity of relationships among the planets of our solar system. The individual person possesses a physiological system of many interrelated parts. A group of people, communicating and interacting, make up a social system. Several of these primary groups can make up a system of such groups which we can call an organization. Our society as a whole can be regarded as a system of organizations.

These illustrations also help to illustrate that systems exist at different levels of abstraction. For example, there are atomic systems, molecular systems, organic systems, and social systems. And these different systems are related to one another.

Students of administration have long recognized that the manager must understand and be able to cope with the realities of pertinent systems. This kind of skill, which can be called conceptual skill, is something required of the manager, or executive, in addition to his technical skill and his managerial skill in planning, organizing, staffing and controlling.

Conceptual skill refers to the ability to perceive the enterprise as a whole with its many parts interrelated. Beyond that ability to perceive the existing pattern of interrelationships, conceptual skill enables the administrator to visualize an improved pattern of relationships among the parts of the enterprise, and to bring about changes in the existing pattern so that the improved pattern is adopted in practice.

For that matter, the conceptual skill blends into the managerial skill required of the administrator. That is, the management process of planning and controlling can be treated as providing feedback control so as to assure that desired goals of the enterprise are accomplished and that there is achieved a desired coordination of activities among personnel.

Systems Approach

A good historical example of a systems approach to administration is found in the case of the DuPont Company. That firm is concerned with relating the different operating divisions to one another so that the interests of the enterprise as a whole are served. DuPont evaluates overall performance in terms of measured rate of return on investment. The arithmetic is simple: Rate of return equals investment turnover multiplied by profits as a percentage of sales. Investment turnover is sales divided by total investment; total investment being fixed investment plus working capital. Profits are calculated by deducting from sales the familiar itemized costs of sales.

While the arithmetic is simple, the framework this scheme provides for top management control is found to be a powerful one. How this can be is illustrated by the following simplified hypothetical example from business:

Ball Manufacturing Company

	Eastern Division	Western Division	Southern Division
Sales	$1,000	$1,200	$1,000
Mill Cost of Sales	500	700	520
Selling Expense	200	180	200
Freight and Delivery	100	100	100
Administrative Expense	100	100	100
Cash	100	100	100
Accounts Receivable	100	150	100
Inventories	200	300	100
Permanent Investment (Fixed Assets)	600	650	500

Source: Dan Voich and Daniel Wren, Principles of Management (New York: Ronald Press, 1968), p. 274.

228

The rate of return on investment for each division happens to be the same 10 percent. That is what each division contributes to return on investment for Ball Manufacturing Company as a whole. Comparisons among the divisions, item-by-item, give clues about possible types of action to take to increase divisional return on investment and to increase the rate of return on investment for the whole company. The $700 Mill Cost of Sales for the Western Division is relatively high in comparison to Sales and to Mill Cost of Sales for the Eastern Division and the Southern Division. What is suggested here is that greater efficiency in production planning and controlling appears called for at the Western Division. Also, more effective inventory control seems necessary at the Eastern Division, as well as the Western Division, when their invetory valuation is compared to the Southern Division.

What is the relevance of all this to the control of operations of a library which is organized on a functional basis -- that is, by circulation department, reference department, periodicals section, cataloguing section, audio-visual aids department, etc. -- rather than a product basis? And what is the pertinence to a library which has no sales revenue or profits corresponding to a profit-making commercial enterprise? These questions are not to be treated as mere rhetorical ones. Rather, they are literal-minded questions, the proper answers to which can have highly significant implications for library administration. Here are the answers: Where it is found that an individual library is not capable of being controlled effectively, by virtue of its functional organization or for other reasons, a system of several college libraries can be used for purposes of achieving a control similar to that type of overall control illustrated above for business.

And, in response to the second question, the sampling of in-library book use and in-circulation book use would provide data which would be analogous to demand and derived sales for the commercial enterprise.

Itemized costs and assets could be assembled library-by-library. Comparisons among the libraries can be made for each item in the cost and assets structure, in relation to book use, to see how the resources of each library can be used more efficiently.

Also, the results of the use studies at each library could be compared to find significant differences among the libraries according to:

> characteristics of readers
> characteristics of books being read
> pattern of reading by time of day and
> day of week
> utilization of facilities, such as carrels
> and other reading places.

From the sample data on use of individual libraries, overall average figures on service use and resource use can be calculated. These averages can serve as standards to which characteristics of individual libraries can be compared.

Forecasting Book Use and Allocating Books Among Libraries

Let us turn from the process of recognizing in the abstract that corrective action of some kind or other might be needed. And let us turn to sophisticated forecasting of book use, which can be brought into play once it is fully understood that such forecasting (and resultant reallocation of books among the libraries) will provide mutual benefits to all the libraries of a library system. Thus, there is being illustrated here the basis for changing and improving interrelationships among parts of a system.

Need for Proper Allocation of Books

One of the major recognized problems of library administrators, from both an individual and a system point of view, is the question of book allocation and acquisition among libraries. Often the standard used is a "books per pupil" one.

Perhaps, better practice would be to allocate books on a "use" basis. Such a standard is ideally suited to a system of libraries. Books by category could be allocated among the libraries of the system according to their relative frequency of use. Those libraries with relatively high demand for Literature books would get a correspondingly large allocation of Literature books. If the demand for Pure Science is relatively low at a library, the allocation of books to that library in this area would be relatively small. There are limitations, of course. Some books, though rarely used, must nevertheless be stocked. Such books must be available if students want them. However, each library of the system need not have its own copy of little-used books. One or two copies for the entire system would be sufficient. A copy could be sent to a member library on demand.

Our discussion of the "use" standard will be limited to in-library reading but the techniques can be extended readily to include books in circulation as well.

Forecasting Demand

In allocating books by use it is essential that there be some means of estimating demand for the various categories of books. Again, our concern is with the in-library demand, let's say on a weekly basis, using Literature books as the category of interest.

To estimate the weekly demand for Literature books, first there is needed an idea of the weekly in-library user traffic. Using statistical techniques discussed earlier in the "Computer Methods" section of this book, carrel occupancy can be simulated by hour of day and by day of the week. These occupancy figures then can be transformed into arrival rate tables. These tables are presented below.

Percent of carrel occupancy found at Rider by day of week.

Day	Percent Occupancy	Rel. Strength of Arrivals
Mon	.136	.136/.840 = .16
Tues	.120	.14
Wed	.111	.13
Thur	.124	.15
Fri	.094	.11
Sat	.056	.07
Sun	.200	.24

Percent of occupancy by hour of day.

Time	Percent Occupancy	Relative Strength
8 – 8:59	.036	.02
9 – 9:59	.076	
10 – 10:59	.109	.05
11 – 11:59	.095	
12 – 12:59	.109	
1 – 1:59	.123	.07
2 – 2:59	.116	
3 – 3:59	.190	
4 – 4:59	.066	
5 – 5:59	.082	
6 – 6:59	.109	
7 – 7:59	.216	.12
8 – 8:59	.271	
9 – 9:59	.174	
10 – 10:59	.064	
	1.836	

Using the relative strength of arrival tables it is possible to estimate the number of in-library readers during the week by counting the arrivals during just one hour. And although a rather substantial error in estimate is involved, this error can be reduced by "smoothing." The sampling plan is simple. Randomly choose a day, then randomly choose an hour and count the arrivals during that hour.

Say, Wednesday from 1:00 p.m. to 2:00 p.m. is chosen for the count and that 14 people enter and occupy carrels at that time. From the arrival-rate table, it can be seen that 7 percent of daily arrivals enter between 1:00 p.m. and 2:00 p.m. Assuming this same percent holds for all days, one can say that the 14 arrivals represent 7 percent of Wednesday's total arrivals. If d = Wednesday's total arrivals, then

$$.07d = 14$$
$$\text{or}$$
$$d = \frac{14}{.07} = 200$$

From the arrival-rate table Wednesday's arrivals account for 13 percent of the weekly arrivals. Let w = weekly arrival total, then

$$.13w = 200$$
$$w = \frac{200}{.13} = 1462$$

Estimated Number of Weekly Arrivals Who Read Books

In the research described in Chapters 3, 4 and 5; of the 268 readers sampled, 64 were reading library books.

i.e., $\frac{64}{268} = 24\%$

∴ Estimated number
weekly readers reading
library books $= .24 (1462) = 351$

Estimated Number of Literature Book Readers

Approximately 17 percent of the in-library readers read Literature books, based on the research sample; hence

est. number of
Literature readers
per week $= .17 (351) = 60$

Similarly on the basis of that single hour's arrival count, one could develop estimates of in-library reading of all categories of books. By replication we could develop a week by week estimate of the number and kind of books being read.

Of course, a weekly estimate of use based on a sample of one hour's activity, is subject to wide error. There are standard errors involved in arrivals per hour, arrivals per week, and the relative frequency of reading by book categories. These relative frequencies must be revised or updated periodically.

The impact of these errors can be reduced by applying to our weekly estimates of in-library book usage the device of "smoothing," a widely used tool in inventory control. "Smoothing" generally deals with a moving average or an exponential average.

Forecasting for Inventory -- Moving Average

Suppose a distributor must stock 10,000 items, each with its own demand and order period. For some items, the period might be daily or weekly; for others, monthly, quarterly or even annually. In any event, the distributor must forecast the demand one period ahead for each item and place his order accordingly.

With so many items to check, it is pointless to look for trends which may fit some well-known distributions except, perhaps, for those items whose cost is disproportionately high. Not only would the effort and expense of such a search be prohibitive, but in many instances it would be a waste of time since for some items demand may have no readily described pattern. Further, even if a pattern exists and can be described, demand may change and an entire re-evaluation would have to be made.

There are several methods for forecasting demand, period-by-period, that avoid curve fitting or probability distribution fitting. One method is the moving average. First, we make a distinction between the trend of demand and the actual demand during a given period. Demand may fluctuate from one period to the next,

but its trend can remain unchanged. For example, the graphs in the figures below
represent the periodic demand for two different items over eight periods. Both
graphs show random fluctuations in demand, but the trend of demand is in each
case unchanged. In the first of the two figures, the trend is essentially constant; in the second figure, the trend is rising. These random fluctuations about
a basic demand pattern are called "noise."

Here, a word of caution must be added. When the fluctuations in demand are
attributed to "noise," one must be sure that it really is "noise" and not a change
in trend, nor some kind of seasonal fluctuation.

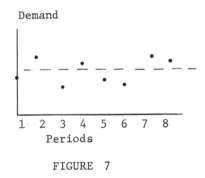

FIGURE 7

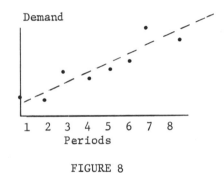

FIGURE 8

Once the distinction between trend and noise has been made, one next must find a way of separating trend from noise. One way of reducing noise and isolating trend is to take a moving average of a sequence of successive demands and attribute this average demand to a specific period, generally the middle period. Then, think of this average as the trend of demand at that particular time. This averaging process is called "smoothing."

To illustrate, suppose we want to smooth the following demand for electric generators, using a 5-period moving average.

Period	Actual Demand	5-Period Moving Average Demand
1	90	
2	120	
3	102	98.4
4	81	100.8
5	99	
6	102	

One can average the demands of five successive periods and attribute this average demand to the middle period. As the average moves from period to period, the oldest demand is dropped and the current one replaces it.

The nature of the demand suggests the choice of the number of periods to use in the moving average. If demand is volatile, a short period for the moving average is indicated; if stable, a longer period.

There are several complaints against this method for projecting demand. First, the moving average stops at the 4th period. If we want to forecast demand for the 7th period, we must extrapolate three periods beyond the one for which we last have the smoothed average. Secondly, the same weight, namely 1/5 or $\frac{1}{n}$ in general, is given to all demands included in the average. Such a weight is unrealistic. One would expect the more distant to be less indicative of the current trend of demand than are the more recent demands; and, consequently, less attention should be paid to the older demand.

Another complaint is a data processing one. For some items, a 20-period moving average might be used which means 20 values must be stored. For other items, a 15-period moving average may be indicated, or a 10, or a 5, etc. With 10,000 items, this becomes a problem on two counts: the first is storage and the second is variability in the amounts of information required.

An alternative to the moving average method for projecting demand is exponential smoothing. Exponential smoothing requires much less information than does the moving average; the information is uniform for all items, and the weights given to past demands decrease exponentially with their age. Further, forecasting with an exponentially smoothed average involves an extrapolation of just one period.

Exponential Smoothing

Let E_n = Exponential average of demand for n^{th} period, which will be the forecasted demand for the $n + 1$ period;

A_n = Actual demand during n^{th} period; and

α = Constant of proportionality between 0 and 1, exclusive.

We define E_n as follows:

$$E_n = E_{n-1} + \alpha(A_n - E_{n-1}).$$

In other words, the projected demand for the $n + 1$ period (E_n) is the projection of the previous period (E_n-1) plus a correction for the error in that projection.

The exponential nature of E_n becomes clear if we re-arrange the terms of the expressions for E_n. E_n can be written:

$$E_n = \alpha A_n + (1 - \alpha) E_{n-1}.$$

From the above equation, it follows that:

$$E_{n-1} = \alpha A_{n-1} + (1 - \alpha) E_{n-2}$$

$$E_{n-2} = \alpha A_{n-1} + (1 - \alpha) E_{n-3},$$

and so on down to E_1, which is:

$$E_1 = \alpha A_1 ,+ (1 - \alpha) E_0.$$

It is left to us to choose E_0. Substituting these results, each in turn, in the expression for E_n, we get

$$E_n = \alpha A_n + \alpha(1 - \alpha)A_{n-1} + (1 - \alpha)^2 A_{n-2} + \ldots + (1 - \alpha)^n E_0.$$

In this form, it can be seen that the projected demand for the n + 1 period is a weighted average of all past demands and that the weights assigned to those demands decrease exponentially with their age.

Average Age of Demand

In order to relate an n period moving average to an exponential average, we must find a correspondence between n and α. This requires a basis for comparison. A convenient basis is that of the average age of demand, which can be defined to be the product of the age of demand and the weight given it summed from age 0 for the current demand to age n − 1 for the most distant of the n demands. (For an exponential average, the most distant demand has age ∞ since the beginning point may be anywhere in the past.)

In a moving average of n periods, the demand of each period has weight $\frac{1}{n}$, thus:

$$\text{Average age of demand of an n-period moving average} = \sum_{m=0}^{n-1} m \frac{1}{n} = \frac{1}{n} \sum_{m=1}^{n-1} m = \frac{n-1}{2}$$

Now in an exponential average, the weight of the current demand is α; that of the preceding period, $\alpha(1 - \alpha)$; the one before that, $\alpha(1 - \alpha)^2$; and so on. Thus:

$$\text{Average age of demand of an exponential average} = \sum_{m=0}^{\infty} m\alpha(1-\alpha)^m = \frac{1-\alpha}{\alpha}$$

Finally, equate the average ages of demand of a moving average and an exponential average, and we have:

$$\frac{n-1}{2} = \frac{1-\alpha}{\alpha}, \text{ or}$$

$$\alpha = \frac{2}{n+1}$$

Thus, a moving average of 2 periods corresponds to an exponential average with $\alpha = \frac{2}{3}$, a moving average of 19 periods corresponds to an exponential average with $\alpha = \frac{1}{10}$.

Choice of α

In choosing α, any value between 0 and 1, exclusive, will do. The choice can be restricted still further, however, if we keep in mind the relationship between an exponential average and a moving average.

The least number of periods that a moving average can have is 2, which corresponds to an exponential average with an α of 2/3. This can be thought of as an upper limit for α. Setting a lower limit is largely arbitrary since there is no maximum number of periods to a moving average. However, an α of .05, which corresponds to a moving average of 39 periods, can be considered minimal.

Between these two extremes, .05 and 2/3, the choice of α is essentially subjective, perhaps even a matter of trial and error. And whatever the choice, it will have its advantages as well as its disadvantages. A large α will respond quickly to changes in the trend of demand, which is good, but it will react just as quickly to sheer noise, which is bad. A smaller α, on the other hand, is less affected by noise, but is also less responsive to essential change.

Generally, α is taken between .1 and 1/3. An α in that range controls noise fairly well and tracks demand satisfactorily. If necessary, a correction for trend can be added to the exponential average.

We now smooth exponentially the demand for generators that was earlier smoothed using a 5-period moving average. First, we must choose α and E_o. Take α to be 1/3, since this is the value that corresponds to a 5-period moving average, and let $E_o = A_1 = 90$. For E_o, we could just as well have taken the average of the previous demands, or the average of some of those demands. It does not matter really. After a time, the exponential average is the same, regardless of the choice of α.

Next, calculate the exponential averages. For example:

$$E_1 = E_o + \frac{1}{3}(A_1 - E_o) = 90 + \frac{1}{3}(90-90) = 90$$
$$E_2 = E_1 + \frac{1}{3}(A_2 - E_1) = 90 + \frac{1}{3}(120-90) = 100$$

and so on. The results, rounded to 1-decimal place, are given in the table below.

Period	Actual Demand	Exponential Average
1	90	90
2	120	100
3	102	100.7
4	81	94.1
5	99	95.7
6	102	97.8

Finally, the forecast for the 7th period is $E_6 = 97.8$.

Measure of Variation

It is recognized that our forecasted demand for the 7th period (namely, 97.8) will either overshoot or undershoot the actual demand by some amount. For one thing, the estimate is a decimal number and actual demand must be an integer. But even if the projection were an integer, one could hardly expect the forecast to be exact.

Hence in making the forecast one should indicate what kind of error to expect. In other words, boundaries should be placed about the estimate. In setting up the boundaries a measure of expected variation is needed. The first kind of measure of variation that comes to mind is standard deviation, but this would involve computational difficulties, requiring as it does, squaring and root-taking. Instead of using standard deviation as a measure of variation, one can use a smoothed form of mean absolute deviation which then can be translated into terms of standard deviation.

Smoothed Mean Deviations

Let M_n = smoothed mean absolute deviation (MAD) at the end of the nth period.

D_n = absolute difference between the actual demand during the mth period, A_n, and the forecasted demand for the nth period, E_{n-1}.

that is, $D_n = \left| A_n - E_{n-1} \right|$.

The smoothed mean absolute deviation at the end of the nth period, M_n, is by the expression

$$M_n = M_{n-1} + \alpha (D_n - M_{n-1})$$

In a normal distribution

$$\sigma \approx 1.25 \ \text{MAD}$$

If we now assume that actual demand is normally distributed about the exponential average, then

$$\sigma_n = 1.25 M_n$$

241

where σ_n = smoothed standard deviation for the nth period.

Confidence Bands

Turning now to the generator illustration, we will find the smoothed MAD and standard deviations for the 7 periods and construct 2σ confidence intervals about or exponential average.

One must choose a value for M_o. It makes no difference what choice is made. In the long run M_n will be the same no matter what initial selections is made for M_o. For convenience let $M_o = 0$.

Then

$$M_1 = M_o + \frac{1}{3}(D_1 - M_o) \text{ where } D_1 = \left| A_1 - E_o \right|$$

$$= 0 + \frac{1}{3}(0 - 0) = 0$$

and

$$\sigma_1 = 1.25M_1 = 0$$

$$M_2 = M_1 + \frac{1}{3}(D_2 - M_1) \text{ where } D_2 = \left| A_2 - E_1 \right|$$

$$= 0 + \frac{1}{3}(30 - 0) = 10$$

$$\sigma_2 = 1.25M_2 = 12.5$$

and so on. Putting the results together in a table we have the following:

n	A_n	E_n	M_n	σ_n	$E_n - 2\sigma_n$	$E_n + 2\sigma_n$
1	90	90	0	0	90	90
2	120	100	10	12.5	75	125
3	102	100.7	8	10	80.7	120.7
4	81	94.1	11.9	14.9	64.3	123.9
5	99	95.7	9.6	12	71.7	119.7
6	102	97.8	8.5	10.6	76.6	119

Thus our forecast for the 7th period is 97.8 and assuming normality of demand about the exponential estimate, we are 95 percent certain that the actual demand will be between 76.6 and 119   i.e., in the range $E_n \pm 2\sigma_n$.

Exponential Smoothing Applied to In-Library Usage

In inventory control we used the exponential average of demand at the end of a given period to forecast demand for the following period. In connection with in-library book usage we use the exponential average in a slightly different way. We will use it to put confidence bands on our estimate of a book usage gained from the single hour's count. We will then use these bands to forecast actual usage during the following period.

Let A_n = estimate of the number of Literature books
read during the nth week

E_n = exponential average of the estimated number
of Literature books read during the nth week.

$$E_n = E_{n-1} + \alpha(A_n - E_{n-1})$$

Suppose the weekly estimate of Literature books for three successive weeks are

Week	Estimate of Lit. Books Read
n	A_n
1	60
2	72
3	58

In smoothing these estimates use an $\alpha = .25$, which corresponds to a moving average of 7 periods. By this choice of α we bring into play, in effect, a week's worth of randomly chosen hourly samples.

Using an $\alpha = .25$ and taking $E_0 = A_1 = 60$, we get the following exponential average of the estimated number of times Literature books are read in the library weekly (rounded to nearest integer).

n	A_n	E_n
1	60	60
2	72	63
3	58	62

Using a smoothed form of mean deviation, i.e.,

$$M_n = M_{n-1} + \alpha(D_n - M_{n-1})$$

and assuming that the actual number of Literature books read is normally distributed about this exponential estimate, E_n, we can use the relation that

$$\sigma_n = 1.25M_n$$

to put, say, 2σ limit confidence bands on our estimate of actual book usage. Taking $M_n = 0$ we get the following (rounded to nearest integer)

n	A_n	E_n	M_n	σ_n	$E_n - 2\sigma_n$	$E_n = 2\sigma_n$
1	60	60	0			
2	72	63	3	4	55	71
3	58	62	3	4	54	70

Thus, we can say, assuming that actual use during the nth week is normally distributed about the exponential average of that week, that the actual number of times that Literature books were read in the 3rd week was between 54 and 70 with 95 percent certainty.

This type of weekly analysis of book use is ideally suited for a system of libraries for purposes of book allocations. Allocations can be made weekly on the basis of these forecasts.

Suppose a system has two libraries, and the second of these libraries is analyzed as was the first with respect to Literature book usage in the library week by week. Suppose the following results held for the same periods.

n	A_n	E_n	M_n	σ_n	$E_n-2\sigma_n$	$E_n + 2\sigma_n$
1	100	100	0			
2	90	98	3	4	90	106
3	130	106	10	13	80	132

Here actual use during the 3rd period was between 80 and 132.

Now combine the two results into weekly usage of Literature books for the system as a whole.

n	A_n	E_n	M_n	σ_n	$E_n-2\sigma_n$	$E_n + 2\sigma_n$
1	160	160	0			
2	162	161	1	1	158	162
3	188	168	8	10	148	188

System use of Literature books during the 3rd week was between 148 and 188. If we now average the upper and lower demand limits of the system, we get

$$\frac{148 \text{ to } 188}{2} = 74 \text{ to } 94 \text{ as the average limits per library}$$

Using the average limits per library as a standard for allocating Literature books among the two libraries the following decision rule might be established. Allocate books on a 1-2-3 basis. Libraries whose usage limits fall entirely below the average limits will be allocated 1/6 of the total inventory of Literature books; those libraries whose usage limits fall within the average limits will be allocated 2/6 of the total Literature books; and those libraries whose usage limits fall entirely above the average limits will receive 3/6 of the total Literature books.

If all libraries fall in the first two categories (that is, their usage limits are either entirely below the average limits, or within the average limits), the allocation would be made on a 1-2 basis; if all libraries fall in the second and third category, then the allocation would be made on a 2-3 basis

In our illustration the usage limits of the first library fall entirely below the average limits and those of the second fall within the average limits. Allocation here will be made on a 1-2 basis; the first library will receive 1/3 of the Literature books, the second library 2/3.

Although in some situations it might not be feasible to shift shelved volumes about in accord with demand, certainly new purchases and book requests from the member libraries could be allocated on this basis.

In addition to serving as the basis of a scheme of overall control of performance, and as the basis for achieving the synergistic effect of improved coordination among libraries, the systemic approach makes feasible the conducting of controlled experiments to determine the improvements to adopt.

Experimentation

An example of the type of experiment which can be conducted when a system of libraries exists, is found in a study among three elementary school libraries in Terre Haute, Indiana.[1] The purpose of the study was to determine the relationship between library supervision and theft (or loss) of books from the collection. At one of the libraries, there was no professional librarian, the students had free access to the open shelves, and there was no charge-out requirement. At the second library, a part-time librarian was on duty. At the third library, a full-time librarian was present whenever the library was open; all books had to be charge out to students who wished to borrow.

The record of book loos was compared for these three libraries. It was con-

---

1. American Libraries, American Library Association Bulletin, 1970, p.924.

cluded that there was no significant difference in book loss per student among the three libraries. The broad implication for library administration is that the presence of a librarian who administers standard procedures for charging-out books has little influence on the rate of book loss.

One might not be prepared to accept the methods and finding of the Terre Haute study uncritically. The point of the illustration is not so much the particular methods and results, but the fact that cooperation among three libraries made possible the conduct of the experiment. When valid results are obtained each library can adopt the improvement.

Chapter 14

Library Standards and
Sampling Library Use

ALA Statement of 1959

Probably, the most authoritative statement of college library standards was promulgated by the American Library Association in 1959.[1] This chapter begins with a summary of the ALA 1959 statement on standards for the college library. The organizational status of the chief librarian is described in the first and third sections of the 1959 ALA statement, as follows: He should report to the college president. The chief librarian should have exclusive administrative authority over the library operations. He should plan and administer the library budget. When a faculty library committee exists, it should be advisory to the librarian. There can be a student library committee, too.

The 1959 ALA statement of standards seems to assume the existence of a hierarchical organization structure. Thus, the college librarian would have at least two assistants, one dealing with reader services and the other with technical processes. There should be at least three professional librarians at a college library. A professional is defined as one who holds a graduate library degree (presumably the M.L.S.).

Principles of organization are incorporated into the discussion of staffing. Thus, lines of authority should be established. Clearcut channels of communication should exist. Subordinates of the chief librarian should be consulted by him, and as a result there would be observed a "staff relationship." Over and above the matters dealing with the "scalar principle," the planning and controlling functions are provided for in the reference to the duties of the

---

1. *Standards for College Libraries*. Reprinted in "Raising the Standards: College Libraries," *Drexel Library Quarterly*, July 1966, pp. 251-263.

chief librarian. He is supposed to be concerned "with statistics on activities, acquisitions, and use of the library."

Quantitative standards having to do with staffing, along with the general features of position descriptions are provided in the "staffing" section, the third section of the rather brief 1959 ALA statement on standards. The report holds that there should be a minimum of three professional members of the staff. Also, there should be at least one professional librarian in charge of reader services and at least one with responsibility for technical processes. Furthermore, at least one professional librarian should be on duty in the library whenever the library is open.

The 1959 ALA statement continues, there should be practiced an appropriate degree of specialization as among professional librarians, clerical employees, and student assistants. It follows that the professional should not engage in clerical work. Competent clerical workers should perform the clerical work, which should not be entrusted to student assistants. The ALA statement of standards asserts that, in general, the larger the size of the library, then the larger the justifiable proportion of nonprofessional to professional employees in the library. Finally, the statement indicates that the professional librarians have a responsibility to educate others at the college in the effective use of library resources.

Quantitative standards are provided on the library budget. The 1959 statement maintains that at a minimum the library budget of the college library should be 5 percent of the total educational and general budget of the college, in order to implement the proposed library standards. This percentage would range upward from the 5 percent figure depending on whether library deficiencies exist to start with; the extent of master's degree programs at the school, and the extent to which independent study is to be emphasized at the school. It is a danger signal if the library budget falls below the median percentage for comparable institutions, it is pointed out. Salaries of library employees should come to about two times the amount of the expenditures on books for the library.

A word of comment will be offered on the 5 percent budget standard, before continuing with the summary. The percentage of the total institutional budget to be earmarked for the library should be derived from the use of the library. For example, there would be different reader profiles for each library and for each system of libraries. Such differences in reader profiles would lead to different amounts being expended on book acquisitions, as well as staff personnel, for instance. Staff personnel characteristics -- the number, ability, training, and interests -- would vary with reader profile. Thus, for the individual library, this budgetary percentage could be a good deal different than 5 percent.

Given the application of the 5 percent standard to a particular library, there remains the question of how the amount, represented by the 5 percent, is to be allocated among different uses. The utility to be obtained from different uses would be a basis that would have merit. The comparative utility of different categories of books in the library could be found by:

> (1) the more-or-less standard questionnaire survey to determine attitudes of students toward the library;
>
> (2) a measurement of physiological processes of the reader while he is reading (a la an extension of the polygraph or lie-detector test); and
>
> (3) tests of comprehension of subject matter of library books which have been read.

This third type of test of utility would relate the library budget to the budget for classroom instruction. If there is greater utility from classroom work by students and less utility from reading library books, then more funds should be allocated to classroom instruction. If there is more utility to be gained from spending more money on library books and less utility lost from reducing expenditures on classroom instruction, then the reallocation appears justified in favor of the library budget.

To resume the summary, in the section dealing with the library collections, the 1959 statement of standards first gives a statement of purpose in qualitative terms. The purposes of the collection are: to meet curriculum needs of the school; to serve the faculty and assist them in professional growth; and to meet independent study needs.

In that section, too, there is presented a series of qualitative statements about the collection; for example:

> there should be a strong and up-to-date reference section
>
> the periodicals should be well balanced and carefully chosen
>
> the librarian should have the right to select books, free of censorship
>
> the library holdings should be compared to standard bibliographies
>
> the main catalog should be a union catalog which observes an accepted scheme of book classification and is revised constantly
>
> the audio-visual aids should be an integral part of the library, and the librarian should use the same high standards of selection as in book selection. Furthermore, adequate staff and facilities are needed for audio-visual aids.

The quantitative standards on the book collection are qualified in two respects. For one thing, it is recognized that the size of the book collection is determined by selected variables. They are:

1. extent and nature of curriculum

2. number and character of graduate programs

3. methods of instruction

4. size of undergraduate and graduate student body

5. need of faculty for more advanced materials.

Secondly, the quantitative standards are regarded as minimal. It is explained that the quantitative standards have been derived from an analysis of statistics in small-college libraries, libraries which could find themselves confronted by resistance to an increase in the number of books in their collection beyond 300,000 volumes.

The quantitative standards state that the minimum number of volumes in a college library should be 50,000. And, for each additional 200 students in the student body beyond 600 students, there should be added 10,000 volumes to the collection.

With respect to the statement of standards on the library building, a similar pattern obtains. That is, general qualitative statements of standards are presented, as well as a few selected quantitative standards. Thus, it is proposed that the library building should be centrally located and functional in design, and that a new building should provide for future expansion. There should be well-planned areas within the library for such functions as the reference activity. Adequate quarters should be provided for the processes of ordering, preparation, cataloguing, etc. Private office space should be available for administrative positions. A staff lounge should be included in the library building which would be equipped with kitchen facilities. Finally, a variety of types of seating should be provided for library users.

The quantitative standards specify that seating capacity should be available for one-third of the present student body, and that seating capacity should be

derived from expected future growth of the library over the next 20 years. Also,
shelf space should allow for a doubling of the existing number of volumes in the
collection. Furthermore, one hundred and twenty-five square feet of floor space
per staff worker should be provided. Table space of six square feet (3 ft. x 2 ft.)
per reader should be available for general library use.

Moving on to the topic of determining the quality of library service and the
evaluation of the service, the 1959 statement explains that there is no topic more
important nor more difficult. The statement recognizes that the analysis of the
statistical records of the circulation department gives only a partial picture,
especially where open shelves are to be found at the library. Nevertheless, it
is thought likely that there is a connection between the library service improving at the same time that per capita figures of books on regular loan are showing an upward trend over a period of time.

In addition, the statement recommends surveys of reading in the library,
studies of books not supplied, reference questions not answered, and the like.
With respect to organizing for conducting such studies, the statement recommends
frequent self-studies by library staff and teaching faculty.

The last topic treated in the 1959 statement is the topic of "Inter-library
Cooperation." The statement recognizes that real benefits can be obtained from
pooling library resources of several libraries. Each library is enabled to give
better service to its own readers. And each can better use its funds. The report
points out that planned purchasing of materials to avoid duplication, is the
source of economies from interlibrary cooperation. On the other hand, it is noted
that one library should not borrow from another library those things that are
basic to the college program of the first library.

In a review of the impact of the 1959 statement of standards, five years
after the standards had been formulated in 1959, it was concluded that there is

(1) a need for an improved objective basis for quantitative standards[3] and (2)
no one set of quantitative library standards that could be applied universally.
For example, library and school accreditational evaluations are relative to
institutional purpose, available resources, and extent to which purpose is accomplished using resources efficiently.[4]

What can be said about the pertinence of sampling book use at a library
to the foregoing summary of library standards for colleges? It should be clear
that the 1959 ALA statement places an obligation on librarians to adopt appropriate statistical methods in order to measure accurately how the library's
resources are being utilized. Furthermore, the librarian as administrator is
obligated to make use of the results of such statistically sound methods.

Specifically, when it comes to the topics of quantitative standards such
as size of book collection, square footage of building, and seating capacity
of library, the ability to measure actual use (as described in this book) provides an improved basis for setting such standards which should come to supersede per capita standards.

Public Library Statement of 1966

When one compares the 1959 statement of standards for college libraries
and the 1966 statement of standards for public libraries one finds interesting
similarities.[5] For example, the standards generally are treated as minimum
standards in both sources. There are extensive qualitative statements of standards in both documents. And there is no little reference to the desirability

3. Helen M. Brown, "The Standards and the College Library in 1965," Drexel
   Library Quarterly, July 1966, pp. 202-206.

4. Albert E. Meder, Jr., "Accrediting Agencies and the Standards," Drexel
   Library Quarterly, July 1966, pp. 213-219.

5. Minimum Standards for Public Library Systems, 1966. (Chicago: American Library
   Association, 1967).

of adopting appropriate management principles in both. Quantitative standards
are stated in per capita terms in both documents; that is, in terms of number
of students enrolled or number of persons in the population served.

A striking difference between the two is the great emphasis given to
library systems in the public libraries statement which is not to be found in
the college libraries standards. The public libraries statement points out the
vital importance of a system of libraries so as to enable the relatively small
local library to provide greater breadth and depth of service to users. It
indicates that centralization of selected functions should be considered and
adopted where appropriate. Here we have the adoption of a strategy on centralization and decentralization similar to General Motors' and Dupont's.

The discussions of sampling a system of libraries could have particular
relevance here. Perhaps there is a greater sense of urgency among public libraries that would lead to the use of a systems approach to evaluate the effectiveness of individual libraries, the construction of improved coordination
among parts of a system to gain a synergistic effect, and the use of a system
to conduct controlled experiments. See Chapter 13 on "Sampling the
Library System."

Generalizing the Quantitative Method

What needs to be avoided in the library field is the type of pitfall into
which planning for outdoor recreation fell at one time. In urban areas, the
land acreage standard of ten acres of land devoted to recreational use per 1,000
persons in the population has been widely adopted by town after town and city
after city. Some consulting agencies have promoted the use of this universal
quantitative standard. After all, it does have the virtues of simplicity and

concreteness. Its use is a substitute for time-consuming and sometimes difficult administrative planning and decision-making.

This acreage standard for urban places has serious deficiencies, however. It is stated in terms of the supply side of the picture. It fails to take into account demand for outdoor recreation of the population at large, and variations in demand according to such variables as age, economic and social status, place of residence, etc. In addition there is a need for intensive empirical observation of the details of recreation behavior of those persons who are using recreation areas.[6] And the technical issue of capacity of the recreation area must be resolved in order to relate to one another supply of and demand for recreation areas.

The general proposition is that it is not the specific quantitative standards which should be generalized in the library field, but it is the methodology of measurement and analysis which can be generalized and standardized. Once this is done, the methodology can be applied to describe the use of one library or many libraries, according to the purpose at hand. And both quantitative and qualitative standards can be brought into play, tentative and relative though they might be, to evaluate the library operations under the special circumstances of the given situation.[7]

---

6. See Robert J. Daiute, "Methods for Determination of Demand for Outdoor Recreation," Land Economics, August, 1966, pp. 327-338.

7. Interestingly, when one traces the history of the acreage standards in outdoor recreation planning, one finds that a few excellent empirical studies were conducted some 60 to 70 years ago. These studies underly the standards that came to prevail unchanged for many years. But, instead of generalizing this methodology, the results were generalized and applied widely regardless of local circumstances.
On the desirability of tentative quantitative standards see Anatol Rapoport, Operational Philosophy (New York: Harper, 1953).

Whatever the basic nature of the quantitative standards, certainly no credence is given to the idea that professional judgment will be superseded somehow. Within the quantitative standards, however formulated, there is still an important place for the exercise of professional judgment in the selection of books to be purchased. For instance, it must be decided what proportions of new books should be new titles, titles published at earlier dates, and titles already in the collection but requiring multiple volumes or replacement. Librarians would refer to selected bibliographies, some of which are derived from the card catalogs of libraries acknowledged to be outstanding libraries. Librarians would also refer to authoritative sources of book reviews, such as the journal Choice. In addition, professors would recommend the purchase of books that they find are needed for their academic purposes.

Quantitative standards serve to supplement the judgment of professional librarians. Statistics cannot (repeat cannot) be used independent of the competent librarian's judgment. Where there appears to be a conflict between judgment based on professional experience and what is suggested by the results of the quantitative analysis, the two must be integrated. The librarian, himself, must integrate the two. This type of problem is not unusual but it is simply a special case of the classic problem of conflict resolution. In order for there to be such an integration it is essential for the librarian to participate directly in a process to resolve the conflict. This process leads to the creation of any required changes by those directly involved in the conflict, and to the acceptance of innovations.[8]

---

8. For a discussion of conflict resolution by integration and by looking at the facts of the situation, see Mary Parker Follett, Dynamic Administration (New York: Harper and Row, 1940).

APPENDICES

RANDOM TIMES AND RANDOM LOCATIONS
FOR FIRST TWO DAYS OF INTERVIEWING

September 11, 1969

September 11, 1969 continued

10:15 a.m.	**3:05 p.m.**
150	129
087	135
167	018
325	262
110	260
10:25 a.m.	**3:20 p.m.**
190	029
169	309
054	365
023	271
271	144
10:30 a.m.	**3:25 p.m.**
082	211
225	005
249	322
344	363
217	337
12:05 p.m.	**3:50 p.m.**
154	319
002	245
380	312
107	030
034	366
1:20 p.m.	**5:40 p.m.**
033	373
337	162
297	378
078	134
258	187
2;25 p.m.	**6:55 p.m.**
262	099
216	200
033	302
098	0911
173	172
8:30 p.m.	**8:55 p.m.**
333	360
014	025
129	238
364	071
315	273
9:30 p.m.	**9:50 p.m.**
110	039
251	116
367	209
041	176
006	245

September 11, 1969 continued

September 12, 1969 continued

10:15 p.m.

175
245
368
238
018

September 12, 1969

8:45 a.m.

209
387
381
174
253

9:45 a.m.

099
358
331
378
205

9:55 a.m.

001
290
041
351
184

10:30 a.m.

337
374
208
094
254

12:25 p.m.

272
020
285
235
158

1:10 p.m.

084
250
386
182
176

3:30 p.m.

027
352
182
342
159

4:00 p.m.

378
166
169
390
359

4:15 p.m.

075
058
160
279
210

5:00 p.m.

038
076
308
160
090

8:05 p.m.

038
235
087
231
159

8:30 p.m.

061
005
231
038
192

8:45

267
192
110
150
395

9:25 p.m.

266
128
357
264
089

INSTRUCTIONS: At the time designated below, report to the first library carrel listed. Before proceeding with the interview, the interviewee must meet the following requirements:
1. Seated at the designated carrel

2. Reading any BOOK.

Then, proceed to obtain the desired information. If reader is a student, obtain student's name, campus address, and full bibliographical description of book, including library call number if book is a library book. Other information on the student can be obtained at the Office of the Dean of Students at a later time. If reader of book is not a student, obtain name and address of the reader, as well as purpose for reading the book. Also, of course, obtain full bibliographical description of book.

REMEMBER: At no time is the normal function of the library to be interrupted. Conduct interviews as QUIETLY and QUICKLY as possible.

SPECIAL NOTE: There is a high probability that you will find a reader at one of the five carrels. If you are unable to find a qualified interviewee at the first carrel listed, proceed to the second listed carrel. If still unable to find a qualified person, proceed to the third listed number, and so forth. If unable to find a suitable interviewee at any of the designated carrels, indicate this fact and the reason at the bottom of this page in the space provided. It should be understood that your interview activities will be monitored.

IT IS OF EXTREME IMPORTANCE THAT THE INTERVIEW BE HELD AT THE DESIGNATED TIME. PLEASE BE PROMPT.

DESIGNATED TIME: _____

DESIGNATED CARRELS: 1. _____ 2. _____ 3. _____

4. _____ 5. _____

UNABLE TO FIND A QUALIFIED INTERVIEWEE: _____

THE UPPER NUMBER ON THE GUMMED LABEL REFERS TO THE NUMBER OF THE INNER CARREL. THE LOWER NUMBER REFERS TO THE OUTER CARREL.

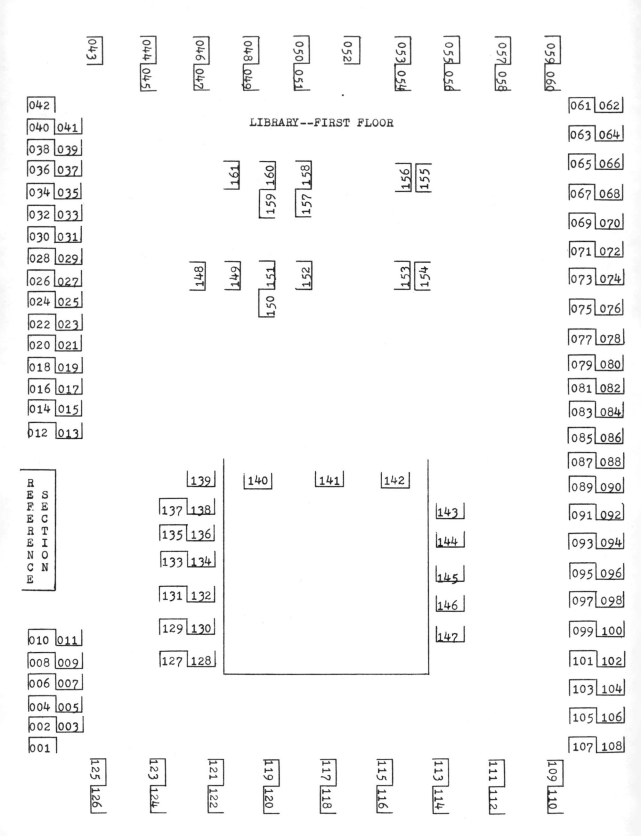

LIBRARY--FIRST FLOOR

Name of Interviewer: _____

Time of Interview: _____

Number of Carrel: _____

Name of Reader: _____

Sex of Reader: _____

_____

Complete Bibliographical Description of Book Being Read : _____

_____

_____

_____

_____

_____

_____

_____

_____

_____

_____

Name of Author : _____

Title of Book: _____

Place of Publication: _____ Name of Publisher: _____

Date of Publication: _____

Library Call Number on Book: _____

Place of Residence: ☐ Dormitory ☐ Sorority ☐ Fraternity or Off-Campus ☐

Academic Average of Reader: _____ Major Field of Study: _____

Freshman ☐   Sophomore ☐   Junior ☐   Senior ☐   Evening School Student ☐

Graduate School Student ☐

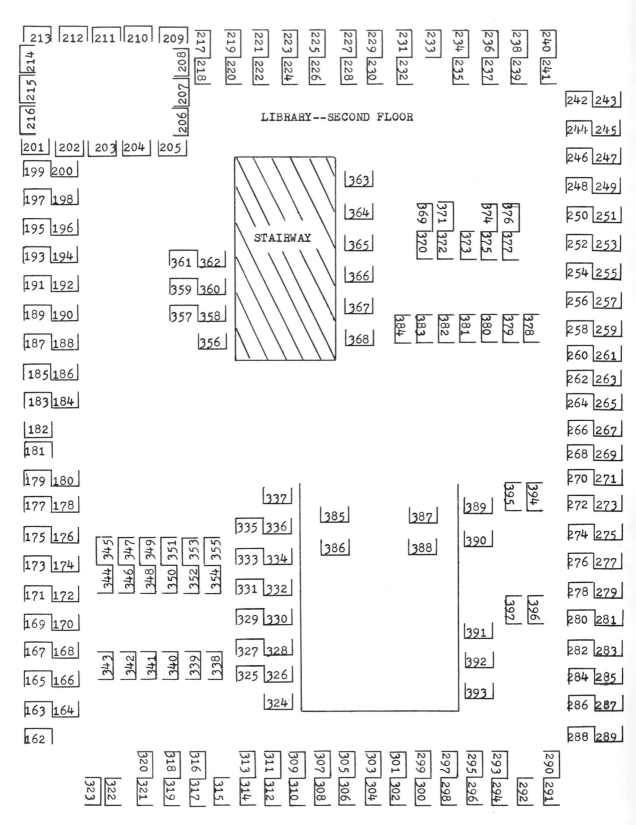

LIBRARY--SECOND FLOOR

STAIRWAY

APPENDIX C
FORM FOR CLASSIFYING AND CODING
BOOKS BEING READ

CLASSIFICATION OF BOOKS

Interview Information	Verbal Description	Program Code Number
No interview conducted	No interview	
Interview conducted but no Rider Library call number	Not Rider Library Book	
300-399 call number	Rider Library Social Sciences Book	
500-599 call number	Rider Library Pure Sciences Book	
600-699 call number	Rider Library Technology (Applied Sciences) Book	
800-899 call number	Rider Library Literature and Rhetoric Book	
000-099 Generalities) 100-199 Philosophy and re-) lated disciplines) 200-299 Religion) 400-499 Language) 700-799 The Arts)	Rider Library Other Book	

NOTE: For a description of the call number classification see:
Melvil Dewey, Dewey Decimal Classification and Relative Index,
Edition 17. (Lake Placid, New York: Forest Press, Inc. of
Lake Placid Club Education Foundation, 1965), especially pp.
109-120.

CODE SHEET FOR RIDER COMPUTER CENTER
DATA BANK ON STUDENTS

REGISTRATION CARD CODES

OCTOBER 1969

Col   A)   RACE
28   1. American Indian
           2. American Negro
           3. Oriental American
           4. Spanish American
           5. Foreign Student
           6. Other (including caucasian)

           SEMESTER
29   B)   No. of semesters completed based on credits passed:

Semester	Credits Passed
1	0 to 16
2	17 to 32
3	33 to 48
4	49 to 64
5	65 to 80
6	81 to 96
7	97 to 112
8	113 –
9	SPECIAL STUDENTS

30   C)   SEX
           1. Male
           2. Female

31   D)   MARITAL STATUS
           1. Single
           2. Married

32   E)   MILITARY
           1. Veteran
           2. Non-Veteran

33   F)   FRATERNITY-SORORITY
           1. PKP   6. AKD
           2. PSE   7. DPE
           3. THE   8. DZ
           4. TC   9. ZTA
           5. ZBT

34   G)   HOUSING
               1. Commute   4. Fraternity
               2. Dormitory 5. Private Home
               3. Sorority

35-36   H)   RELIGION   BLANK IF NO PREFERENCE

10. Baptist	20. Reformed Jewish	40. Other
11. Lutheran	21. Conservative Jewish	41. Christian Science
12. Methodist	22. Orthodox Jewish	
13. Reformed		
14. Presbyterian	30. Roman Catholic	
15. Episcopalian	31. Eastern Orthodox	
16. United Church of Christ		

37   I)   ENTERING COLLEGE
               1. First Time
               2. Transfer
               3. Re-enteringRider (continuing or readmit)

38-40   J)   CURRICULUM CODES

1) Bus. Admin
   1-01 A.A. Bus Adm
   1-02 A.A. Med Sci
   1-03 A.A. Sec. Sci
   1-41 B.S. Acct
   1-42 B.S. Ind Rel
   1-43 B.S. Bus Adm
   1-46 B.S. Finance
   1-48 B.S. Insurance
   1-49 B.S. Management
   1-50 B.S. Marketing
   1-51 B.S. Real Estate
   1-52 B.S. Sec Sci
   1-59 Basic Business Curr

2) Liberal Arts
   2-10 B.A. General L.A.
   2-11 B.A. American Studies
   2-12 B.A. Biology
   2-13 B.A. Chemistry
   2-14 B.A. English
   2-15 B.A. Fine Arts
   2-17 B.A. History
   2-18 B.A. Journalism
   2-19 B.A. Math
   2-20 B.A. Philosophy
   2-21 B.A. Pol Sci
   2-22 B.A. Psychology
   2-24 B.A. Sociology
   2-25 B.A. Spanish
   2-42 B.S. Biology
   2-45 B.S. Chemistry
   2-26 B.A. German
   2-27 B.A. Communications
   2-28 B.A. Physics

3) Education
   3-53 B.S. Dist Education
   3-44 B.S. Bus Education
   3-23 B.A. Sec Education
   3-25 B.A. Elem Education

4) Special (non-degree Candidates)
   4-99 Special

K)   GRADUATION
Expected year of Graduation...if Graduation is 1970
   70-1 January Grad.
   70-2 June Grad.
   70-3 Summer Grad.

Col

L) <u>STATE CODES</u>

44-45
01 ALA	11 IDAHO	22 MINN	33 N.D.	44 VT
50 ALASKA	12 ILL	23 MISS	34 OHIO	45 VA
02 ARIZ	13 IND	24 MO	35 OKLA	46 WASH
03 ARK	14 IOWA	25 MONT	36 ORE	47 W. VA.
04 CALIF	15 KANS	26 NEB	37 PENNA	48 WISC
05 COLO	16 KY	27 NEV	38 R.I.	49 WYO
06 CONN	17 LA	28 N.H.	39 S.C.	
07 DEL	18 ME	29 N.J.	40 S.D.	
08 D.C.	19 MD	30 N.M.	41 TENN	
09 FLA	20 MASS	31 N.Y.	42 TEX	
10 GA	21 MICH	32 N.C.	43 UTAH	
50 HAWAII				

M) <u>COUNTY CODES</u>   N.J. ONLY
<u>Blank if State is not N.J.</u>

46-47
01 ATLANTIC	15 GLOUCESTER	29 OCEAN
03 BERGEN	17 HUDSON	31 PASSAIC
05 BURLINGTON	19 HUNTERDON	33 SALEM
07 CAMDEN	21 MERCER	35 SOMERSET
09 CAPE MAY	23 MIDDLESEX	37 SUSSEX
11 CUMBERLAND	25 MONMOUTH	39 UNION
13 ESSEX	27 MORRIS	41 WARREN

N) <u>SCHOLARSHIP</u> - Blank if none

48
1. Fellowship   5. Work-Study Program
2. Scholarship   6. Research or Teaching Assistantship
3. Loan Fund   7. Athletic Scholarship
4. Education   8. Other
   opportunity
   Grant

49-60 O) SELECTIVE SERVICE NUMBER

61-66 P) BIRTH DATE

CODING SYSTEM OF RESEARCH PROJECT

C C 1-3

Interview form number.

C C 4

0 If no interview because all 5 carrels unoccupied.
1 If no interviews because carrel occupant is not reading a book.
2 If interview.

C C 5

1 If male.
2 If female.

C C 6

1 If reader found on Monday.
2 If reader   "   " Tuesday.
3 If reader   "   " Wednesday.
4 If reader   "   " Thursday.
5 If reader   "   " Friday.
6. If reader   "   " Saturday.
7 If reader   "   " Sunday.

C C 7-8

1 If reader found between 8 and 8/59 am.
2 If reader   "   "   9 and 9:59 am.
3. If reader   "   "   10 and 10:59 am.
4 If reader   "   "   11 and 11:59 am.
5 If reader   "   "   12 and 12:59 pm.
6 If reader   "   "   1 and 1:59 pm.
7 If reader   "   "   2 and 2:59 pm.
8 If reader   "   "   3 and 3:59 pm.
9 If reader   "   "   4 and 4:59 pm.
10 If reader   "   "   5 and 5:59 pm.
11 If reader   "   "   6 and 6:59 pm.
12 If reader   "   "   7 and 7:59 pm.
13 If reader   "   "   8 and 8:59 pm.
14 If reader   "   "   9 and 9:59 pm.
15 If reader   "   "   10 and 10:30 pm.

C C 9

0 If not Rider library book.
1 If Rider library book.

C C 10

0 If not Rider student.
1 If Rider student.

C C 11

1 If social science library book.
2 If pure science library book.
3 If technology (applied science) library book.
4 If literature library book.
5 If geography or history library book.
6 If other library book.

C C 12

1 If Rider Freshman.
2 If Rider Sophomore.
3 If Rider Junior.
4 If Rider Senior.
5 If Rider graduate student.
6 If Rider evening student (non-matriculated).

NOTE: If Rider evening student is matriculated,
       translate his status, by means of credit hours
       completed, into terms of freshman, sophomore etc.

C C 13

1 If Liberal Arts major.
] If Education major.
3 If Business major.
4 If Education master.
5 If Business master.

NOTE: If Rider evening student is matriculated, his
       major is Business.

C C 14

1 If Rider dormitory student.
] If Rider commuter.
3 If Rider fraternity or sorority.

C C 15-18

Cumulative average in form X.XX.
Count only Rider undergraduates (day and
matriculated evening students).

APPENDIX F
VALIDATION OF INTERVIEW PROCEDURE

A random sample of 50 interview occasions was selected from the original sample of 700 planned interview attempts. Members of the women's fraternity served as validators. The validators were supposed to conduct themselves just as regular interviewers would, except that the validators would give the right-of-way to the regular interviewers.

The 50-item validating sample is listed below:

Schedule of Validating Interviews

	Date and Time			Date and Time	
1.	9-11-69	12:05 p.m.	26.	10-9-69	9:15 a.m.
2.	9-11-69	10:15 p.m.	27.	10-10-69	9:25 a.m.
3.	9-19-69	11:15 a.m.	28.	10-12-69	2:20 p.m.
4.	9-18-69	3:15 p.m.	29.	10-14-69	10:15 a.m.
5.	9-19-69	12:10 p.m.	30.	10-14-69	2:55 p.m.
6.	9-23-69	10:45 a.m.	31.	10-14-69	9:35 p.m.
7.	9-23-69	2:45 p.m.	32.	10-16-69	9:15 a.m.
8.	9-]4-69	99:15 a.m.	33.	10-16-69	7:55 p.m.
9.	9-]3-69	1:00 p.m.	34.	10-16-69	9:35 p.m.
10.	9-24-69	7:50 p.m.	35.	10-17-69	8:25 a.m.
11.	9-25-69	2:30 p.m.	36.	10-18-69	1:00 p.m.
12.	9-25-69	7:45 p.m.	37.	10-18-69	4:10 p.m.
13.	9-26-69	9:50 a.m.	38.	10-20-69	11:30 a.m.
14.	9-26-69	12:25 p.m.	39.	10-20-69	12:05 p.m.
15.	9-29-69	10:20 a.m.	40.	10-20-69	4:15 p.m.
16.	9-29-69	3:10 p.m.	41.	10-22-69	2:35 p.m.
17.	9-29-69	8:30 p.m.	42.	10-22-69	6:55 p.m.
18.	9-30-69	10:15 a.m.	43.	10-28-69	6:40 p.m.
19.	9-30-69	6:40 p.m.	44.	10-28-69	1:00 p.m.
20.	10-1 -69	12:30 p.m.	45.	10-29-69	8:00 a.m.
21.	10-2 -69	9:30 p.m.	46.	10-29-69	5:40 p.m.
22.	10-3 -69	10:00 a.m.	47.	10-31-69	3:50 p.m.
23.	10-3 -69	10:15 a.m.	48.	11- 3-69	12:20 p.m.
24.	10-4 -69	2:05 p.m.	49.	11- 4-69	1:15 p.m.
25.	10-6 -69	11:35 a.m.	50.	11- 7-69	10:00 a.m.

A discrepancy of one kind or other has been found between the validator's report and the regular interviewer's report for eleven interviews. The interview dates and times for the discrepancies are:

273

1.	9–18–69	11:15 a.m.
2.	9–23–69	10:45 a.m.
3.	9–23–69	2:45 p.m.
4.	9–24–69	9:15 a.m.
5.	9–24–69	7:50 p.m.
6.	9–29–69	10:20 a.m.
7.	10–16–69	9:15 a.m.
8.	10–18–69	1:00 p.m.
9.	10–22–69	6:55 p.m.
10.	10–26–69	6:40 p.m.
11.	11– 3–69	12:20 p.m.

Seven of the discrepancies are reconcilable; however, four of the discrepancies stand as identified invalidated interviews. This result means that 8 percent (4 ÷ 50) of the interviews conducted should be regarded as not being validated.

The validation procedure used has been an effective instrument for measuring the extent to which interviews conducted by regular interviewers were not validated as having observed the requirements of the sample design.

EXCERPT FROM <u>WORK SAMPLING</u> BY BARNES

STUDY NO. 1:   A DELAY-ALLOWANCE STUDY OF COMMON

MACHINE SHOP OPERATIONS

The purpose of this study was to determine personal and delay allowances for common machine shop operations.

This machine shop department consisted of 64 machines and 40 operators.
The machines were of 15 different classes common to most machine shops. All
employees who worked with these machines were paid on an incentive basis.

Observations were taken at random during a period of 11 days, and a
sufficient number of observations were obtained on five operations to draw
conclusive results concerning allowances. These operations were single
turret lathes, ordinary single drills, ordinary gang drills, gang turret
lathes, and single speed drills. Observations were also recorded on other
miscellaneous operations in the same department.

JOB INTERRUPTION KEY

No. Description of Interruption

1 Talk about job to foreman,

   clerks, truckers, or supervisors.

2 Get started--prepare and arrange

   work area, start machines or

   equipment.

3 Change jobs--get and aside

   supplies, tools, prints, and

   other equipment

4 Secure inspector's approval

5 Check work--measurement or

   gauging of work.

6 Work, count, arrange, or record

No. Description of Interruption

11 Oil machines or equipment --

   get oil, oil machine, aside oil

12 Minor repair of tools, machines,

   or equipment.

13 Alignment of jigs, fixtures,

   gages, stops.

14 Wait for tools, trucks, stock,

   foreman, or supplies.

15 Add coolant or processing

   materials.

16 Help another worker.

17 Shut down at end of shift --

material, production, or scrap.

7 Load or move material on trucks.

8 Clean equipment or work area --remove chips and shavings, want for cleanup man.

9 Minor mechanical or electrical difficulties.

10 Maintain process--adjust equipment, sharpen tools, change broaches.

aside equipment or cleanup of workplace, make out time slip.

18 Miscellaneous--open and close windows, turn lights on or off, clean right-of-way.

19 Personal--lunch periods, get drink, smoke, washroom, and other personal needs.

20 Avoidable delay--arrive late, leave early, idle.

The first step in this study consisted of securing the cooperation of the departmental foreman. Since the shop was unionized, the unio stewards were told the purpose and nature of the study. Through these means, the employees were informed of the observer's actions.

A data sheet was constructed which listed each of the 15 various operations. A job interruption key was also made for use in keying the causes of delay.

Results and conclusions of Study No. 1 are included in Study No. 2 for purposes of comparison.

STUDY NO. 2: A DELAY-ALLOWANCE STUDY OF COMMON MACHINE SHOP OPERATIONS

The purpose of this study was to determine the reliability of the ratio-delay method by comparison of the results of Study No. 1 with Study No. 2.

TABLE 22. COMPARISON OF RESULTS OF STUDY NO. 1 AND STUDY NO. 2

	Study No. 1, %	Study No. 2, %	Composite Allowance, %
Average delay allowance	7.3	7.9	
Average personal allowance	4.1	4.5	
Total allowance	11.4	12.4	
Delay allowances for individual operations			
Turret lathe (single)	8.3	8.4	8.4
Single drill (ordinary)	10.2	9.0	9.5
Gang drill (ordinary)	5.8	5.7	5.7
Drill and tap (single drill)	..	6.6	8.5
Single speed drill	4.4	..	7.6
Turret lathe (gang)	4.2	..	5.6
Bore and ream (single drill)	..	7.9	7.1
Milling machine	..	..	5.0

*Based on results of a total of 7380 observations.

The blank spaces indicate operations on which insufficient observations were recorded to obtain results within the desired limits of accuracy for each of the studies. When the number of observations from each study was totaled, the composite gave a sufficient number for accurate results.

Both of these studies were taken in the same machine shop, covering the same operations under similar conditions. These studies were taken one month apart. Production records were checked as a measure of assurance that the conditions were similar. The procedure followed was the same as was employed in Study No. 1. The composite results of the two studies made it possible to obtain delay-allowance percentages on eight different operations.

A comparison of results of Study No. 1 and Study No. 2, for the purpose of determining reliability, is shown in Table 22.

The delay analysis summary (Table 23) is the tool for use in improving
methods and eliminating delays. This summary shows the frequency with which
the individual delays occur. For example: In

TABLE 23. DELAY ANALYSIS SUMMARY

Key No.	Description of Interruption	No. of Delays	Per Cent of Total Delay
14	Wait for tools, truck, stock, foreman, or supplies	101	19.6
8	Clean equipment, work area	90	17.5
17	Shut down at end of shift	76	14.5
2	Get started	72	14.0
1	Talk about job to foreman, clerks, truckers, or supervisors	38	7.3
10	Maintain process	36	7.0
4	Secure inspector's approval	33	6.4
15	Add coolant or processing material	24	4.7
12	Minor repair of tools, machines, or equipment	14	2.7
17	Make out time slip or production record	7	1.4
16	Help another worker	6	1.2
11	Oil machines or equipment	5	1.0
2	Change jobs	4	0.8
9	Minor mechanical or electrical difficulties	4	0.8
18	Miscellaneous	4	0.8
	Total	514	100.0

Studies No. 1 and No. 2, the largest delay occurence was Key No. 14 --
"Wait for tools, truck, stock, foreman, or supplies." Thus, to improve

departmental efficiency and decrease delays, better methods might be
employed in routing, scheduling, and trucking. The next most frequent
delay was Key No. 8 -- "Clean equipment or work area." This delay might
be decreased by use of a cleanup crew.

RELIABILITY AND ECONOMY

The conclusions based upon the results of Studies No. 1 and No. 2
are briefly as follows. The obtained point difference between the
average departmental delay allowances was 0.6%, and the point difference
between average departmental personal allowances was 0.4%. The maximum
difference of any one operations was 1.2%. Differences as small as these
may certainly be attributed to chance variations in delay occurence.
Thus, these studies indicate a reliability of measurement by the ratio-
delay method.

In addition to evidencing, reliability, the ratio-delay method also
showed a great economy of time consumed in obtaining the results.

It took approximately 34 hours to obtain results for these two studies.
Eight hours in addition were spent in computing the results. This made a
total of 42 hours spent in covering eight operations by ratio-delay.

Assuming that it is only necessary to take one eight-hour production
time study of each operation to obtain reliable values, it would take 8
hours to study one operation, plus about 2 hours to complete the results,
or a total of 10 hours per operation. This assumption is a bare minimum,
and more than one eight-hour time study should probably be taken for
accurate results.

It took only 42 hours to obtain allowances for 8 operations by the
ratio-delay method. In comparison, it would take an estimated 8 x 10
hours or 80 hours to obtain allowances for 8 operations by time study.
The ratio-delay method took only one half the time that it is estimated

would be necessary by time study. Thus, the economy of the method is clearly demonstrated.

STUDY NO. 3:

A DELAY-ALLOWANCE STUDY OF BENCH AND MACHINE CORE-MAKING OPERATIONS

A further industrial plant study of the reliability and validity of this technique was made, covering bench and machine core-making operations. Comparisons were obtained between studies taken by the ratio-delay method and those of stop-watch time study when both methods were used simultaneously on the same operations.

As a measure of reliability, comparison was made between results of two independent ratio-delay studies taken on successive days. A comparison of the results of both of these studies with time study was also made as a check on validity.

The resulting comparisons are shown in Table 24.

From these comparisons the ratio-delay method evidences both reliability and validity of measurement.

GENERAL CONCLUSIONS

As a result of this investigation and others made by the writers, using the ratio-delay method, the following conclusions seem to be evident.

The proper use of the ratio-delay method will result in reliable and valid allowances, in an economical manner, for common industrial operations.

Certain advantages appeared in the use of the ratio-delay method over all-day production time studies.

(1) Less time is consumed in determining the allowances, especially where there are many similar operations so that several observations may be obtained each round. The estimated cost of determining allowances by ratio-delay is about one fourth to one half that of time study.

280

TABLE 24. COMPARISON OF RESULTS OBTAINED FROM

RATIO-DELAY STUDIES AND FROM TIME STUDIES

	Ratio-Delay Method, %		
Operation	Study A	Study B	Time Study
Bench coremaker			
Delay allowance	8.7	7.6	6.4
Personal allowance	3.9	4.7	5.2
Total allowance	12.6	12.3	11.6
Core blowing machine operator			
Delay allowance	7.7	7.7	6.4
Personal allowance	4.5	5.4	5.4
Total allowance	12.2	13.1	11.8

(2) There is less chance of obtaining misleading results, as the operators are not under close observation for long periods of time.

(3) Observations may be taken over a period of days or weeks, thus decreasing the chance of day-to-day or week-to-week variation affecting the results.

(4) This type of study may be interrupted at any time without affecting the results.

(5) The ratio-delay method may be used to analyze an entire department for the purpose of methods improvement.

(6) It is possible by this method to obtain delay allowances on operations where time study is not feasible. Examples of operations such as these are: assembly lines, multiple-man molding units, and other group operations. All members of the group may be included in

one study by ratio-delay, but numerous studies may be required by

time study for equally accurate results.

Source: Advanced Management, Vol. 15,No. 8 and 9,Aug. Sept.,1950.
           Reprinted with permission . of Society for the Advancement
           of Management

EXCERPT FROM <u>WORK</u> <u>SAMPLING</u> <u>FOR</u> <u>MODERN</u> <u>MANAGEMENT</u> BY HANSEN

SELECTION OF RANDOM TIMES FOR READINGS:

During most of the study, the sample was stratified by taking two read-ings each hour. The selection of times within the hour was made by assign-ing five-minute increments to the first 12 digits of a table of 16-digit random numbers. The numbers were read from the table and the appropriate time indicated on the data sheet.

Since the office manager's route for data collection was varied from trip to trip and took approximately two minutes, it was felt that setting up the readings at random five-minute periods did nothing to detract from the statistical validity of the study.

The purpose in stratifying the sample was to obtain a true picture of the time distribution of the clerical force with fewer readings than would have to be taken to obtain the same reliability with an unstratified sample.

Spot checks made after the second reading in an hour to determine if anyone was taking advantage of the "unobservable" time indicated that no one was doing so. However, near the end of the study, stratifying the sample was discontinued and the readings were taken at completely random times during the day.

The times were selected at five-minute intervals by assigning a combi-nation of numbers from the 16-digit random numbers to each interval. The numbers were then read from the table and the appropriate observation time indicated on the data sheet.

PERIODS OF THE STUDY AND CATEGORY DEFINITIONS:

The observed activity was divided into 10 categories. These were: Using telephone, Librarian duties, Productive work other than typing, Typing, Typing for students, Interruptions by staff, Interruptions by students, Interruptions by others, Personal, Other. The categories were further defined as follows:

1 Telephone: All telephone activity except personal calls.

2 Librarian: All activity connected with the book and film library.
Does not include talking to anyone, even if in regard to librarian
duties.

3 Typing for Staff: All activity connected with typing for official
purposes. Insertion and removal of paper from machine. Does not
include typing for students.

4 Productive Operations: All official activity other than work for
students and not indicated elsewhere. For example: filing, collating,
and operating ditto machine.

5 Typing for Students: All typing of material developed by students
for course purposes.

6 Contact with Staff: All official oral contact with other members of
the staff. For example: answering and asking questions.

7 Contact with Students: All oral contact with students. For example:
answering requests for information, delivering messages, checking
books at library (only when student is present).

8 Contact with Other Persons: All oral contact with persons other than
staff and students. For example: other Rock Island Arsenal employees,
salesmen.

9 Personal: All activity other than official business or official contact
with staff, students, or others. For example: Rest room, coffee break,
personal conversations, getting a drink.

10 Other: Any activity not covered in 1-9. Record at 10a, 10b, 10c, etc.,
and list under a, b, c, etc., in space for description of 10 on data
sheet.

PRELIMINARY RESULTS

After six weeks, results for the entire group were: Using telephone --
3.5%, Librarian duties--4%, Productinve work other than typing -- 51.0%,
Typing -- 14.5%, Typing for students -- 9.9%, Interruption by staff-- 6.1%,
Interruption by students -- 0.4%, Interruption by others -- 0.9%, Personal --
23.2%, Other -- 0.0%.

Since many of the percentages for the categories were so small, it
would take an excessive number of readings to validate them. Also, the aim
of the study was re-evaluated in terms of an office work-measurement program. The jobs upon which standards would be set were determined, and a
new category of nonstandard work was provided. The original categories were r
re-grouped as follows: (1) Interruptions--Formerly: Using telephone, Interruption by staff, Interruption by students, Interruption by others;
(2) Personal; (3) Standard production; and (4) Nonstandard production --
Formerly: Typing, Productive work other than typing, Typing for students,
Librarian, and Other. The data for period "A" were adjusted for the new
categories. Also, during the entire study, a record was kept of all productive time, standard and nonstandard. Period "B" began with the week
ending 27 May, when the observations were divided into the four categories.

When, according to the study, the personal time showed a marked increase, this was called to the attention of the clerical staff. The girls
expressed the opinion that the data were not being recorded accurately. To
provide for a check, data sheets were distributed to each member of the
clerical staff, and the girls indicated which activity they were engaged in
when the office manager made his observation. The office manager's data
sheets and the individual recordings were compared daily. After nonstandard

work was more clearly defined, there was very little disagreement.

Source: Bertrand L. Hansen, WORK SAMPLING FOR MODERN MANAGEMENT,
          (C) 1960, pp. 128-130. By permission of Prentice-Hall,
          Inc., Englewood Cliffs, N. J.

APPENDIX I

COMPUTER PROGRAMS

All of the computer programs which were prepared for the in-library book readership research are included in Appendix I. These programs are written in Fortran IV language for programming an IBM 1130 computer. The programs are the working programs which were used in actual practice.

PRINT-OUT OF DATA, INTERNAL VALIDATION OF DATA AND RANDOM CHECK

LOG DRIVE   CART SPEC   CART AVAIL   PHY DRIVE
  0000   0008   0008   0000

V2 M06   ACTUAL 8K   CONFIG 8K

```
// FOR
*LIST SOURCE PROGRAM
*IOCS (CARD,1403 PRINTER,TYPEWRITER,KEYBOARD)
*EXTENDED PRECISION
*ONE WORD INTEGERS
C-----PRINT-OUT OF DATA,INTERNAL VALIDATION OF DATA AND RANDOM CHECK
      INTEGER R,ERROR
      DIMENSION NR(100),KEEP(700)
      ERROR =0
      KARD  =0
      MATCH =0
C-----READ 100 RANDOM NUMBERS
      READ(2,100)NR
  100 FORMAT(25I3)
    1 IPP=0
      WRITE(5,2)
    2 FORMAT(1H1,2X,'LINE  INTW.  INTW.  SEX  DAY  TIME  LBRY BK.  RIDER
     1  KIND OF   CLASS  MAJOR  RES.  CUM.',/,3X,'NO.   TRY',27X,'OR NOT'
     2,4X,'STDNT  LIB.BK.  YEAR',16X,'AVG.',//)
    3 IF(IPP-15)4,1,1
    4 READ(2,5)IFORM,INT,I,J,K,LIB,IST,L,N,M,R,AVG
    5 FORMAT(I3,I1,I1,I1,I2,I1,I1,I1,I1,I1,I1,F4.2)
      IF(IFORM)6,6,8
C-----SUMMARY
    6 WRITE(5,7)KARD,ERROR
    7 FORMAT(3X,'INTERNAL VALIDATION OF THE',1X,I3,1X,'DATA CARDS COMPLE
     1TED.',//,2X,I3,'ERRORS HAVE BEEN FOUND,AND SO INDICATED.',//)
C-----MAKE 95 PERCENT OF THE CARDS AN INTEGER FOR HYPER-GEOM. FORMULA
      IB=0.95*KARD
      PROB=1.0
      DO101 LP=1,MATCH
  101 PROB=PROB*(IB-(LP-1))/(KARD-(LP-1))
      CERTY=(1. -PROB)*100
      WRITE(5,102)MATCH,KARD,CERTY
  102 FORMAT(3X,I2,1X,'OF THE',1X,I3,1X,'DATA CARDS HAVE BEEN RANDOMLY C
     1HOSEN FOR CODING ERROR CHECKS.',//,3X,'IF THE RANDOMLY SAMPLED CAR
     2DS ARE OK,THEN IT IS',1X,F9.5,1X,'PERCENT CERTAIN',//,3X,'THAT AT
     3MOST 5 PERCENT OF THE CARDS HAVE ERRORS.')
      CALL EXIT
    8 KARD=KARD+1
      IPP=IPP+1
C-----MATCH CARD NUMBER WITH ASSIGNED RANDOM NUMBERS
      IF(MATCH-75)200,204,204
  200 DO203NB=1,100
      KALL=KARD-NR(NB)
      IF(KALL)203,201,203
  201 WRITE(5,202)KARD,IFORM,INT,I,J,K,LIB,IST,L,N,M,R,AVG
  202 FORMAT(3X,I3,3X,I3,6X,I1,5X,I1,4X,I1,4X,I2,6X,I1,8X,I1,7X,I1,7X,I1
     1,6X,I1,5X,I1,5X,F4.2,4X,'CHECK',//)
      MATCH=MATCH+1
```

```
      GO TO 206
  203 CONTINUE
  204 WRITE(5,205)KARD,IFORM,INT,I,J,K,LIB,IST,L,N,M,R,AVG
  205 FORMAT(3X,I3,3X,I3,6X,I1,5X,I1,4X,I1,4X,I2,6X,I1,8X,I1,7X,I1,7X,I1
     1,6X,I1,5X,I1,5X,F4.2,//)
C-----CHECK FOR DUPLICATES
  206 KEEP(KARD)=IFORM
      INDEX=KARD-1
      IF(INDEX-1)211,211,207
  207 DO210 LIKE=1,INDEX
      IF(KEEP(KARD)-KEEP(LIKE))210,208,210
  208 WRITE(5,209)LIKE
  209 FORMAT(3X,'DUPLICATE OF CARD LISTED ON LINE',1X,I3)
      ERROR=ERROR+1
      GO TO 211
  210 CONTINUE
C-----CONTINUING WITH THE INTERNAL VALIDATION
  211 IF(AVG-5.00)212,400,212
  400 WRITE(5,401)
  401 FORMAT(3X,'EVENING STUDENT-CHECH HIS MATRICULATION STATUS.',//)
      ERROR=ERROR+1
      IF(I-5)213,300,213
  300 WRITE(5,301)
  301 FORMAT(3X,'VALIDATOR FOUND NO INTERVIEW TOOK PLACE.',//)
      ERROR=ERROR+1
      GO TO 3
  212 IF(N-9)213,402,213
  402 WRITE(5,403)
  403 FORMAT(3X,'ERROR BY INTERVIEWER OR UNCERTAIN INFORMATION.',//)
      ERROR=ERROR+1
      GO TO 3
  213 IF(INT-1)10,10,14
   10 SUM=I+J+K+LIB+IST+L+N+M+R+AVG
      IF(SUM)11,11,12
   11 GO TO 3
   12 WRITE(5,13)
   13 FORMAT(3X,'ALL COLUMNS FROM SEX ON SHOULD BE ZERO IF NO INTERVIEW
     1TOOK PLACE.',//)
      ERROR=ERROR+1
      GO TO 3
   14 IF(INT-2)17,17,15
   15 WRITE(5,16)
   16 FORMAT(3X,'NUMBER OUTSIDE SET.',//)
      ERROR=ERROR+1
      GO TO 32
   17 IF(I-2)18,18,15
   18 IF(J-7)19,19,15
   19 IF(K-15)20,20,15
   20 IF(LIB-1)21,21,15
   21 IF(IST-1)22,22,15
   22 IF(L-6)23,23,15
   23 IF(N-6)24,24,15
   24 IF(M-5)25,25,15
   25 IF(R-3)26,26,15
   26 IF(AVG-4.00)27,27,15
   27 IF(I)28,28,30
   28 WRITE(5,29)
```

```
   29 FORMAT(3X,'INCONSISTENT COLUMN ENTRIES.',//)
      ERROR=ERROR+1
      GO TO 40
   30 IF(J)28,28,31
   31 IF(K)28,28,32
   32 IF(LIB)34,34,33
   33 IF(L)28,28,35
   34 IF(L)35,35,28
   35 IF(N)3,3,36
   36 IF(IST)28,28,37
   37 IF(R)28,28,38
   38 IF(N-5)39,39,3
   39 IF(M)28,28,40
   40 IF(N-1)3,3,41
   41 IF(N-4)42,42,3
   42 IF(AVG)43,43,3
   43 WRITE(5,44)
   44 FORMAT(3X,'CUM. AVERAGE MISSING.',//)
      ERROR=ERROR+1
      GO TO 3
      END

FEATURES SUPPORTED
 ONE WORD INTEGERS
 EXTENDED PRECISION
 IOCS

CORE REQUIREMENTS FOR
 COMMON        0  VARIABLES     842  PROGRAM    1162

 END OF COMPILATION

// XEQ
```

```
      INTEGER R,RIDER,UNDER,OTHER,RECC
      DIMENSION ISX(2),IDY(7),ITM(15),IBK(6),MAJ(5),IRS(3),IRD(6),LEVEL(
     18),PER(8),STDP(15),BER(15),FER(7),SFER(7),CONB(15),CONF(7)
      DO 1I=1,2
   1  ISX(I)=0
      DO2J=1,7
   2  IDY(J)=0
      DO3K=1,15
   3  ITM(K)=0
      DO4L=1,6
   4  IBK(L)=0
      DO5N=1,6
   5  IRD(N)=0
      DO6R=1,3
   6  IRS(R)=0
      DO13 M=1,5
  13  MAJ(M)=0
      DO126MA=1,8
 126  LEVEL(MA)=0
      WOMM=0
      MANM=0
      WOMA=0
      CUAM=0
      CUAM2=0
      CUAF=0
      CUAF2=0
      MANA=0
      FCCL2=0
      FCCL=0
      PCCL2=0
      PCCL=0
      ICC=0
      NCAR=0
      NBK=0
      INTW=0
      NLBRY=0
      LBRY=0
      NORID=0
      RIDER=0
      UNDER=0
      OTHER=0
      RECC=0
      KRID=0
      MATR=0
      CUMA=0
```

```
        CUMA2=0
        CUMCL=0
        CUMC2=0
  12 READ(2,7)IFORM,INT,I,J,K,LIB,IST,L,N,M,R,AVG
   7 FORMAT(I3,I1,I1,I1,I2,I1,I1,I1,I1,I1,I1,F4.2)
        IF(IFORM)80,80,8
   8 ICC=ICC+1
        IF(INT-1)9,10,11
   9 NCAR=NCAR+1
        GO TO 12
  10 NBK=NBK+1
        GO TO 12
  11 INTW=INTW+1
        ISX(I)=ISX(I)+1
        IDY(J)=IDY(J)+1
        ITM(K)=ITM(K)+1
        IF(LIB)14,14,15
  14 NLBRY=NLBRY+1
        GO TO 16
  15 LBRY=LBRY+1
        IBK(L)=IBK(L)+1
  16 IF(IST)17,17,18
  17 NORID =NORID +1
        GO TO 12
  18 RIDER=RIDER+1
        IF(N)12,12,30
  30 KRID=KRID+1
        IRD(N)=IRD(N)+1
        IRS(R)=IRS(R)+1
        IF(M-3)20,20,19
  19 OTHER=OTHER+1
        GO TO 22
  20 UNDER=UNDER+1
        IF(AVG)22,22,21
  21 RECC=RECC+1
        CUMA=CUMA+AVG
        CUMA2=CUMA2+AVG**2
        IF(I-2)321,322,322
 321 CUAM=CUAM+AVG
        CUAM2=CUAM2+AVG**2
        MANA=MANA+1
        GO TO 323
 322 CUAF=CUAF+AVG
        CUAF2=CUAF2+AVG**2
        WOMA=WOMA+1
 323 IF(AVG-.5)200,201,201
 200 LEVEL(1)=LEVEL(1)+1
        GO TO 22
 201 IF(AVG-1.)202,203,203
 202 LEVEL(2)=LEVEL(2)+1
        GO TO 22
 203 IF(AVG-1.5)204,205,205
 204 LEVEL(3)=LEVEL(3)+1
        GO TO 22
 205 IF(AVG-2.)206,207,207
 206 LEVEL(4)=LEVEL(4)+1
        GO TO 22
```

```
207 IF(AVG-2.5)208,209,209
208 LEVEL(5)=LEVEL(5)+1
    GO TO 22
209 IF(AVG-3.)210,211,211
210 LEVEL(6)=LEVEL(6)+1
    GO TO 22
211 IF(AVG-3.5)212,213,213
212 LEVEL(7)=LEVEL(7)+1
    GO TO 22
213 LEVEL(8)=LEVEL(8)+1
 22 IF(N-5)24,24,23
 23 GO TO 12
 24 MATR = MATR+1
    MAJ(M)=MAJ(M)+1
    CUMCL=CUMCL +N
    CUMC2=CUMC2 +N**2
    IF(I-2)324,325,325
324 PCCL=PCCL+N
    PCCL2=PCCL2+N**2
    MANM=MANM+1
    GO TO 12
325 FCCL=FCCL+N
    FCCL2=FCCL2+N**2
    WOMM=WOMM+1
    GO TO 12
 80 A = NCAR*1.  /ICC
    B = ISX(1)*1.   /INTW
    C=LBRY*1./(NBK+INTW)
    Y=NBK*1./(NBK+INTW)
    EA=((A*(1-A))/ICC)**.5
    CONEA=1.96*EA
    EB=((B*(1-B))/INTW)**.5
    CONFB=1.96*EB
    EC=((C*(1-C))/(NBK+INTW))**.5
    CONFE=1.96*EC
    EY=((Y*(1-Y))/(NBK+INTW))**.5
    CONFY=1.96*EY
    WRITE(5,500)ICC,INTW,NBK,LBRY,NLBRY
500 FORMAT(1H1,2X,'INTERVIEW ATTEMPTS ',I3,//,2X,'INTERVIEWS COMPLETED
   1 ',I3,//,2X,'NON-BOOK READERS ',I3,//,2X,'LIBRARY BOOK READERS ',I
   23,//,2X,'OTHER BOOK READERS ',I3,//)
    WRITE(5,501)
501 FORMAT(2X,'NOTE. NON-BOOK READERS NOT INCLUDED IN INTERVIEWS COMPL
   1ETED.',/,2X,'THEY WERE NOT INTERVIEWED.',//)
    WRITE(5,181)
181 FORMAT(2X,'LIBRARY BOOK CODES AS FOLLOWS',//,3X,'1-SOCIAL SCIENCE'
   1,//,3X,'2-PURE SCIENCE',//,3X,'3-TECH. OR APPLIED SCI.',//,3X,
   2'4-LITERATURE',//,3X,'5-GEOG. OR HIST',//,3X,'6-OTHER',//)
    WRITE(5,182)
182 FORMAT(2X,'CODE',6X,'RELATIVE FREQUENCY',6X,'STANDARD',6X,'95 PERC
   1ENT CONFIDENCE',/,12X,'OF USE',18X,'ERROR',9X,'INTERVAL(PLUS-MINUS
   2)',//)
    DO184 L=1,6
    BOOK =IBK(L)*1.  /LBRY
    EBK=((BOOK*(1-BOOK))/LBRY)**.5
    CONBK=1.98*EBK
    WRITE(5,183)L,BOOK,EBK,CONBK
```

```
183 FORMAT(3X,I1,14X,F5.3,14X,F5.3,14X,F5.3,//)
184 CONTINUE
    WRITE(5,185)
185 FORMAT(2X,'DAY OF THE WEEK CODES AS FOLLOWS',//,3X,'MONDAY-1,
   1TUES-2, ETC.'//)
    WRITE(5,186)
186 FORMAT(2X,'DAY IN WEEK',8X,'REL. FREQUENCY READER FOUND',//)
    DO187 J=1,7
    DAY =IDY(J)*1.  /INTW
    WRITE(5,189)J,DAY
189 FORMAT(7X,I1,19X,F5.3,//)
187 CONTINUE
    F= RIDER*1.  /INTW
    EF=((F*(1-F))/INTW)**.5
    CONEF=1.96*EF
    WRITE(5.95)
 95 FORMAT(2X,'PERCENT OF RIDER READERS BY CLASS YEAR'//)
    WRITE(5,110)
110 FORMAT(2X,'CLASS YEAR CODES AS FOLLOWS',//,3X,'1-FRESHMAN',//,3X,'
   12-SOPHMORE',//,3X,'3-JUNIOR',//,3X,'4-SENIOR',//,3X,'5-GRADUATE',/
   2/,3X,'6-OTHER',//)
    WRITE(5,182)
    DO113N=1,6
    CLASS=IRD(N)*1.0/KRID
    ECL=((CLASS*(1-CLASS))/KRID)**.5
    CONCL=1.96*ECL
    WRITE(5,183)N,CLASS,ECL,CONCL
113 CONTINUE
    WRITE(5,154)
154 FORMAT(2X,'PERCENT OF RIDER READERS BY RESIDENCE',//)
    WRITE (5,150)
150 FORMAT(2X,'PLACE OF RESIDENCE CODES AS FOLLOWS',//,2X,'1-DORMITORY
   1',//,2X,'2-COMMUTER',//,2X,'3-SORORITY OR FRATERNITY',//)
    WRITE(5,182)
    DO152LET=1,3
    H=IRS(LET)*1./RIDER
    EH=((H*(1-H))/RIDER)**.5
    CONEH=1.96*EH
    WRITE(5,183)LET,H,EH,CONEH
152 CONTINUE
    WRITE(5,98)
 98 FORMAT(2X,'PERCENT OF RIDER READERS BY MAJOR'//)
    WRITE(5,99)
 99 FORMAT(2X,'MAJOR FIELD CODES AS FOLLOWS',//,3X,'1-LIBERAL ARTS',//
   1,3X,'2-EDUCATION',//,3X,'3-BUSINESS',//,3X,'4-EDUCATION MASTER',//
   2,3X,'5-BUSINESS MASTER',//)
    WRITE(5,182)
    DO106M=1,5
    FIELD=MAJ(M)*1.0/MATR
    EFL=((FIELD*(1-FIELD))/MATR)**.5
    CONFL=1.96*EFL
    WRITE(5,183)M,FIELD,EFL,CONFL
106 CONTINUE
    AVE = CUMA/RECC
    STDA =((RECC*CUMA2 -CUMA**2)/(RECC*(RECC-1)))**.5
    AVC = CUMCL/MATR
    STDC=((MATR*CUMC2-CUMCL**2)/(1.*MATR*(MATR-1)))**.5
```

```
      AVEM=CUAM/MANA
      AVEF=CUAF/WOMA
      AVCM=PCCL/MANM
      AVCF=FCCL/WOMM
      STDAM=((MANA*CUAM2-CUAM**2)/(1.*MANA*(MANA-1)))**.5
      STDAF=((WOMA*CUAF2-CUAF**2)/(1.*WOMA*(WOMA-1)))**.5
      STDCM=((MANM*PCCL2-PCCL**2)/(1.*MANM*(MANM-1)))**.5
      STDCF=((WOMM*FCCL2-FCCL**2)/(1.*WOMM*(WOMM-1)))**.5
      WRITE(5,250)
  250 FORMAT(2X,'OTHER RESULTS CODES AS FOLLOWS',//,3X,'1-READERS WHO AR
     1E RIDER STUDENTS',//,3X,'-2SAMPLE CARRELS UNOCCUPIED',//,3X,'3-MAL
     2E READERS',//,3X,'4-READING THAT IS LIBRARY BOOKS',//,3X,'5-READIN
     3G THAT IS OTHER THAN BOOKS',//)
      WRITE(5,182)
      IM=1
      WRITE(5,183)IM,F,EF,CONEF
      IM=2
      WRITE(5,183)IM,A,EA,CONEA
      TM=3
      WRITE(5,183)IM,B,EB,CONFB
      IM=4
      WRITE(5,183)IM,C,EC,CONFE
      IM=5
      WRITE(5,183)IM,Y,EY,CONFY
      WRITE(5,114)
  114 FORMAT(2X,'TIME OF DAY CODES AS FOLLOWS',//,3X,'1-8 00 TO 8 59AM',
     1//,3X,'2-9 00 TO 9 59AM',//,3X,'ETC.',//)
      WRITE(5,115)
  115 FORMAT(2X,'TIME OF DAY',8X,'REL. FREQUENCY OF READERS',//)
      DO117K =1,15
      TIME = ITM(K)*1.  /INTW
      WRITE(5,116)K,TIME
  116 FORMAT(6X,I2,19X,F5.3,//)
  117 CONTINUE
      WRITE(5,300)
  300 FORMAT(2X,'LIBRARY READERS BY CUM. AVG.',//)
      WRITE(5,301)
  301 FORMAT(2X,'CUM. AVERAGE',10X,'RELATIVE FREQUENCY',6X,'STANDARD',6X
     1,'95 PERCENT CONFIDENCE',/,48X,'ERROR',9X,'INTERVAL',//)
      DO220LET=1,8
      RLOW=(LET-1)/2.
      RHIGH=RLOW+.49
      PER(LET)=LEVEL(LET)*1./RECC
      EP=((PER(LET)*(1-PER(LET)))/RECC)**.5
      CONEP=1.96*EP
      WRITE(5,219)RLOW,RHIGH,PER(LET),EP,CONEP
  219 FORMAT(2X,F4.2,1X,'TO',1X,F4.2,16X,F5.3,14X,F5.3,13X,F5.3,//)
  220 CONTINUE
C----ESTIMATE OF OCCUPANCY BY TIME OF DAY USING BINOMIAL APPROX.
      WRITE(5,50)
   50 FORMAT(3X,'TIME OF  ',4X,"PERCENT OF  ",4X,'STANDARD',6X,'95 PERCE
     1NT CONFIDENCE',/,3X,'DAY',10X,'OCCUPANCY',7X,'ERROR',9X,'INTERVAL'
     2,//)
C----STANDARD DEVIATION OF OCCUPANCY
      CUMPP=0
      CUMPR=0
      DO60KN=1,15
```

```
      IF(KN-2)56,56,57
   56 BER(KN)=1-(1-(ITM(KN)+5.*NBK/88)/((5.*ICC)/88))**.2
      STDP(KN)=((BER(KN)*(1-BER(KN)))/((5.*ICC)/88))**.5
      GO TO 58
   57 IF(KN-6)550,550,551
  550 BER(KN)=1-(1-(ITM(KN)+6.*NBK/88)/((6.*ICC)/88))**.2
      STDP(KN)=((BER(KN)*(1-BER(KN)))/((6.*ICC)/88))**.5
      GO TO 58
  551 IF(KN-9)552,552,553
  552 BER(KN)=1-(1-(ITM(KN)+7.*NBK/88)/((7.*ICC)/88))**.2
      STDP(KN)=((BER(KN)*(1-BER(KN)))/((7.*ICC)/88))**.5
      GO TO 58
  553 IF(KN-15)550,64,64
   64 BER(KN)=1-(1-(ITM(KN)+3.*NBK/88)/((3.*ICC)/88))**.2
      STDP(KN)=((BER(KN)*(1-BER(KN)))/((3.*ICC)/88))**.5
   58 CONB(KN)=1.96*STDP(KN)
      WRITE(5,59)KN,BER(KN),STDP(KN),CONB(KN)
   59 FORMAT(4X,I2,12X,F5.3,10X,F5.3,12X,F5.3,//)
      CUMPR=CUMPR+BER(KN)
   60 CUMPP=CUMPP+(BER(KN))**2
      AVRGE=CUMPR/15.
      STANP=(15*CUMPP-CUMPR**2)**.5/15.
      CONNP=1.96*STANP/15**.5
C----ESTIMATE OF OCCUPANCY BY DAY OF WEEK
      WRITE(5,66)
   66 FORMAT(3X,'DAY OF  ',5X,'PERCENT OF  ',5X,'STANDARD ',5X,'95 PERCEN
     1T CONFIDENCE',/,3X,'WEEK',9X,'OCCUPANCY',7X,'ERROR',9X,'INTERVAL',
     2//)
      CUMDR=0
      CUMDP=0
      DO40ME=1,7
      IF(ME-6)70,71,79
   70 FER(ME)=1-(1-(IDY(ME)+14.5*NBK/88)/((14.5*ICC)/88))**.2
      SFER(ME)=((FER(ME)*(1-FER(ME)))/((14.5*ICC)/88))**.5
      GO TO 78
   71 FER(ME)=1-(1-(IDY(ME)+07.0*NBK/88)/((07.0*ICC)/88))**.2
      SFER(ME)=((FER(ME)*(1-FER(ME)))/((07.0*ICC)/88))**.5
      GO TO 78
   79 FER(ME)=1-(1-(IDY(ME)+08.5*NBK/88)/((08.5*ICC)/88))**.2
      SFER(ME)=((FER(ME)*(1-FER(ME)))/((08.5*ICC)/88))**.5
   78 CONF(ME)=1.96*SFER(ME)
      WRITE(5,59)ME,FER(ME),SFER(ME),CONF(ME)
      CUMDR=CUMDR+FER(ME)
   40 CUMDP=CUMDP+(FER(ME))**2
      STAND=(7*CUMDP-CUMDR**2)**.5/7.
      AVDGE=CUMDR/7.
      WRITE(5,61)AVRGE,STANP,CONNP
   61 FORMAT(2X,'AVERAGE PERCENTAGE OF OCCUPANCY',F5.3,//,2X,'STANDARD D
     1EVIATION OF OCCUPANCY',F5.3,//,2X,'95 PERCENT CONFIDENCE INTERVAL
     2FOR OCCUPANCY',F5.3,//)
      WRITE(5,100)
  100 FORMAT(2X,'STATISTICS RELATING TO CUM. AVG. AND CLASS YEAR.',//)
      WRITE(5,101)
  101 FORMAT(15X,'SAMPLE',5X,'STANDARD',6X,'STANDARD ERROR',5X,'95 PERCE
     1NT CONFIDENCE',/,15X,'MEAN',7X,'DEVIATION',5X,'OF SAMPLE MEAN',5X,
     2'INTERVAL FOR SAMPLE MEAN',//)
      EAVE=STDA/RECC**.5
```

```
      CEAVE=1.96*EAVE
      EAVC=STDC/MATR**.5
      CEAVC=1.96*EAVC
      EAVM=STDAM/MANA**.5
      CEAVM=1.96*EAVM
      EAVF=STDAF/WOMA**.5
      CEAVF=1.96*EAVF
      EACM-STDCM/MANM**.5
      CEACM=1.96*EACM
      EACF=STDCF/WOMM**.5
      CEACF=1.96*EACF
      WRITE(5,102)AVE,STDA,EAVE,CEAVE
  102 FORMAT(2X,'CUM. AVG.',6X,F4.2,8X,F4.2,13X,F4.2,15X,F4.2,//)
      WRITE(5,103)AVC,STDC,EAVC,CEAVC
  103 FORMAT(2X,'CLASS YEAR',4X,F4.2,8X,F4.2,13X,F4.2,15X,F4.2,//)
      WRITE(5,404)AVEM,STDAM,EAVM,CEAVM
  404 FORMAT(2X,'CUM.MALE',7X,F4.2,8X,F4.2,13X,F4.2,15X,F4.2,//)
      WRITE(5,405)AVEF,STDAF,EAVF,CEAVF
  405 FORMAT(2X,'CUM.FEMALE',5X,F4.2,8X,F4.2,13X,F4.2,15X,F4.2,//)
      WRITE(5,406)AVCM,STDCM,EACM,CEACM
  406 FORMAT(2X,'CL.MALE',7X,F4.2,8X,F4.2,13X,F4.2,15X,F4.2,//)
      WRITE(5,407)AVCF,STDCF,EACF,CEACF
  407 FORMAT(2X,'CL,FEMALE',5X,F4.2,8X,F4.2,13X,F4.2,15X,F4.2,//)
      CALL EXIT
      END

FEATURES SUPPORTED
 ONE WORD INTEGERS
 EXTENDED PRECISION
 10CS

CORE REQUIREMENTS FOR
 COMMON      0  VARIABLES    564   PROGRAM    4408

 END OF COMPILATION

 // XEQ
```

```
C       CHI-SQUARE TESTS FOR LIBRARY BOOK OR NOT BY VARIOUS CATEGORIES
        INTEGER R,RIDER,RECC
        DIMENSION ASMX(6,7),ALMX(6,7),AYMX(6,/),ARMX(6,7),ANMX(6,7),AMMX(6
       1,7),AAMX(6,7),ATMX(6,7),EMX(6,7),TROW(6),TCOL(7),P(7),(CHI(30),AMX(
       26,7),RTMX(1,2),RLMX(6,7)
        DATA CHI/3.84,5.99,7.82,9.49,11.07,12.59,14.06,15.51,16.92,18.31,1
       19.68,21.03,22.36,23.69,25.00,26.3,27.59,28.87,30.14,31.41,32.67,33
       2.92,35.17,36.42,37.65,38.89,40.11,41.34,42.56,43.77/
C-----INIALIZE COUNTERS AND MATRICES
        INTW=0
        RIDER=0
        MATR=0
        RECC=0
        DO1IN=1,6
        DO1JN=1,7
        ASMX(IN,JN)=0
        ALMX(IN,JN)=0
        AYMX(IN,JN)=0
        ARMX(IN,JN)=0
        RLMX(IN,JN)=0
        ANMX(IN,JN)=0
        AMMX(IN,JN)=0
        AAMX(IN,JN)=0
      1 ATMX(IN,JN)=0
      2 READ(2,3)IFORM,INT,I,LIB,K,J,IST,L,N,M,R,AVG
      3 FORMAT(I3,I1,I1,I1,I2,I1,I1,I1,I1,I1,I1,F4.2)
        IF(IFORM)18,18,4
      4 IF(INT-1)2,2,5
      5 INTW=INTW+1
        AYMX(IST+1,J+1)=AYMC(IST+1,J+1)+1
        ASMX(I,J+1)=ASMX(I,J+1)+1
        IF(LIB-5)300,300,301
    300 RLMX(1,J+1)=RLMX(1,J+1)+1
        GO TO 302
    301 RLMX(2,J+1)=RLMX(2,J+1)+1
        GOT TO 302
    302 CONTINUE
        IF(IST)13,13,6
      6 RIDER=RIDER+1
        ARMX(R,J+1)=ARMX(R,J+1)+1
        ANNX(N,J+1)=ANMX(N,J+1)+1
        IF(N-5)7,7,13
      7 MATR=MATR+1
        AMMX(M,J+1)=AMMX(M,J+1)+1
        IF(AVG)13,13,8
```

```
    8 RECC=RECC+1
      IF(AVG-2.)9,10,10
    9 AAMX(1,J+1)=AAMX(1,J+1)+1
      GO TO 13
   10 IF(AVG-3.)11,12,12
   11 AAMX(2,J+1)=AAMX(1,J+1)+1
      GO TO 13
   12 AAMX(3,J+1)=AAMX(3,J+1)+1
   13 IF(K-6)14,15,15
   14 ATMX(1,J+1)=ATMX(1,J+1)+1
      GO TO 2
   15 IF(K-11)16,17,17
   16 ATMX(2,J+1)=ATMX(2,J+1)+1
      GO TO 2
   17 ATMX(3,J+1)=ATMX(3,J+1)+1
      GO TO 2
   18 KALL=0
   19 KALL=KALL+1
      GO TO (20,30,40,60,80,90,290,130),KALL
C     LIBRARY BOOK OR NOT SEX
   20 WRITE(5,21)
   21 FORMAT(1H1,22X,'LIBRARY BOOK OR NOT BY SEX OF READER MATRIX',///)
      WRITE(5,22)
   22 FORMAT(20X,'NON-LIBRARY BOOK',4X,'LIBRARY BOOK',//)
      WRITE(5,23)(ASMX(1,J),J=1,2)
   23 FORMAT(4X,'MALE',7X,2(9X,F6.2),//)
      WRITE(5,24)(ASMX(2,J),J=1,2)
   24 FORMAT(4X,'FEMALE',5X,2(9X,F6.2),//)
      WRITE(5,25)
   25 FORMAT(22X,'NULL HYPOTHESIS',/,4X,'THERE IS NO RELATIONSHIP BETWEE
     1N THE KIND OF BOOK, THAT IS LIBRARY BOOK OR NOT AND',//)
      WRITE(5,27)
   27 FORMAT(4X,'THE SEX OF THE LIBRARY READER.',//)
      LIMR=2
      LIMC=2
      DO26IROW-1,LIMR
      DO26JCOL-1,LIMC
   26 AMX(IROW,JCOL)=ASMX(IROW,JCOL)
      GO TO 99
C   LIBRARY BOOK OR NOT BY TIME OF WEEK
   30 WRITE(5,31)
   31 FORMAT(1H1,22X,'LIBRARY BOOK OR NOT BY TIME OF WEEK MATRIX',//)
      WRITE(5,22)
      WRITE(5,32)(RLMX(1,J),J=1,2)
   32 FORMAT(4X,'WEEKDAY',4X,2(9X,F6.2),//)
      WRITE(5,33)(RLMX(2,J),J=1,2)
   33 FORMAT(4X,'WEEKEND',4X,2(9X,F6.2),//)
      WRITE(5,25)
      WRITE(5,270)
  270 FORMAT(4X,'THE DAY OF THE WEEK',//)
      LIMR=2
      LIMC=2
      DO35IROW=1,LIMR
      DO35JCOL=1,LIMC
   35 AMX(IROW,JCOL)=RLMX(IROW,JCOL)
      GO TO 99
C     LIBRARY BOOK OR NOT BY STUDENT OR NOT
```

```
   40 WRITE(5,41)
   41 FORMAT(20X,'LIBRARY BOOK OR NOT BY STUDENT READER OR NOT',////)
      WRITE(5,22)
      WRITE(5,42)(AYMX(1,J),J=1,2)
   42 FORMAT(4X,'NON-RIDER',2X,2(9X,F6.2),//)
      WRITE(5,43)(AYMX(2,J),J=1,2)
   43 FORMAT(4X,'RIDER',6X,2(9X,F6.2),//)
      WRITE(5,25)
      WRITE(5,44)
   44 FORMAT(4X,'THE BOOK READERS CONNECTION WITH RIDER COLLEGE.',//)
      LIMR=2
      LIMC=2
      DO45IROW=1,LIMR
      DO45JCOL=1,LIMC
   45 AMX(IROW,JCOL)=AYMX(IROW,JCOL)
      GO TO 99
C     LIBRARY BOOK OR NOT BY CLASS YEAR
   60 WRITE(5,61)
   61 FORMAT(20X,'LIBRARY BOOK OR NOT BY CLASS YEAR OF READER',////)
      WRITE(5,22)
      Write(5,62)(ANMX(1,J),J=1,2)
   62 FORMAT(4X,'FRESHMAN',3X,2(7X,F6.2),//)
      WRITE(5,63)(ANMX(2,J),J=1,2)
   63 FORMAT(4X,'SOPHMORE',3X,2(9X,F6.2),//)
      WRITE(5,64)(ANMX(3,J),J=1,2)
   64 FORMAT(4X,'JUNIOR',5X,2(7X,F6.2),//)
      WRITE(5,65)(ANMX(4,J),J=1,2)
   65 FORMAT(4X,'SENIOR',5X,2(7X,F6.2),//)
      WRITE(5,25)
      WRITE(5,68)
   68 FORMAT(4X,'THE CLASS YEAR OF THE READER.',//)
      LIMR=4
      LIMC=2
      DO69IROW=1,LIMR
      DO69JCOL=1,LIMC
   69 AMX(IROW,JCOL)=ANMX(IROW,JCOL)
      GO TO 99
C     LIBRARY BOOK OR NOT BY CUM. AVG.
   80 WRITE(5,81)
   81 FORMAT(20X,'LIBRARY BOOK OR NOT BY CUM. AVG. OR READER',////)
      WRITE(5,22)
      WRITE(5,82)(AAMX(1,J),J=1,2)
   82 FORMAT(4X,'0 TO 1.99',2X,2(9X,F6.2),//)
      WRITE(5,82)(AAMX(2,J),J=1,2)
   83 FORMAT(4X,'2 to 2.99',2X,2(9X,F6.2),//)
      WRITE(5,84)(AAMX(3,J),J=1,2)
   84 FORMAT(4X,'3 TO 4.00',2X,2(9X,F6.2),//)
      WRITE(5,25)
      WRITE(5,85)
   85 FORMAT(4X,'THE CUM. AVERAGE OF THE READER.',//)
      LIMR=3
      LIMC=2
      DO86IROW=1,LIMR
      DO86JCOL=1,LIMC
   86 AMX(IROW,JCOL)=AAMX(IROW,JCOL)
      GO TO 99
C     LIBRARY BOOK OR NOT BY TIME OF DAY
```

```
   90 WRITE(5,91)
   91 FORMAT(20X,'LIBRARY BOOK OR NOT BY TIME OF DAY READER FOUND',///)
      WRITE(5,22)
      WRITE(5,92)(ATMX(1,J),J=1,2)
   92 FORMAT(4X,'MORNING',4X,2(9X,F6.2),/)
      WRITE(5,93)(ATMX(2,J),J=1,2)
   93 FORMAT(4X,'AFTERNOON',2X,2(9X,F6.2),//)
      WRITE(5,94)(ATMX(3,J),J=1,2)
   94 FORMAT(4X,'EVENING',4X,2(9X,F6.2),//)
      WRITE(5,95)
   95 FORMAT(4X,'BY MORNING IS MEANT 8 00 AM. TO 12 59 PM.,AFTERNOON,1 0
     10 TO 5 59 PM.',//,4X,'AND EVENING.6 00 TO 10 30 PM.',//)
      WRITE(5,25)
      WRITE(5,96)
   96 FORMAT(4X,'THE TIME OF DAY OF LIBRARY READING.',//)
      LIMR=3
      LIMC=2
      DO97IROW=1,LIMR
      DO97JCOL=1,LIMC
   97 AMX(IROW,JCOL)=ATMX(IROW,JCOL)
      GO TO 99
  290 WRITE(5,91)
      WRITE(5,22)
      DO 291 J=1,2
  291 RTMX(1,J)=ATMX(1,J)+ATMX(2,J)
      WRITE(5,292)(RTMX(1,J),J=1,2)
  292 FORMAT(4X,'8 TO 5 59PM',2(9X,F6.2),//)
      WRITE(5,293)(ATMX(3,J),J=1,2)
  293 FORMAT(4X,'6 TO END',3X,2(9X,F6.2),//)
      WRITE(5,25)
      WRITE(5,96)
      LIMC=2
      LIMR=2
      DO 294 JCOL=1,2
      AMX(1,JCOL)=RTMX(1,JCOL)
  294 AMX(2,JCOL)=ATMX(3,JCOL)
      GO TO 99
C-----SUBROUTINE FOR CHI-SQUARE ANALYSIS
C-----CALCULATE EXPECTED MATRIX IF NULL HYPOTHESES IF TRUE.
   99 DO100IROW=1,LIMR
      DO100JCOL=1,LIMC
C-----CHECK CELLS FOR 5 OR MOR FREQUENCIES.
      IF(AMX(IROW,JCOL)-5)119,100,100
  100 CONTINUE
C-----INITIALIZE ROW TOTALLS AND TOTAL OF THE REW TOTALS.
      DO101IROW=1,LIMR
  101 TROW(IROW)=0
      ALLR=0
C-----TOTAL ROWS
      DO103IROW=1,LIMR
      DO102JCOL=1,LIMC
  102 TROW(IROW)=TROW(IROW)+AMX(IROW,JCOL)
C-----TOTAL ALL ROWS
  103 ALLR=ALLR+TROW(IROW)
C-----INITIALIZE COLUMN TOTALS AND TOTAL OF THE COLUMN TOTALS.
      DO104JCOL=1,LIMC
  104 TCOL(JCOL)=0
```

```
      ALLC=0
C-----TOTAL COLUMNS.
      DO106JCOL=1,LIMC
      DO105IROW=1,LIMR
  105 TCOL(JCOL)=TCOL(JCOL)+AMX(IROW,JCOL)
C-----TOTAL ALL COLUMNS
  106 ALLC=ALLC+TCOL(JCOL)
C-----CHECK FOR ERROR
      IF(ALLC-ALLR)121,107,121
C-----CALCULATE EXPECTED CELL VALUES
  107 DO108JCOL=1,LIMC
      DO108IROW=1,LIMR
      P(JCOL)=TCOL(JCOL)/ALLC
  108 EMX(IROW,JCOL)=P(JCOL)*TROW(IROW)
C-----WRITE EXPECTED MATRIX
      WRITE(5,109)
  109 FORMAT(22X,'EXPECTED MATRIX IF NULL HYP. TRUE.',//)
      WRITE(5,22)
      WRITE(5,110)((EMX(IROW,JCOL),JCOL=1,LIMC),IROW=1,LIMR)
  110 FORMAT(2(7X,F6.2),//)
C-----STATE SAMPLE SIZE
      WRITE(5,111)ALLC
  111 FORMAT(4X,'SAMPLE SIZE IS',1X,F4.0,//)
C-----GET CRITICAL VALUE FOR CHI-SQUARE TEST.
      ICDF=(LIMR-1)*(LIMC-1)
      CHICR=CHI(ICDF)
      WRITE(5,112)ICDF,CHICR
  112 FORMAT(4X,'TEST HYPOTHESIS USING CHI-SQUARE AT A 5 PERCENT LEVEL O
     1F SIGNIFICANCE.',//,4X,'THE NUMBER OF DEGREES OF FREEDOM IS',1X,I2
     2,',AND THE CRITICAL VALUE FOR THE TEST IS',1X,F5.2,//)
C-----CALCULATE CHI-SQUARE
      CHISQ=0
      DO113IROW=1,LIMR
      DO113JCOL=1,LIMC
      DIFF2=(AMX(IROW,JCOL)-EMX(IROW,JCOL)**2/EMX(IROW,JCOL)
  113 CHISQ=CHISQ+DIFF2
      WRITE(5,114)CHISQ
  114 FORMAT(4X,'CHI-SQUARE VALUE=',1X,F6.2,//)
C-----COMPARE CRITICAL VALUE WITH CHI-SQUARE VALUE.
      IF(CHISQ-CHICR)115,115,117
  115 WRITE(5,116)
  116 FORMAT(4X,'NO SIGNIFICANT DIFFERENCE AT 5 PERCENT LEVEL BETWEEN AC
     1TUAL',//,4X,'RESULTS AND EXPECTED RESULTS.ACCEPT THE NULL HYPOTHES
     2ES.',//)
      GO TO 123
  117 WRITE(5,118)
  118 FORMAT(4X,'SIGNIFICANT DIFFERENCE AT 5 PERCENT LEVEL BETWEEN ACTUA
     1L RESULTS',//,4X,'AND EXPECTED RESULTS.REJECT THE NULL HYPOTHESIS.
     2',//)
      GO TO 123
  119 WRITE(5,120)
  120 FORMAT(4X,'NO CHI-SQUARE TEST POSSIBLE WITHOUT REGROUPING.',//)
      GO TO 123
  121 WRITE(5,122)
  122 FORMAT(4X,'MATH ERROR.HALT.')
      CALL EXIT
  123 CONTINUE
```

```
      GO TO 19
130 CALL EXIT
    END

FEATURES SUPPORTED
 ONE WORD INTEGERS
 EXTENDED PRECISION
 IOCS

CORE REQUIREMENTS FOR
 COMMON      0  VARIABLES    1590  PROGRAM    2852

END OF COMPILATION

// XEQ
```

PROGRAM OF THE CHI-SQUARE TEST OF THE NULL HYPOTHESES THAT THERE IS NO RELATIONSHIP
BETWEEN KIND OF LIBRARY BOOK BEING READ AND THE SEVERAL CHARACTERISTICS OF THE READER

```
C-----CHI SQ. TESTS FOR LIBRARY BOOKS BY VARIOUS CATEGORIES
      INTEGER R,RIDER,RECC
      DIMENSION ASMX(6,7),ALMX(6,7),AYMX(6,7),ARMX(6,7),ANMX(6,7),AMMX(6
     1,7),AAMX(6,7),ATMX(6,7),EMX(6,7),TROW(6),TCOL(7),P(7),CHI(30),AMX(
     26,7),RNMX(1,5)
      DATA CHI/3.84,5.99,7.82,9.49,11.07,12.59,14.06,15.51,16.92,18,31,1
     119.68,21.03,22.36,23.69,25.00,26.3,27.59,28.87,30.14,31.41,32.67,33
     22.92,35.17,36.42,37.65,38.89,40.11,41.34,42.56,43.77/
C-----INIALIZE COUNTERS AND MATRICES
      INTW=0
      RIDER=0
      MATR=0
      RECC=0
      DO1IN=1,6
      DO1JN=1,7
      ASMX(IN,JN)=0
      ALMX(IN,JN)=0
      AYMX(IN,JN)=0
      ANMX(IN,JN)=0
      AMMX(IN,JN)=0
      ARMX(IN,JN)=0
      AAMX(IN,JN)=0
    1 ATMX(IN,JN)=0
    2 READ(2,3)IFORM,INT,I,L,L,LIB,IST,J,N,M,R,AVG
    3 FORMAT(I3,I1,I1,I1,I2,I1,I1,I1,I1,I1,I1,F4.2)
      IF(IFORM)18,18,4
    4 IF(INT-1)2,2,5
    5 INTW=INTW+1
      IF(LIB)2,2,200
  200 CONTINUE
      IF(J-1)2,201,202
  201 ASMX(I,1)=ASMX(I,1)+1
      AYMX(IST=1,1)=AYMX(IST+1,1)+1
      GO TO 204
  202 ASMX(I,2)=ASMX(I,2)+1
      AYMX(IST+1,2)=AYMX(IST+1,2)+1
  204 CONTINUE
      IF(IST)13,13,6
    6 RIDER=RIDER+1
      IF(J-1)2,205,206
  205 ARMX(R,1)=ARMX(R,1)+1
      ANMX(N,1)=ANMX(N,1)+1
      GO TO 207
  206 ARMX(R,2)=ARMX(R,2)+1
      ANMX(N,2)=ANMX(N,2)+1
```

```
  207 CONTINUE
      IF(N-5)7,7,13
    7 MATR=MATR+1
      IF(J-1)2,208,209
  208 AMMX(M,1)=AMMX(M,1)+1
      GO TO 210
  209 AMMX(M,2)=AMMX(M,2)+1
  210 CONTINUE
      IF(AVG)13,13,8
    8 RECC=RECC+1
      IF(AVG-2.49)9,9,11
    9 IF(J-1)2,211,212
  211 AAMX(1,1)=AAMX(1,1)+1
      GO TO 13
  212 AAMX(1,2)=AAMX(1,2)+1
      GO TO 13
   11 IF(J-1)2,213,214
  213 AAMX(2,1)=AAMX(2,1)+1
      GO TO 13
  214 AAMX(2,2)=AAMX(2,2)+1
      GO TO 13
   13 IF(K-6)14,15,15
   14 IF(J-1)2,217,218
  217 ATMX(1,1)=ATMX(1,1)+1
      GO TO 2
  218 ATMX(1,2)=ATMX(1,2)+1
      GO TO 2
   15 IF(K-11)16,17,17
   16 IF(J-1)2,219,220
  219 ATMX(2,1)=ATMX(2,1)+1
      GO TO 2
  220 ATMX(2,2)=ATMX(2,2)+1
      GO TO 2
   17 IF(J-1)2,221,222
  221 ATMX(3,1)=ATMX(3,1)+1
      GO TO 2
  222 ATMX(3,2)=ATMX(3,2)+1
      GO TO 2
   18 KALL=0
   19 KALL=KALL+1
      GO TO (20,40,50,60,70,80,90,120),KALL
C-----LIB. BK BY SEX
   20 WRITE(5,21)
   21 FORMAT(1H1,22X,'LIBRARY BOOK BY SEX OF READER MATRIX',///)
      WRITE(5,22)
   22 FORMAT(20X,'SOCIAL SCIENCE     OTHER',//)
      WRITE(5,23)(ASMX(1,J),J=1,2)
   23 FORMAT(4X,'MALE'7X,2(7X,F6.2),//)
      WRITE(5,24)(ASMX(2,J),J=1,2)
   24 FORMAT(4X,'FEMALE',5X,2(7X,F6.2),//)
   25 FORMAT(22X,'NULL HYPOTHESES',/,4X,'THERE IS NO RELATIONSHIP BETWEE
     1N THE KIND OF LIBRARY BOOK AND',//)
      WRITE(5,27)
   27 FORMAT(4X,'THE SEX OF THE LIBRARY READER.',//)
      LIMR=2
      LIMC=2
      DO26IROW=1,LIMR
```

```
          DO26JCOL=1,LIMC
   26 AMX(IROW,JCOL)=ASMX(IROW,JCOL)
          GO TO 99
C-----LIB. BK BY STUDENT OR NON STUDENT
   40 WRITE(5,41)
   41 FORMAT(1H1,22X,'LIBRARY BOOK BY RIDER STUDENT OR NOT MATRIX',///)
          WRITE(5,22)
          WRITE(5,42)(AYMX(1,J),J=1,2)
   42 FORMAT(4X,'NON-RIDER',2X,2(9X,F6.2),//)
          WRITE(5,43)(AYMX(2,J),J=1,2)
   43 FORMAT(4X,'RIDER',6X,2(9X,F6.2),//)
          WRITE(5,25)
          WRITE(5,44)
   44 FORMAT(4X,'THE BOOK READERS CONNECTION WITH RIDER COLLEGE.',//)
          LIMR=2
          LIMC=2
          DO45IROW=1,LIMR
          DO45JCOL=1,LIMC
   45 AMX(IROW,JCOL)=AYMX(IROW,JCOL)
          GO TO 99
C-----LIB. BK. BY RESIDENCE
   50 WRITE(5,51)
   51 FORMAT(1H1,22X,'6IBRARY BOOK BY RESIDENCE OF STUDENT MATRIX',///)
          WRITE(5,22)
          WRITE(5,52)(ARMX(1,J),J=1,2)
   52 FORMAT(4X,'DORMITORY',2X,2(9X,F6.2),//)
          WRITE(5,53)(ARMX(2,J),J=1,2)
   53 FORMAT(4X,'COMMUTER',3X,2(9X,F6.2),//)
          WRITE(5,25)
          WRITE(5,55)
   55 FORMAT(4X,'THE RESIDENCE OF THE STUDENT.',//)
          LIMC=2
          DO56IROW=1,LIMR
          DO56JCOL=1,LIMC
   56 AMX(IROW,JCOL)=ARMX(IROW,JCOL)
          GO TO 99
C-----LIB. BK BY CLASS YEAR
   60 WRITE(5,61)
   61 FORMAT(1H1,22X,'LIBRARY BOOK BY CLASS OF RIDER READER MATRIX',///)
          DO261J=1,2
  261 RNMX(1,J)=ANMX(3,J)+ANMX(4,J)
          WRITE(5,22)
          WRITE(5,62)(ANMX(1,J),J=1,2)
   62 FORMAT(4X,'FRESHMAN',3X,2(9X,F6.2),//)
          WRITE(5,63)(ANMX(2,J),J=1,2)
   63 FORMAT(4X,'SOPHMORE',3X,2(9X,F6.2),//)
          WRITE(5,64)(RNMX(1,J),J=1,2)
   64 FORMAT(4X,'JUN-SEN',4X,2(9X,F6.2),//)
          WRITE(5,25)
          WRITE(5.68)
   68 FORMAT(4X,'THE CLASS YEAR OF THE READER.',//)
          LIMR=3
          LIMC=2
          DO69IROW=1,2
          DO69JCOL=1,LIMC
   69 AMX(IROW,JCOL)=ANMX(IROW,JCOL)
          DO269JCOL=1,LIMC
```

```
   269 AMX(3,JCOL)=RNMX(1,JCOL)
       GO TO 99
C-----LIB.BK BY MAJOR
    70 WRITE(5,71)
    71 FORMAT(1H1,22X,'LIBRARY BOOK BY MAJOR FIELD OF RIDER READER MATRIX
      1',///)
       WRITE(5,22)
       WRITE(5,72)(AMMX(1,J),J=1,2)
    72 FORMAT(4X,'LIB. ARTS',2X,2(9X,F6.2),//)
       WRITE(5,73)(AMMX(2,J),J=1,2)
    73 FORMAT(4X,'EDUCATION',2X,2(9X,F6.2),//)
       WRITE(5,74)(AMMX(3,J),J=1,2)
    74 FORMAT(4X,'BUSINESS',3X,2(9X,F6.2),//)
       WRITE(5,25)
       WRITE(5,77)
    77 FORMAT(4X,'THE MAJOR OF THE READER.',//)
       LIMR=3
       LIMC=2
       DO78IROW=1,LIMR
       DO78JCOL=1,LIMC
    78 AMX(IROW,JCOL)=AMMX(IROW,JCOL)
       GO TO 99
C-----LIB. BK. BY CUM AVE.
    80 WRITE(5,81)
    81 FORMAT(1H1,22X,'LIBRARY BOOK BY CUM. AVG. OF RIDER READER',///)
       WRITE(5,22)
       WRITE(5,82)(AAMX(1,J),J=1,2)
    82 FORMAT(4X,'0 YO 2.49',2X,2(9X,F6.2),//)
       WRITE(5,83)(AAMX(2,J),J=1,2)
    83 FORMAT(4X,'2.5 TO 4.0',1X,2(9X,F6.2),//)
       WRITE(5,25)
       WRITE(5,85)
    85 FORMAT(4X,'THE CUM. AVERAGE OF THE READER.',//)
       LIMR=2
       LIMC=2
       LIMC=3
       LIMR=3
       DO86IROW=1,LIMR
       DO86JCOL=1,LIMC
    86 AMX(IROW,JCOL)=AAMX(IROW,JCOL)
       GO TO 99
C-----LIB. BK. BY TIME OF DAY
    90 WRITE(5,91)
    91 FORMAT(1H1,22X,'LIBRARY BOOK BY TIME OF DAY MATRIX',///)
       WRITE(5,22)
       WRITE(5,92)(ATMX(1,J),J=1,2)
    92 FORMAT(4X,'MORNING',4X,2(9X,F6.2),/)
       WRITE(5,93)(ATMX(2,J),J=1,2)
    93 FORMAT(4X,'AFTERNOON',2X,2(9X,F6.2),//)
       WRITE(5,94)(ATMX(3,J),J=1,2)
    94 FORMAT(4X,'EVENING',4X,2(9X,F6.2),//)
       WRITE(5,95)
    95 FORMAT(4X,'BY MORNING IS MEANT 8&00 AM. TO 12&59 PM.,AFTERNOON,1&0
      10 TO 5&59 PM.',//,4X,'AND EVENING,6&00 TO 10&30 PM.',//)
       WRITE(5,25)
       WRITE(5,96)
    96 FORMAT(4X,'THE TIME OF DAY OF LIBRARY READING.',//)
```

```
      LIMR=3
      LIMC=2
      DO97IROW=1,LIMR
      DO97JCOL=1,LIMC
   97 AMX(IROW,JCOL)=ATMX(IROW,JCOL)
      GO TO 99
C-----SUBROUTINE FOR CHI-SQUARE ANALYSIS
C-----CALCULATE EXPECTED MATRIX IF NULL HYPOTHESES IF TRUE.
   99 DO100IROW=1,LIMR
      DO100JCOL=1,LIMC
C-----CHECK CELLS FOR 5 OR MOR FREQUENCIES.
      IF(AMX(IROW,JCOL)-5)119,100,100
  100 CONTINUE
C-----INITIALIZE ROW TOTALS AND TOTAL OF THE REW TOTALS.
      DO101IROW=1,LIMR
  101 TROW(IROW)=0
      ALLR=0
C-----TOTAL ROWS
      DO103IROW=1,LIMR
      DO102JCOL=1,LIMC
  102 TROW(IROW)=TROW(IROW)+AMX(IROW,JCOL)
C-----TOTAL ALL ROWS
  103 ALLR=ALLR+TROW(IROW)
C-----INITIALIZE COLUMN TOTALS AND TOTAL OF THE COLUMN TOTALS.
      DO104JCOL=1,LIMC
  104 TCOL(JCOL)=0
      ALLC=0
C-----TOTAL COLUMNS.
      DO106JCOL=1,LIMC
      DO105IROW=1,LIMR
  105 TCOL(JCOL)=TCOL)JCOL)+AMX(IROW,JCOL)
C-----TOTAL ALL COLUMNS
  106 ALLC=ALLC+TCOL(JCOL)
C-----CHECK FOR ERROR
      IF(ALLC-ALLR)121,107,121
C-----CALCULATE EXPECTED CELL VALUES
  107 DO108JCOL=1,LIMC
      DO108IROW=1,LIMR
      P(JCOL)=TCOL(JCOL)/ALLC
  108 EMX(IROW,JCOL)=P(JCOL)*TROW(IROW)
C-----WRITE EXPECTED MATRIX
      WRITE(5,109)
  109 FORMAT(22X,'EXPECTED MATRIX IF NULL HYP. TRUE.',//)
      WRITE(5,22)
      WRITE(5,110)((EMX(IROW,JCOL),JCOL=1,LIMC),IROW=1,LIMR)
  110 FORMAT(2(7X,F6.2),//)
C-----STATE SAMPLE SIZE
      WRITE(5,111)ALLC
  111 FORMAT(4X,'SAMPLE SIZE IS',1X,F4.0,//)
C-----GET CRITICAL VALUE FOR CHI-SQUARE TEST.
      ICDF=(LIMR-1)*(LIMC-1)
      CHICR=CHI(ICDF)
      WRITE(5,112)ICDF,CHICR
  112 FORMAT(4X,'TEST HYPOTHESIS USING CHI-SQUARE AT A 5 PERCENT LEVEL O
     1F SIGNIFICANCE.',//,4X,'THE NUMBER OF DEGREES OF FREEDOM IS',1X,I2
     2,',AND THE CRITICAL VALUE FOR THE TEST IS',1X,F5.2,//)
C-----CALCULATE CHI-SQUARE
```

```
      CHISQ=0
      DO113IROW=1,LIMR
      DO113JCOL=1,LIMC
      DIFF2=(AMX(IROW,JCOL)-EMX(IROW,JCOL))**2/EMX(IROW,JCOL)
  113 CHISQ=CHISQ+DIFF2
      WRITE(5,114)CHISQ
  114 FORMAT(4X,'CHI-SQURAE VALUE=',1X,F6.2,//)
C-----COMPARE CRITICAL VALUE WITH CHI-SQUARE VALUE.
      IF(CHISQ-CHICR)115,115,117
  115 WRITE(5,116)
  116 FORMAT(4X,'NO SIGNIFICANT DIFFERENCE AT 5 PERCENT LEVEL BETWEEN AC
     1TUAL',//,4X,'RESULTS AND EXPECTED RESULTS.ACCEPT THE NULL HYPOTHES
     2ES.',//)
      GO TO 123
  117 WRITE(5,118)
  118 FORMAT(4X,'SIGNIFICANT DIFFERENCE AT 5 PERCENT LEVEL BETWEEN ACTUA
     1L RESULTS',//,4X,'AND EXPECTED RESULTS.REJECT THE NULL HYPOTHESIS.
     2',//)
      GO TO 123
  119 WRITE(5,120)
  120 FORMAT(4X,'NO CHI-SQUARE TEST POSSIBLE WITHOUT REGROUPING.',//)
      GO TO 123
  121 WRITE(5,122)
  122 FORMAT(4X,'MATH ERROR.HALT.')
      CALL EXIT
  123 CONTINUE
      GO TO 19
  130 CALL EXIT
      END

FEATURES SUPPORTED
 ONE WORD INTEGERS
 EXTENDED PRECISION
 IDCS

CORE REQUIREMENTS FOR
 COMMON       0  VARIABLES   1472   PROGRAM   2972

 END OF COMPILATION

// XEQ
```

PROGRAM OF THE CHI-SQUARE TEST OF THE NULL HYPOTHESES THAT THERE IS NO RELATIONSHIP
BETWEEN THE MAJOR FIELD OF STUDY OF THE READER AND THE SEVERAL CHARACTERISTICS OF
OF THE READER

```
C      CHI-SQUARE TEST FOR MAJOR BY VARIOUS CATEGORIES
       INTEGER R,RIDER,RECC
       DIMENSION ASMX(6,7),ALMX(6,7),AYMX(6,7),ARMX(6,7),ANMX(6,7),AMMX(6
      1,7),AAMX(6,7),ATMX(6,7),EMX(6,7),TROW(6),TCOL(7),P(7),CHI(30),AMX(
      26,7)
       DATA CHI/3.84,5.99,7.82,9.49,11.07,12.59,14.06,15.51,16.92,18.31,1
      19.68,21.03,22.36,23.69,25.00,26.3,27.59,28.87,30.14,31.41,32.67,33
      2.92,35.17,36.42,37.65,38.89,40.11,41.34,43.56,43.77/
C-----INITIALIZE COUNTERS AND MATRICES
       INTW=0
       RIDER=0
       MATR=0
       RECC=0
       DO1IN=1,6
       DO1JN=1,7
       ASMX(IN,JN)=0
       ALMX(IN,JN)=0
       AYMX(IN,JN)=0
       ANMX(IN,JN)=0
       AMMX(IN,JN)=0
       ARMX(IN,JN)=0
       AAMX(IN,JN)=0
    1  ATMX(IN,JN)=0
    2  READ(2,3)IFORM,INT,I,M,K,LIB,LST,L,N,J,R,AVG
    3  FORMAT(I3,I1,I1,I1,I2,I1,I1,I1,I1,I1,I1,F4.2)
       IF(IFORM)18,18,4
    4  IF(INT-1)2,2,5
    5  INTW=INTW+1
       AYMX(IST+1,J)=AYMX(IST+1,J)+1
       IF(IST)13,13,6
    6  RIDER=RIDER+1
       IF(N-5)7,7,13
    7  MATR=MATR+1
       ASMX(I,J)=ASMX(I,J)+1
       ALMX(LIB+1,J)=ALMX(LIB+1,J)+1
       ARMX(R,J)=ARMX(R,J)+1
       ANMX(N,J)=ANMX(N,J)+1
       AMMX(M,J)=AMMX(M,J)+1
       IF(AVG)13,13,8
    8  RECC=RECC+1
       IF(AVG=2.)9,10,10
    9  AAMX(1,J)=AAMX(1,J)+1
       GO TO 13
   10  IF(AVG-3.)11,12,12
   11  AAMX(2,J)=AAMX(2,J)+1
```

```
        GO TO 13
   12 AAMX(3,J)=AAMX(3,J)+1
   13 IF(K-6)14,15,15
   14 ATMX(1,J)=ATMX(1,J)+1
        GO TO 2
   15 IF(K-11)16,17,17
   16 ATMX(2,J)=ATMX(2,J)+1
        GO TO 2
   17 ATMX(3,J)=ATMX(3,J)+1
        GO TO 2
   18 KALL=0
   19 KALL=KALL+1
        GO TO (20,30,50,60,80,130),KALL
C-----MAJOR BY SEX OF READER
   20 WRITE(5,21)
   21 FORMAT(1H1,22X,'MAJOR BY SEX OF READER MATRIX',///)
        WRITE(5,22)
   22 FORMAT(20X,'LIBERAL ARTS',4X,'EDUCATION',4X,'BUSINESS',//)
        WRITE(5,23)(ASMX(1,J),J=1,3)
   23 FORMAT(4X,'MALE',7X,3(8X,F6.2))
        WRITE(5,24)(ASMX(2,J),J=1,3)
   24 FORMAT(4X,'FEMALE',5X,3(8X,F6.2))
        WRITE(5,25)
   25 FORMAT(22X,'NULL HYPOTHESIS',/,4X,'THERE IS NO RELATIONSHIP BETWEE
       1N THE MAJOR FIELD AND',//)
        WRITE(5,27)
   27 FORMAT(4X,'THE SEX OF THE LIBRARY READER.',//)
        LIMR=2
        LINC=3
        DO26IROW=1,LIMR
        DO26JCOL=1,LIMC
   26 AMX(IROW,JCOL)=ASMX(IROW,JCOL)
        GO TO 99
C-----MAJOR BY KIND OF BOOK
   30 WRITE(5,31)
   31 FORMAT(1H1,22X,'MAJOR BY KIND OF BOOK MATRIX',//)
        WRITE(5,22)
        WRITE(5,32)(ALMX(1,J),J=1,3)
   32 FORMAT(4X,'NON-LIBRARY',398X,F6.2))
        WRITE(5,33)(ALMX(2,J),J=1,3)
   33 FORMAT(4X,'LIBRARY',4X,3(8X,F6.2))
        WRITE(5,25)
        WRITE(5,34)
   34 FORMAT(4X,'THE KIND OF BOOKS READ IN THE LIBRARY, THAT IS LIBRARY
       1BOOK OR NON-LIBRARY BOOK.',//)
        LIMR=2
        LIMC=3
        DO35IROW=1,LIMR
        DO35JCOL=1,LIMC
   35 AMX(IROW,JCOL)=ALMX(IROW,JCOL)
        GO TO 99
C-----MAJOR BY RESIDENCE OF STUDENT MATRIX
   50 WRITE(5,51)
   51 FORMAT(1H1,22X,'MAJOR BY RESIDENCE OF STUDENT MATRIX',///)
        WRITE(5,22)
        WRITE(5,52)(ARMX(1,J),J=1,3)
   52 FORMAT(4X,'DORMITORY',2X,3(8X,F6.2))
```

```
      WRITE(5,53)(ARMX(2,J),J=1,3)
   53 FORMAT(4X,'COMMUTER',3X,3(8X,F6.2))
      WRITE(5,54)(ARMX(3,J),J=1,3)
   54 FORMAT(4X,'FRAT OR SOR',3(8X,F6.2))
      WRITE(5,25)
      WRITE(5,55)
   55 FORMAT(4X,'THE RESIDENCE OF THE STUDENT.',//)
      LIMR=3
      LIMC=3
      DO56IROW=1,LIMR
      DO56JCOL=1,LIMC
   56 AMX(IROW,JCOL)=ARMX(IROW,JCOL)
      GO TO 99
C-----MAJOR BY CLASS YEAR
   60 WRITE(5,61)
   61 FORMAT(1H1,22X,'MAJOR BY CLASS YEAR OF STUDENT MATRIX',///)
      WRITE(5,22)
      WRITE(5,62)(ANMX(1,J),J=1,3)
   62 FORMAT(4X,'FRESHMAN',3X,3(8X,F6.2))
      WRITE(5,63)(ANMX(2,J),J=1,3)
   63 FORMAT(4X,'SOPHMORE',3X,3(8X,F6.2))
      WRITE(5,64)(ANMX(3,J),J=1,3)
   64 FORMAT(4X,'JUNIOR',5X,3(8X,F6.2))
      WRITE(5,65)(ANMX(4,J),J=1,3)
   65 FORMAT(4X,'SENIOR',5X,3(8X,F6.2))
      WRITE(5,25)
      WRITE(5,68)
   68 FORMAT(4X,'THE CLASS YEAR OF THE READER.',//)
      LIMR=4
      LIMC=3
      DO69IROW=1,LIMR
      DO69JCOL=1,LIMC
   69 AMX(IROW,JCOL)=ANMX(IROW,JCOL)
      GO TO 99
C-----MAJOR BY CUM. AVG.
   80 WRITE(5,81)
   81 FORMAT(1H1,22X,'MAJOR BY CUM. AVG. OF RIDER READER MATRIX',///)
      WRITE(5,22)
      WRITE(5,82)(AAMX(1,J),J=1,3)
   82 FORMAT(4X,'0 TO 1.59',2X,3(8X,F6.2))
      WRITE(5,83)(AAMX(2,J),J=1,3)
   83 FORMAT(4X,'2 TO 2.59',2X,3(8X,F6.2))
      WRITE(5,84)(AAMX(3,J),J=1,3)
   84 FORMAT(4X,'3 TO 4.00',2X,3(8X,F6.2))
      LIMC=3
      LIMR=3
      DO86IROW=1,LIMR
      DO86JCOL=1,LIMC
   86 AMX(IROW,JCOL)=AAMX(IROW,JCOL)
      GO TO 99
C-----SUBROUTINE FOR CHI-SQUARE ANALYSIS
C-----CALCULATE EXPECTED MATRIX IF NULL HYPOTHESES IF TRUE.
   99 DO100IROW=1,LIMR
      DO100JCOL=1,LIMC
C-----CHECK CELLS FOR 5 OR MOR FREQUENCIES.
      IF(AMX(IROW,JCOL)-5)119,100,100
  100 CONTINUE
```

```
C-----INITIALIZE ROW TOTALS AND TOTAL OF THE REW TOTALS.
      DO101IROW=1,LIMR
  101 TROW(IROW)=0
      ALLR=0
C-----TOTAL ROWS
      DO103IROW=1,LIMR
      DO102JCOL=1,LIMC
  102 TROW(IROW)=TROW(IROW)+AMX(IROW,JCOL)
C-----TOTAL ALL ROWS
  103 ALLR=ALLR+TROW(IROW)
C-----INITIALIZE COLUMN TOTALS AND TOTAL OF THE COLUMN TOTALS.
      DO104JCOL=1,LIMC
  104 TCOL(JCOL)=0
      ALLC=0
C-----TOTAL COLUMNS.
      DO106JCOL=1,LIMC
      DO105IROW=1,LIMR
  105 TCOL(JCOL)=TCOL(JCOL)+AMX(IROW,JCOL)
C-----TOTAL ALL COLUMNS
  106 ALLC=ALLC+TCOL(JCOL)
C-----CHECK FOR ERROR
      IF(ALLC-ALLR)121,107,12
C-----CALCULATE EXPECTED CELL VALUES
  107 DO108JCOL=1,LIMC
      DO108IROW=1,LIMR
      P(JCOL)=TCOL(JCOL)/ALLC
  108 EMX(IROW,JCOL)=P(JCOL)+TROW(IROW)
C-----WRITE EXPECTED MATRIX
      WRITE(5,109)
  109 FORMAT(22X,'EXPECTED MATRIX IF NULL HYP. TRUE.',//)
      WRITE(5,22)
      WRITE(5,110)((8MX(IROW,JCOL),JCOL=1,LIMC),IROW=1,LIMR)
  110 FORMAT(17X,3(8X,F6.2),//)
C-----STATE SAMPLE SIZE
      WRITE(5,111)ALLC
  111 FORMAT(4X,'SAMPLE SIZE IS',1X,F4.0,//)
C-----GET CRITICAL VALUE FOR CHI-SQUARE TEST.
      ICDF=(LIMR-1)*(LIMC-1)
      CHICR=CHI(ICDF)
      WRITE(5,112)ICDF,CHICR
  112 FORMAT(4X,'TEST HYPOTHESIS USING CHI-SQUARE AT A 5 PERCENT LEVEL O
     1F SIGNIFICANCE.',//,4X,'THE NUMBER OF DEGREES OF FREEDOM IS',1X,I2
     2,',AND THE CRITICAL VALUE FOR THE TEST IS',1X,F5.2,//)
C-----CALCULATE CHI-SQUARE
      CHISQ=0
      DO113IROW=1,LIMR
      DO113JCOL=1,LIMC
      DIFF2=(AMX(IROW,JCOL)-EMX(IROW,JCOL))**2/EMX(IROW,JCOL)
  113 CHISQ=CHISQ+DIFF2
      WRITE(5,114)CHISQ
  114 FORMAT(4X,'CHI-SQURAE VALUE=',1X,F6.2,//)
C-----COMPARE CRITICAL VALUE WITH CHI-SQUARE VALUE.
      IF(CHISQ-CHICR)115,115,117
  115 WRITE(5,116)
  116 FORMAT(4X,'NO SIGNIFICANT DIFFERENCE AT 5 PERCENT LEVEL BETWEEN AC
     1TUAL',//,4X,'RESULTS AND EXPECTED RESULTS.ACCEPT THE NULL HYPOTHES
     2ES.',//)
```

```
      GO TO 123
117 WRITE(5,118)
118 FORMAT(4X,'SIGNIFICANT DIFFERENCE AT 5 PERCENT LEVEL BETWEEN ACTUA
   1L RESULTS',//,4X,'AND EXPECTED RESULTS.REJECT THE NULL HYPOTHESIS.
   2',//)
      GO TO 123
119 WRITE(5,120)
120 FORMAT(4X,'NO CHI-SQUARE TEST POSSIBLE WITHOUT REGROUPING.',//)
      GO TO 123
121 WRITE(5,122)
122 FORMAT(4X,'MATH ERROR.HALT.')
      CALL EXIT
123 CONTINUE
      GO TO 19
130 CALL EXIT
      END
```

FEATURES SUPPORTED
 ONE WORD INTEGERS
 EXTENDED PRECISION
 IOCS

CORE REQUIREMENTS FOR
 COMMON   0 VARIABLES   1460   PROGRAM   2320

END OF COMPILATION

// XEQ

```
C     CHI-SQUARE TESTS FOR RESIDENCE BY VARIOUS CATEGORIES
      INTEGER R,RIDER,RECC
      DIMENSION ASMX(6,7),ALMX(6,7),AYMX(6,7),ARMX(6,7),ANMX(6,7),AMMX(6
     1,7),AAMX(6,7),ATMX(6,7),EMX(6,7),TROW(6),TCOL(7),P(7),CHI(30),AMX(
     26,7),RTMX(1,2),RRMX(2,2)
      DATA CHI/3.84,5.99,7.82,9.49,11.07,12.59,14.06,15.51,16.92,18.31,1
     19.68,21.03,22.36,23.69,25.00,26.3,27.59,28.87,30.14,31.41,32.67,33
     2.92,35.17,36.42,37.65,38.89,40.11,41.34,42.56,43.77/
C-----INITIALIZE COUNTERS AND MATRICES
      INTW=0
      RIDER=0
      MATR=0
      RECC=0
      DO1IN=1,6
      DO1JN=1,7
      ASMX(IN,JN)=0
      ALMX(IN,JN)=0
      AYMX(IN,JN)=0
      ARMX(IN,JN)=0
      ANMX(IN,JN)=0
      AMMX(IN,JN)=0
      AAMX(IN,JN)=0
    1 ATMX(IN,JN)=0
    2 READ(2,3)IFORM,INT,I,R,K,LIB,IST,L,N,M,J,AVG
    3 FORMAT(I3,I1,I1,I1,I2,I1,I1,I1,I1,I1,I1,F4.2)
      IF(IFORM)18,18,4
    4 IF(INT-1)2,2,5
    5 INTW=INTW+1
      ASMX(I,J)=ASMX(I,J)+1
      ALMX(LIB+1,J)=ALMX(LIB+1,J)+1
      AYMX(IST+1,J)=AYMX(IST+1,J)+1
      IF(IST)13,13,6
    6 RIDER=RIDER+1
      ARMX(R,J)=ARMX(R,J)+1
      ANMX(N,J)=ANMX(N,J)+1
      IF(N-5)7,7,13
    7 MATR=MATR+1
      AMMX(M,J)=ANMX(M,J)+1
      IF(AVG)13,13,8
    8 RECC=RECC+1
      IF(AVG-2.49)9,9,11
    9 AAMX(1,J)=AAMX(1,J)+1
      GO TO 13
   11 AAMX(2,J)=AAMX(2,J)+1
   13 IF(K-6)14,15,15
```

```
   14 ATMX(1,J)=ATMX(1,J)+1
      GO TO 2
   15 IF(K-11)16,17,17
   16 ATMX(2,J)=ATMX(2,J)+1
      GO TO 2
   17 ATMX(3,J)=ATMX(3,J)+1
      GO TO 2
   18 KALL=0
   19 KALL=KALL+1
      GO TO (20,30,50,60,70,80,90,290,130), KALL
C     RESIDENCE BY SEX
   20 WRITE(5,21)
   21 FORMAT(1H1,22X,'RESIDENCE BY SEX OF READER MATRIX',///)
      WRITE(5,22)
   22 FORMAT(20X,'DORMITORY    COMMUTER',//)
      WRITE(5,23)(ASMX(1,J),J=1,2)
   23 FORMAT(4X,'MALE'7X,2(7X,F6.2),//)
      WRITE(5,24)(ASMX(2,J),J=1,2)
   24 FORMAT(4X,'FEMALE',5X,2(7X,F6.2),//)
      WRITE(5,205)
  205 FORMAT(22X,'MULL HYPOTHESES',/,4X,'THERE IS NO RELATIONSHIP BETWEE
     1N THE RESIDENCE AND',//)
      WRITE(5,27)
   27 FORMAT(4X,'THE SEX OF THE LIBRARY READER.',//)
      LIMR=2
      LIMC=2
      DO26IROW=1,LIMR
      DO26JCOL=1,LIMC
   26 AMX(IROW,JCOL)=ASMX(IROW,JCOL)
      GO TO 99
C-----RESIDENCE BY KIND OF BOOK
   30 WRITE(5,31)
   31 FORMAT(1H1,22X,'RESIDENCE BY LIBRARY BOOK OR NOT MATRIX',///)
      WRITE(5,22)
      WRITE(5,33)(ALMX(1,J),J=1,2)
   33 FORMAT(4X,'NON-LIBRARY',2(7X,F6.2),//)
      WRITE(5,32)(ALMX(2,J),J=1,2)
   32 FORMAT(4X,'LIBRARY',4X,2(7X,F6.2),//)
      WRITE(5,205)
      WRITE(5,34)
   34 FORMAT(4X,'THE KIND OF BOOKS READ IN THE LIBRARY, THAT IS LIBRARY
     1BOOK OR NON-LIBRARY BOOK.',//)
      LIMR=2
      LIMC=2
      DO35IROW=1,LIMR
      DO35JCOL=1,LIMC
   35 AMX(IROW,JCOL)=ALMX(IROW,JCOL)
      GO TO 99
C     RESIDENCE BY BY WEEKDAY OR WEEKEND
   50 WRITE(5,51)
   51 FORMAT(1H1,22X,'RESIDENCE OF READER RELATIVE TO WEEK MATRIX',///)
      WRITE(5,22)
      DO 251 J=1,2
      RRMX(1,J)=ARMX(1,J)+ARMX(2,J)+ARMX(3,J)+ARMX(4,J)+ARMX(5,J)
  251 RRMX(2,J)=ARMX(6,J)+ARMX(7,J)
      WRITE(5,52)(RRMX(1,J),J=1,2)
   52 FORMAT(4X,'WEEKDAY',4X,2(7X,F6.2),//)
```

```
      WRITE(5,53)(RRMX(2,J),J=1,2)
   53 FORMAT(4X,'WEEKEND',4X,2(7X,F6.2),//)
      WRITE(5,205)
      WRITE(5,55)
   55 FORMAT(4X,'THE TIME OF THE WEEK OF READING',//)
      LIMR=2
      LIMC=2
      DO56IROW=1,LIMR
      DO56JCOL=1,LIMC
   56 AMX(IROW,JCOL)=RRMX(IROW,JCOL)
      GO TO 99
C     RESIDENCE BY CLASS YEAR
   60 WRITE(5,61)
   61 FORMAT(1H1,22X,'RESIDENCE OF READER BY CLASS YEAR MATRIX',///)
      WRITE(5,22)
      WRITE(5,62)(ANMX(1,J),J=1,2)
   62 FORMAT(4X,'FRESHMAN',3X,2(7X,F6.2),//)
      WRITE(5,63)(ANMX(2,J),J=1,2)
   63 FORMAT(4X,'SOPHMORE',3X,2(9X,F6.2),//)
      WRITE(5,64)(ANMX(3,J),J=1,2)
   64 FORMAT(4X,'JUNIOR',5X,2(7X,F6.2),//)
      WRITE(5,65)(ANMX(4,J),J=1,2)
   65 FORMAT(4X,'SENIOR',5X,2(7X,F6.2),//)
      WRITE(5,205)
      WRITE(5,68)
   68 FORMAT(4X,'THE CLASS YEAR OF THE READER.',//)
      LIMR=4
      LIMC=2
      DO69IROW=1,LIMR
      DO69JCOL=1,LIMC
   69 AMX(IROW,JCOL)=ANMX(IROW,JCOL)
      GO TO 99
C     RESIDENCE BY MAJOR OF READER
   70 WRITE(5,71)
   71 FORMAT(1H1,22X,'RESIDENCE OF READER BY MAJOR MATRIX',//)
      WRITE(5,22)
      WRITE(5,72)(AMMX(1,J),J=1,2)
   72 FORMAT(4X,'LIB. ARTS',2X,2(7X,F6.2),//)
      WRITE(5,73)(AMMX(2,J),J=1,2)
   73 FORMAT(4X,'EDUCATION',2X,2(7X,F6.2),//)
      WRITE(5,74)(AMMX(3,J),J=1,2)
   74 FORMAT(4X,'BUSINESS',3X,2(7X,F6.2),//)
      WRITE(5,205)
      WRITE(5,77)
   77 FORMAT(4X,'THE MAJOR OF THE READER.',//)
      LIMR=3
      LIMC=2
      DO78IROW=1,LIMR
      DO78JCOL=1,LIMC
   78 AMX(IROW,JCOL)=AMMX(IROW,JCOL)
      GO TO 99
C-----RESIDENCE BY CUM. AVE.
   80 WRITE(5,81)
   81 FORMAT(1H1,22X,'RESIDENCE BY CUM. AVE. OF RIDER READER',///)
      WRITE(5,22)
      WRITE(5,82)(AAMX(1,J),J=1,2)
   82 FORMAT(4X,'0 TO 2.49',2X,2(7X,F6.2),//)
```

```
      WRITE(5,83)(AAMX(2,J),J=1,2)
   83 FORMAT(4X,'2.5 TO 4.0',1X,2(7X,F6.2),//)
      WRITE(5,205)
      WRITE(5,85)
   85 FORMAT(4X,'THE CUM. AVERAGE OF THE READER.',//)
      LIMR=2
      LIMC=2
      DO86IROW=1,LIMR
      DO86JCOL=1,LIMC
   86 AMX(IROW,JCOL)=AAMX(IROW,JCOL)
      GO TO 99
C-----RESIDENCE BY TIME OF DAY
   90 WRITE(5,91)
   91 FORMAT(1H1,22X,'RESIDENCE BY TIME OF DAY OF LIBRARY READING',///)
      WRITE(5,22)
      WRITE(5,92)(ATMX(1,J),J=1,2)
   92 FORMAT(4X,'MORNING',4X,2(7X,F6.2),//)
      WRITE(5,93)(ATMX(2,J),J=1,2)
   93 FORMAT(4X,'AFTERNOON',2X,2(7X,F6.2),//)
      WRITE(5,94)(ATMX(3,J),J=1,2)
   94 FORMAT(4X,'EVENING',4X,2(7X,F6.2),//)
      WRITE(5,95)
   95 FORMAT(4X,'BY MORNING IS MEANT 8 00 AM. TO 12 59 PM.,AFTERNOON,1 0
     10 TO 5 59 PM.',//,4X,'AND EVENING,6 00 TO 10 30 PM.',//)
      WRITE(5,205)
      WRITE(5,96)
   96 FORMAT(4X,'THE TIME OF DAY OF LIBRARY READING.',//)
      LIMR=3
      LIMC=2
      DO97IROW=1,LIMR
      DO97JCOL=1,LIMC
   97 AMX(IROW,JCOL)=ATMX(IROW,JCOL)
      GO TO 99
  290 WRITE(5,91)
      WRITE(5,22)
      DO 291 J=1,2
  291 RTMX(1,J)=ATMX(1,J)+ATMX(2,J)
      WRITE(5,292)(RTMX(1,J),J=1,2)
  292 FORMAT(4X,'8 TO 3.59',2X,2(7X,F6.2),//)
      WRITE(5,293)(ATMX(3,J),J=1,2)
  293 FORMAT(4X,'4 TO END',3X,2(7X,F6.2),//)
      WRITE(5,96)
      LIMR=2
      LIMC=2
      DO 294 JCOL=1,2
      AMX(1,JCOL)=RTMX(1,JCOL)
  294 AMX(2,JCOL)=ATMX(3,JCOL)
      GO TO 99
C-----SUBROUTINE FOR CHI-SQUARE ANALYSIS
C-----CALCULATE EXPECTED MATRIX IF NULL HYPOTHESES IF TRUE.
   99 DO100IROW=1,LIMR
      DO100JCOL=1,LIMC
C-----CHECK CELLS FOR 5 OR MOR FREQUENCIES.
      IF(AMX(IROW,JCOL)-5)119,100,100
  100 CONTINUE
C-----INITIALIZE ROW TOTALS AND TOTAL OF THE REW TOTALS.
      DO101IROW=1,LIMR
```

```
  101 TROW(IROW)=0
      ALLR=0
C-----TOTAL ROWS
      DO103IROW=1,LIMR
      DO102JCOL=1,LIMC
  102 TROW(IROW)=TROW(IROW)+AMX(IROW,JCOL)
C-----TOTAL ALL ROWS
  103 ALLR=ALLR+TROW(IROW)
C-----INITIALIZE COLUMN TOTALS AND TOTAL OF THE COLUMN TOTALS.
      DO104JCOL=1,LIMC
  104 TCOL(JCOL)=0
      ALLC=0
C-----TOTAL COLUMNS.
      DO106JCOL=1,LIMC
      DO105IROW=1,LIMR
  105 TCOL(JCOL)=TCOL(JCOL)+AMX(IROW,JCOL)
C-----TOTAL ALL COLUMNS
  106 ALLC=ALLC+TCOL(JCOL)
C-----CHECK FOR ERROR
      IF(ALLC-ALLR)121,107,121
C-----CALCULATE EXPECTED CELL VALUES
  107 DO108JCOL=1,LIMC
      DO108IROW=1,LIMR
      P(JCOL)=TCOL(JCOL)/ALLC
  108 EMX(IROW,JCOL)=P(JCOL)*TROW(IROW)
C-----WRITE EXPECTED MATRIX
      WRITE(5,109)
  109 FORMAT(22X,'EXPECTED MATRIX IF NULL HYP. TRUE.',//)
      WRITE(5,22)
      WRITE(5,110)((EMX(IROW,JCOL),JCDL=1,LIMC),IROW=1,LIMR)
  110 FORMAT(2(7X,F6.2),//)
C-----STATE SAMPLE SIZE
      WRITE(5,111)ALLC
  111 FORMAT(4X,'SAMPLE SIZE IS',1X,F4.0,//)
C-----GET CRITICAL VALUE FOR CHI-SQUARE TEST.
      ICDF=(LIMR-1)*(LIMC-1)
      CHICR=CHI(ICDF)
      WRITE(5,112)ICDF,CHICR
  112 FORMAT(4X,'TEST HYPOTHESIS USING CHI-SQUARE AT A 5 PERCENT LEVEL O
     1F SIGNIFICANCE.',//,4X,'THE NUMBER OF DEGREES OF FREEDOM IS',1X,I2
     2,',AND THE CRITICAL VALUE FOR THE TEST IS',1X,F5.2,//)
C-----CALCULATE CHI-SQUARE
      CHISQ=0
      DO113IROW-1,LIMR
      DO113JCOL=1,LIMC
      DIFF2=(AMX(IROW,JCOL)-EMX(IROW,JCOL))**2/EMX(IROW,JCOL)
  113 CHISQ=CHISQ+DIFF2
      WRITE(5,114)CHISQ
  114 FORMAT(4X,'CHI-SQURAE VALUE=',1X,F6.2,//)
C-----COMPARE CRITICAL VALUE WITH CHI-SQUARE VALUE.
      IF(CHISQ-CHICR)115,115,117
  115 WRITE(5,116)
  116 FORMAT(4X,'NO SIGNIFICANT DIFFERENCE AT 5 PERCENT LEVEL BETWEEN AC
     1TUAL',//,4X,'RESULTS AND EXPECTED RESULTS.ACCEPT THE NULL HYPOTHES
     2ES.',//)
      GO TO 123
  117 WRITE(5,118)
```

319

```
118 FORMAT(4X,'SIGNIFICANT DIFFERENCE AT 5 PERCENT LEVEL BETWEEN ACTUA
   1L RESULTS',//,4X,'AND EXPECTED RESULTS.REJECT THE NULL HYPOTHESIS.
   2',//)
119 WRITE(5,120)
120 FORMAT(4X,'NO CHI-SQUARE TEST POSSIBLE WITHOUT REGROUPING.',//)
   GO TO 123
121 WRITE(5,122)
122 FORMAT(4X,'MATH ERROR.HALT.')
   CALL EXIT
123 CONTINUE
   GO TO 19
130 CALL EXIT
   END

FEATURES SUPPORTED
 ONE WORD INTEGERS
 EXTENDED PRECISION
 IDCS

CORE REQUIREMENTS FOR
 COMMON     0  VARIABLES   1482   PROGRAM   3068

 END OF COMPILATION

// XEQ
```

PROGRAM OF THE CHI-SQUARE TEST OF THE NULL HYPOTHESES THAT THERE IS NO RELATIONSHIP
BETWEEN DAY OF WEEK* OF READING AND THE SEVERAL CHARACTERISTICS OF THE READER

```
C-----CHI-SQUARE TESTS FOR DAY BY VARIOUS CATEGORIES
      INTEGER R,RIDER,RECC
      DIMENSION ASMX(6,7),ALMX(6,7),AYMX(6,7),ARMX(6,7),ANMX(6,7),AMMX(6
     1,7),AAMX(6,7),ATMX(6,7),EMX(6,7),TROW(6),TCOL(7),P(7),CHI(30),AMX(
     26,7)
      DATE CHI/3.84,5.99,7.82,9.49,11.07,12.59,14.06,15.51,16.92,18.31,1
     119.68,21.03,22.36,23.69,25.00,26.3,27.59,28.87,30.14,31.41,32.67,33
     22.92,35.17,36.42,37.65,38.89,40.11,41.34,42.56,43.77/
C-----INITIALIZE COUNTERS AND MATRICES
      INTW=0
      RIDER=0
      MATR=0
      RECC=0
      DO1IN=1,6
      DO1JN=1,7
      ASMX(IN,JN)=0
      ALMX(IN,JN)=0
      AYMX(IN,JN)=0
      ARMX(IN,JN)=0
      ANMX(IN,JN)=0
      AMMX(IN,JN)=0
      AAMX(IN,JN)=0
    1 ATMX(IN,JN)=0
    2 READ(2,3)IFORM,INT,I,J,K,LIB,IST,L,N,M,R,AVG
    3 FORMAT(I3,I1,I1,I1,I2,I1,I1,I1,I1,I1,I1,F4.2)
      IF(IFORM)18,18,4
    4 IF(INT-1)2,2,5
    5 INTW=INTW+1
      ASMX(I,J)=ASMX(I,J)+1
      ALMX(LIB+1,J)=ALMX(LIB+1,J)+1
      AYMX(IST+1,J)=AYMX(IST+1,J)+1
      IF(IST)13,13,6
    6 RIDER=RIDER+1
      ARMX(R,J)=ARMX(R,J)+1
      ANMX(N,J)=ANMX(N,J)+1
      IF(N-5)7,7,13
    7 MATR=MATR+1
      AMMX(M,J)=AMMX(M,J)+1
      IF(AVG)13,13,8
    8 RECC=RECC+1
      IF(AVG-2.)9,10,10
    9 AAMX(1,J)=AAMX(1,J)+1
      GO TO 13
   10 IF(AVG-3.)11,12,12
   11 AAMX(2,J)=AAMX(2,J)+1
```

---

*In this Appendix, the first print-out deals with a 5-day week; the
second, a 7-day week.

```
      GO TO 13
   12 AAMX(3,J)=AAMX(3,J)+1
   13 IF(K-6)14,15,15
   14 ATMX(1,J)=ATMX(1,J)+1
      GO TO 2
   15 IF(K-11)16,17,17
   16 ATMX(2,J)=ATMX(2,J)+1
      GO TO 2
   17 ATMX(3,J)=ATMX(3,J)+1
      GO TO 2
   18 KALL=0
   19 KALL=KALL+1
      GO TO (20,30,40,50,60,70,80,90,130),KALL
C-----DAY BY SEX MATRIX
   20 WRITE(5,21)
   21 FORMAT(1H1,22X,'DAY BY SEX OF READER MATRIX',///)
      WRITE(5,22)
   22 FORMAT(20X,'MONDAY  TUESDAY  WEDNESDAY  THURSDAY  FRIDAY  SATURDAY
     1  SUNDAY',//)
      WRITE(5,23)(ASMX(1,J),J=1,7)
   23 FORMAT(4X,'MALE',9X,3(3X,F6.2),5X,F6.2,3(3X,F6.2),//)
      WRITE(5,24)(ASMX(2,J),J=1,7)
   24 FORMAT(4X,'FEMALE',7X,3(3X,F6.2),5X,F6.2,3(6X,F6.2),//)
      WRITE(5,25)
   25 FORMAT(22X,'NULL HYPOTHESIS',/,4X,'THERE IS NO RELATIONSHIP BETWEE
     1N THE DAY OF THE WEEK AND',//)
      WRITE(5,27)
   27 FORMAT(4X,'THE SEX OF THE LIBRARY READER.',//)
      LIMR=2
      LIMC=7
      DO26IROW=1,LIMR
      DO26JCOL=1,LIMC
   26 AMX(IROW,JCOL)=ASMX(IROW,JCOL)
      GO TO 99
C---- DAY BY LIB. BK VS. NON-LIB. BK. MATRIX
   30 WRITE(5,31)
   31 FORMAT(1H1,22X,'DAY BY LIBRARY BOOK VS. NON-LIBRARY BOOK MATRIX',/
     1/)
      WRITE(5,22)
      WRITE(5,33)(ALMX(1,J),J=1,7)
   32 FORMAT(4X,'LIBRARY',6X,3(3X,F6.2),5X,F6.2,3(3X,F6.2),//)
      WRITE(5,32)(ALMX(2,J),J=1,7)
   33 FORMAT(4X,'NON-LIBRARY',2X,3(3X,F6.2),5X,F6.2,3(3X,F6.2),//)
      WRITE(5,25)
      WRITE(5,34)
   34 FORMAT(4X,'THE KIND OF BOOKS READ IN THE LIBRARY, THAT IS LIBRARY
     1BOOK OR NON-LIBRARY BOOK.',//)
      LIMR=2
      LIMC=7
      DO35IROW=1,LIMR
      DO35JCOL=1,LIMC
   35 AMX(IROW,JCOL)=ALMX(IROW,JCOL)
      GO TO 99
C-----DAY BY STUDENT OR NON-STUDENT MATRIX
   40 WRITE(5,41)
   41 FORMAT(1H1,22X,'DAY BY STUDENT VS. NON-STUDENT MATRIX',//)
      WRITE(5,22)
```

```
      WRITE(5,42)(AYMX(1,J),J=1,7)
   42 FORMAT(4X,'NON-RIDER',4X,3(3X,F6.2),5X,F6.2,3(3X,F6.2),//)
      WRITE(5,43)(AYMX(2,J),J=1,7)
   43 FORMAT(4X,'RIDER',8X,3(3X,F6.2),5X,F6.2,3(3X,F6.2),//)
      WRITE(5,25)
      WRITE(5,44)
   44 FORMAT(4X,'THE BOOK READERS CONNECTION WITH RIDER COLLEGE.',//)
      LIMR=2
      LIMC=7
      DO45IROW=1,LIMR
      DO45JCOL=1,LIMC
   45 AMX(IROW,JCOL)=AYMX(IROW,JCOL)
      GO TO 99
C-----DAY BY CLASS YEAR OF RIDER STUDENT MATRIX
   60 WRITE(5,61)
   61 FORMAT(1H1,22X,'DAY BY CLASS YEAR OF STUDENT MATRIX',//)
      WRITE(5,22)
      WRITE(5,62)(ANMX(1,J),J=1,7)
   62 FORMAT(4X,'FRESHMAN',5X,3(3X,F6.2),5X,F6.2,3(3X,F6.2),//)
      WRITE(5,63)(ANMX(2,J),J=1,7)
   63 FORMAT(4X,'SOPHMORE',5X,3(3X,F6.2),5X,F6.2,3(3X,F6.2),//)
      WRITE(5,64)(ANMX(3,J),J=1,7)
   64 FORMAT(4X,'JUNIOR',7X,3(3X,F6.2),5X,F6.2,3(3X,F6.2),//)
      WRITE(5,65)(ANMX(4,J),J=1,7)
   65 FORMAT(4X,'SENIOR',7X,3(3X,F6.2),5X,F6.2,3(3X,F6.2),//)
      WRITE(5,66)(ANMX(5,J),J=1,7)
   66 FORMAT(4X,'GRADUATE',5X,3(3X,F6.2),5X,F6.2,3(3X,F6.2),//)
      WRITE(5,67)(ANMX(6,7),J=1,7)
   67 FORMAT(4X,'OTHER',8X,3(3X,F6.2),5X,F6.2,3(3X,F6.2),//)
      WRITE(5,25)
      WRITE(5,68)
   68 FORMAT(4X,'THE CLASS YEAR OF THE READER.',//)
      LIMR=6
      LIMC=7
      DO69IROW=1,LIMR
      DO69JCOL=1,LIMC
   69 AMX(IROW,JCOL)=ANMX(IROW,JCOL)
      GO TO 99
C-----DAY BY MAJOR OF RIDER READER MATRIX
   70 WRITE(5,71)
   71 FORMAT(1H1,22X,'DAY BY MAJOR OF RIDER READER MATRIX',//)
      WRITE(5,22)
      WRITE(5,72)(AMMX(1,J),J=1,7)
   72 FORMAT(4X,'LIB. ARTS',4X,3(3X,F6.2),5X,F6.2,3(3X,F6.2),//)
      WRITE(5,73)(AMMX(2,J),J=1,7)
   73 FORMAT(4X,'EDUCATION',4X,3(3X,F6.2),5X,F6.2,3(3X,F6.2),//)
      WRITE(5,74)(AMMX(3,J),J=1,7)
   74 FORMAT(4X,'BUSINESS',5X,3(3X,F6.2),5X,F6.2,3(3X,F6.2),//)
      WRITE(5,75)(AMMX(4,J),J=1,7)
   75 FORMAT(4X,'ED. MASTER',3X,3(3X,F6.2),5X,F6.2,3(3X,F6.2),//)
      WRITE(5,76)(AMMX(5,J),J=1,7)
   76 FORMAT(4X,'BUS. MASTER',2X,3(3X,F6.2),5X,F6.2,3(3X,F6.2),//)
      WRITE(5,25)
      WRITE(5,77)
   77 FORMAT(4X,'THE MAJOR OF THE READER.',//)
      LIMR=5
      LIMC=7
```

```
        DO78IROW=1,LIMR
        DO78JCOL=1,LIMC
 78 AMX(IROW,JCOL)=AMMX(IROW,JCOL)
        GO TO 99
C-----DAY BY CUM. AVERAGE OF RIDER READER MATRIX
 80 WRITE(5,81)
 81 FORMAT(1H1,22X,'DAY BY CUM. AVERAGE OF RIDER READER MATRIX',//)
        WRITE(5,22)
        WRITE(5,82)(AAMX(1,J),J=1,7)
 82 FORMAT(4X,'0 TO 1.59',4X,3(3X,F6.2),5X,F6.2,3(3X,F6.2),//)
        WRITE(5,83)(AAMX(2,J),J=1,7)
 83 FORMAT(4X,'2 TO 2.59',4X,3(3X,F6.2),5X,F6.2,3(3X,F6.2),//)
        WRITE(5,84)(AAMX(3,J),J=1,7)
 84 FORMAT(4X,'3 TO 4.00',4X,3(3X,F6.2),5X,F6.2,3(3X,F6.2),//)
        LIMR=3
        LIMC=7
        DO86IROW=1,LIMR
        DO86JCOL=1,LIMC
 86 AMX(IROW,JCOL)=AAMX(IROW,JCOL)
        GO TO 99
C-----DAY BY TIME OF DAY MATRIX
 90 WRITE(5,91)
 91 FORMAT(1H1,22X,'DAY BY TIME OF DAY OF LIBRARY READING',//)
        WRITE(5,22)
        WRITE(5,92)(ATMX(1,J),J=1,7)
 92 FORMAT(4X,'MORNING',6X,3(3X,F6.2),5X,F6.2,3(3X,F6.2),//)
        WRITE(5,93)(ATMX(2,J),J=1,7)
 93 FORMAT(4X,'AFTERNOON',4X,3(3X,F6.2),5X,F6.2,3(3X,F6.2),//)
        WRITE(5,94)(ATMX(3,J),J=1,7)
 94 FORMAT(4X,'EVENING',6X,3(3X,F6.2),5X,F6.2,3(3X,F6.2),//)
        WRITE(5,95)
 95 FORMAT(4X,'BY MORNING IS MEANT 8 00 AM. TO 12 59 PM.,AFTERNOON,1 0
   10 TO 5 59 PM.',//,4X,'AND EVENING.6 00 TO 10 30 PM.',//)
        WRITE(5,25)
        WRITE(5,96)
 96 FORMAT(4X,'THE TIME OF DAY OF LIBRARY READING.',//)
        LIMR=3
        LIMC=7
        DO97IROW=1,LIMR
        DO97JCOL=1,LIMC
 97 AMX(IROW,JCOL)=ATMX(IROW,JCOL)
        GO TO 99
C-----DAY BY RESIDENCE OF STUDENT
 50 WRITE(5,51)
 51 FORMAT(1H1,22X,'DAY BY RESIDENCE OF STUDENT MATRIX',//)
        WRITE(5,22)
        WRITE(5,52)(ARMX(1,J),J=1,7)
 52 FORMAT(4X,'DORMITORY',4X,3(3X,F6.2),5X,F6.2,3(3X,F6.2),//)
        WRITE(5,53)(ARMX(2,J),J=1,7)
 53 FORMAT(4X,'COMMUTER',5X,3(3X,F6.2),5X,F6.2,3(3X,F6.2),//)
        WRITE(5,54)(ARMX(3,J),J=1,7)
 54 FORMAT(4X,'FRAT OR SOR',2X,3(3X,F6.2),5X,F6.2,3(3X,F6.2),//)
        WRITE(5,25)
        WRITE(5,55)
 55 FORMAT(4X,'THE RESIDENCE OF THE STUDENT.',//)
        LIMR=3
        LIMC=7
```

```
      DO56IROW=1,LIMR
      DO56JCOL=1,LIMC
   56 AMX(IROW,JCOL)=ARMX(IROW,JCOL)
      GO TO 99
C-----SUBROUTINE FOR CHI-SQUARE ANALYSIS
C-----CALCULATE EXPECTED MATRIX IF NULL HYPOTHESES IF TRUE.
   99 DO100IROW=1,LIMR
      DO100JCOL=1,LIMC
C-----CHECK CELLS FOR 5 OR MOR FREQUENCIES.
      IF(AMX(IROW,JCOL)-5)119,100,100
  100 CONTINUE
C-----INITIALIZE ROW TOTALS AND TOTAL OF THE ROW TOTALS.
      DO101IROW=1,LIMR
  101 TROW(IROW)=0
      ALLR=0
C-----TOTAL ROWS
      DO103IROW=1,LIMR
      DO102JCOL=1,LIMC
  102 TROW(IROW)=TROW(IROW)+AMX(IROW,JCOL)
C-----TOTAL ALL ROWS
  103 ALLR=ALLR+TROW(IROW)
C-----INITIALIZE COLUMN TOTALS AND TOTAL OF THE COLUMN TOTALS.
      DO104JCOL=1,LIMC
  104 TCOL(JCOL)=0
      ALLC=0
C-----TOTAL COLUMNS.
      DO106JCOL=1,LIMC
      DO105IROW=1,LIMR
  105 TCOL(JCOL)=TCOL(JCOL)+AMX(IROW,JCOL)
C-----TOTAL ALL COLUMNS
  106 ALLC=ALLC+TCOL(JCOL)
C-----CHECK FOR ERROR
      IF(ALLC-ALLR)121,107,121
C-----CALCULATE EXPECTED CELL VALUES
  107 DO108JCOL=1,LIMC
      DO108IROW=1,LIMR
      P(JCOL)=TCOL(JCOL)/ALLC
  108 EMX(IROW,JCOL)=P(JCOL)*TROW(IROW)
C-----WRITE EXPECTED MATRIX
      WRITE(5,109)
  109 FORMAT(22X,'EXPECTED MATRIX IF NULL HYP. TRUE.',//)
      WRITE(5,22)
      WRITE(5,110)((EMX(IROW,JCOL),JCOL=1,LIMC),IROW=1,LIMR)
  110 FORMAT(17X,3(3X,F6.2),5X,F6.2,3X,F6.2,//)
C-----STATE SAMPLE SIZE
      WRITE(5,111)ALLC
  111 FORMAT(4X,'SAMPLE SIZE IS',1X,F4.0,//)
C-----GET CRITICAL VALUE FOR CHI-SQUARE TEST.
      ICDF=(LIMR-1)*(LIMC-1)
      CHICR=CHI(ICDF)
      WRITE(5,112)ICDF,CHICR
  112 FORMAT(4X,'TEST HYPOTHESIS USING CHI-SQUARE AT A 5 PERCENT LEVEL O
     1F SIGNIFICANCE.',//,4X,'THE NUMBER OF DEGREES OF FREEDOM IS',1X,I2
     2,',AND THE CRITICAL VALUE FOR THE TEST IS',1X,F5.2,//)
C-----CALCULATE CHI-SQUARE
      CHISQ=0
      DO113IROW=1,LIMR
```

```
      DO113JCOL=1,LIMC
      DIFF2=(AMX(IROW,JCOL)-EMX(IROW,JCOL)**2/EMX(IROW,JCOL)
  113 CHISQ=CHISQ+DIFF2
      WRITE(5,114)CHISQ
  114 FORMAT(4X,'CHI-SQURAE VALUE=',1X,F6.2,//)
C-----COMPARE CRITICAL VALUE WITH CHI-SQUARE VALUE.
      IF(CHISQ-CHICR)115,115,117
  115 WRITE(5,116)
  116 FORMAT(4X,'NO SIGNIFICANT DIFFERENCE AT 5 PERCENT LEVEL BETWEEN AC
     1TUAL',//,4X,'RESULTS AND EXPECTED RESULTS.ACCEPT THE NULL HYPOTHES
     2ES.',//)
      GO TO 123
  117 WRITE(5,118)
  118 FORMAT(4X,'SIGNIFICANT DIFFERENCE AT 5 PERCENT LEVEL BETWEEN ACTUA
     1L RESULTS',//,4X,'AND EXPECTED RESULTS.REJECT THE NULL HYPOTHESIS.
     2',//)
      GO TO 123
  119 WRITE(5,120)
  120 FORMAT(4X,'NO CHI-SQUARE TEST POSSIBLE WITHOUT REGROUPING.',//)
      GO TO 123
  121 WRITE(5,122)
  122 FORMAT(4X,'MATH ERROR.HALT.')
      CALL EXIT
  123 CONTINUE
      GO TO 19
  130 CALL EXIT
      END

FEATURES SUPPORTED
 ONE WORD INTEGERS
 EXTENDED PRECISION
 IOCS

 C ORE REQUIREMENTS FOR
 COMMON        0  VARIABLES   1458  PROGRAM   3372

 END OF COMPILATION

 // XEQ
```

Note: 7-day week

```
// JOB

LOG DRIVE    CART SPEC    CART AVAIL    PHY DRIVE
  0000         0008         0008          0000

V2 M06   ACTUAL   8K   CONFIG   8K

// FOR
*LIST SOURCE PROGRAM
*IDCS (CARD,1403 PRINTER,TYPEWRITER,KEYBOARD)
*EXTENDED PRECISION
*ONE WORD INTEGERS
C-----CHI-SQUARE TESTS FOR DAY BY VARIOUS CATEGORIES
      INTEGER R,RIDER,RECC
      DIMENSION ASMX(6,7),ALMX(6,7),AYMX(6,7),ARMX(6,7),ANMX(6,7),AMMX(6
     1,7),AAMX(6,7),ATMX(6,7),EMX(6,7),TROW(6),TCOL(7),P(7),CHI(30),AMX(
     26,7)
      DATA CHI/3.84,5.99,7.82,9.49,11.07,12.59,14.06,15.51,16.92,18.31,1
     19.68,21.03,22.36,23.69,25.00,26.3,27.59,28.87,30.14,31.41,32.67,33
     2.92,35.17,36.42,37.65,38.89,40.11,41.34,42.56,43.77/
C-----INITIALIZE COUNTERS AND MATRICES
      INTW=0
      RIDER=0
      MATR=0
      RECC=0
      DO1IN=1,6
      DO1JN=1,7
      ASMX(IN,JN)=0
      ALMX(IN,JN)=0
      AYMX(IN,JN)=0
      ARMX(IN,JN)=0
      ANMX(IN,JN)=0
      AMMX(IN,JN)=0
      AAMX(IN,JN)=0
    1 ATMX(IN,JN)=0
    2 READ(2,3)IFORM,INT,I,J,K,LIB,IST,L,N,M,R,AVG
    3 FORMAT(I3,I1,I1,I1,I2,I1,I1,I1,I1,I1,I1,F4.2)
      IF(IFORM)18,18,4
    4 IF(INT-1)2,2,5
    5 INTW=INTW+1
      ASMX(I,J)=ASMX(I,J)+1
      ALMX(LIB+1,J)=ALMX(LIB+1,J)+1
      AYMX(IST+1,J)=AYMX(IST+1,J)+1
      IF(IST)13,13,6
    6 RIDER=RIDER+1
      ARMX(R,J)=ARMX(R,J)+1
      ANMX(N,J)=ANMX(N,J)+1
      IF(N-5)7,7,13
    7 MATR=MATR+1
      AMMX(M,J)=AMMX(M,J)+1
      IF(AVG)13,13,8
    8 RECC=RECC+1
      IF(AVG-2.)9,10,10
    9 AAMX(1,J)=AAMX(1,J)+1
      GO TO 13
   10 IF(AVG-3.)11,12,12
   11 AAMX(2,J)=AAMX(2,J)+1
```

```
      GO TO 13
   12 AAMX(3,J)=AAMX(3,J)+1
   13 IF(K-6)14,15,15
   14 ATMX(1,J)=ATMX(1,J)+1
      GO TO 2
   15 IF(K-11)16,17,17
   16 ATMX(2,J)=ATMX(2,J)+1
      GO TO 2
   17 ATMX(3,J)=ATMX(3,J)+1
      GO TO 2
   18 KALL=0
   19 KALL=KALL+1
      GO TO (20,30,40,50,60,70,80,90,130),KALL
C-----DAY BY SEX MATRIX
   20 WRITE(5,21)
   21 FORMAT(1H1,22X,'DAY BY SEX OF READER MATRIX',///)
      WRITE(5,22)
   22 FORMAT(20X,'MONDAY  TUESDAY  WEDNESDAY  THURSDAY  FRIDAY',//)
      WRITE(5,23)(ASMX(1,J),J=1,5)
   23 FORMAT(4X,'MALE',9X,3(3X,F6.2),5X,F6.2,3X,F6.2,//)
      WRITE(5,24)(ASMX(2,J),J=1,5)
   24 FORMAT(4X,'FEMALE',7X,3(3X,F6.2),5X,F6.2,3X,F6.2,//)
      WRITE(5,25)
   25 FORMAT(22X,'NULL HYPOTHESIS',/,4X,'THERE IS NO RELATIONSHIP BETWEE
     1N THE DAY OF THE WEEK AND',//)
      WRITE(5,27)
   27 FORMAT(4X,'THE SEX OF THE LIBRARY READER.',//)
      LIMR=2
      LIMC=5
      DO26IROW=1,LIMR
      DO26JCOL=1,LIMC
   26 AMX(IROW,JCOL)=ASMX(IROW,JCOL)
      GO TO 99
C---- DAY BY LIB. BK VS. NON-LIB. BK. MATRIX
   30 WRITE(5,31)
   31 FORMAT(1H1,22X,'DAY BY LIBRARY BOOK VS. NON-LIBRARY BOOK MATRIX',/
     1/)
      WRITE(5,22)
      WRITE(5,33)(ALMX(1,J),J=1,5)
   32 FORMAT(4X,'LIBRARY',6X,3(3X,F6.2),5X,F6.2,3X,F6.2,//)
      WRITE(5,32)(ALMX(2,J),J=1,5)
   33 FORMAT(4X,'NON-LIBRARY',2X,3(3X,F6.2),5X,F6.2,3X,F6.2,//)
      WRITE(5,25)
      WRITE(5,34)
   34 FORMAT(4X,'THE KIND OF BOOKS READ IN THE LIBRARY, THAT IS LIBRARY
     1BOOK OR NON-LIBRARY BOOK.',//)
      LIMR=2
      LIMC=5
      DO35IROW=1,LIMR
      DO35JCOL=1,LIMC
   35 AMX(IROW,JCOL)=ALMX(IROW,JCOL)
      GO TO 99
C-----DAY BY STUDENT OR NON-STUDENT MATRIX
   40 WRITE(5,41)
   41 FORMAT(1H1,22X,'DAY BY STUDENT VS. NON-STUDENT MATRIX',//)
      WRITE(5,22)
```

```
      WRITE(5,42)(AYMX(1,J),J=1,5)
   42 FORMAT(4X,'NON-RIDER',4X,3(3X,F6.2),5X,F6.2,3X,F6.2,//)
      WRITE(5,43)(AYMX(2,J),J=1,5)
   43 FORMAT(4X,'RIDER',8X,3(3X,F6.2),5X,F6.2,3X,F6.2,//)
      WRITE(5,25)
      WRITE(5,44)
   44 FORMAT(4X,'THE BOOK READERS CONNECTION WITH RIDER COLLEGE.',//)
      LIMR=2
      LIMC=5
      DO45IROW=1,LIMR
      DO45JCOL=1,LIMC
   45 AMX(IROW,JCOL)=AYMX(IROW,JCOL)
      GO TO 99
C-----DAY BY CLASS YEAR OF RIDER STUDENT MATRIX
   60 WRITE(5,61)
   61 FORMAT(1H1,22X,'DAY BY CLASS YEAR OF STUDENT MATRIX',//)
      WRITE(5,22)
      WRITE(5,62)(ANMX(1,J),J=1,5)
   62 FORMAT(4X,'FRESHMAN',5X,3(3X,F6.2),5X,F6.2,3X,F6.2,//)
      WRITE(5,63)(ANMX(2,J),J=1,5)
   63 FORMAT(4X,'SOPHMORE',5X,3(3X,F6.2),5X,F6.2,3X,F6.2,//)
      WRITE(5,64)(ANMX(3,J),J=1,5)
   64 FORMAT(4X,'JUNIOR',7X,3(3X,F6.2),5X,F6.2,3X,F6.2,//)
      WRITE(5,65)(ANMX(4,J),J=1,5)
   65 FORMAT(4X,'SENIOR',7X,3(3X,F6.2),5X,F6.2,3X,F6.2,//)
      WRITE(5,25)
      WRITE(5,68)
   68 FORMAT(4X,'THE CLASS YEAR OF THE READER.',//)
      LIMR=4
      LIMC=5
      DO69IROW=1,LIMR
      DO69JCOL=1,LIMC
   69 AMX(IROW,JCOL)=ANMX(IROW,JCOL)
      GO TO 99
C-----DAY BY MAJOR OF RIDER READER MATRIX
   70 WRITE(5,71)
   71 FORMAT(1H1,22X,'DAY BY MAJOR OF RIDER READER MATRIX',//)
      WRITE(5,22)
      WRITE(5,72)(AMMX(1,J),J=1,5)
   72 FORMAT(4X,'LIB. ARTS',4X,3(3X,F6.2),5X,F6.2,3X,F6.2,//)
      WRITE(5,73)(AMMX(2,J),J=1,5)
   73 FORMAT(4X,'EDUCATION',4X,3(3X,F6.2),5X,F6.2,3X,F6.2,//)
      WRITE(5,74)(AMMX(3,J),J=1,5)
   74 FORMAT(4X,'BUSINESS',5X,3(3X,F6.2),5X,F6.2,3X,F6.2,//)
      WRITE(5,25)
      WRITE(5,77)
   77 FORMAT(4X,'THE MAJOR OF THE READER.',//)
      LIMR=3
      LIMC=5
      DO78IROW=1,LIMR
      DO78JCOL=1,LIMC
   78 AMX(IROW,JCOL)=AMMX(IROW,JCOL)
      GO TO 99
C-----DAY BY CUM. AVERAGE OF RIDER READER MATRIX
   80 WRITE(5,81)
   81 FORMAT(1H1,22X,'DAY BY CUM. AVERAGE OF RIDER READER MATRIX',//)
      WRITE(5,22)
```

```
      WRITE(5,82)(AAMX(1,J),J=1,5)
   82 FORMAT(4X,'0 TO 1.99',4X,3(3X,F6.2),5X,F6.2,3X,F6.2,//)
      WRITE(5,83)(AAMX(2,J),J=1,5)
   83 FORMAT(4X,'2 TO 2.99',4X,3(3X,F6.2),5X,F6.2,3X,F6.2,//)
      WRITE(5,84)(AAMX(3,J),J=1,5)
   84 FORMAT(4X,'3 TO 4.00',4X,3(3X,F6.2),5X,F6.2,3X,F6.2,//)
      LIMR=3
      LIMC=5
      DO86IROW=1,LIMR
      DO86JCOL=1,LIMC
   86 AMX(IROW,JCOL)=AAMX(IROW,JCOL)
      GO TO 99
C-----DAY BY TIME OF DAY MATRIX
   90 WRITE(5,91)
   91 FORMAT(1H1,22X,'DAY BY TIME OF DAY OF LIBRARY READING',//)
      WRITE(5,22)
      WRITE(5,92)(ATMX(1,J),J=1,5)
   92 FORMAT(4X,'MORNING',6X,3(3X,F6.2),5X,F6.2,3X,F6.2,//)
      WRITE(5,93)(ATMX(2,J),J=1,5)
   93 FORMAT(4X,'AFTERNOON',4X,3(3X,F6.2),5X,F6.2,3X,F6.2,//)
      WRITE(5,94)(ATMX(3,J),J=1,5)
   94 FORMAT(4X,'EVENING',6X,3(3X,F6.2),5X,F6.2,3X,F6.2,//)
      WRITE(5,95)
   95 FORMAT(4X,'BY MORNING IS MEANT 8 00 AM. TO 12 59 PM.,AFTERNOON,1 0
     1 10 TO 5 59 PM.',//,4X,'AND EVENING,6 00 TO 10 30 PM.',//)
      WRITE(5,25)
      WRITE(5,96)
   96 FORMAT(4X,'THE TIME OF DAY OF LIBRARY READING.',//)
      LIMR=3
      LIMC=5
      DO97IROW=1,LIMR
      DO97JCOL=1,LIMC
   97 AMX(IROW,JCOL)=ATMX(IROW,JCOL)
      GO TO 99
C-----DAY BY RESIDENCE OF STUDENT
   50 WRITE(5,51)
   51 FORMAT(1H1,22X,'DAY BY RESIDENCE OF STUDENT MATRIX',//)
      WRITE(5,22)
      WRITE(5,52)(ARMX(1,J),J=1,5)
   52 FORMAT(4X,'DORMITORY',4X,3(3X,F6.2),5X,F6.2,3X,F6.2,//)
      WRITE(5,53)(ARMX(2,J),J=1,5)
   53 FORMAT(4X,'COMMUTER',5X,3(3X,F6.2),5X,F6.2,3X,F6.2,//)
      WRITE(5,54)(ARMX(3,J),J=1,5)
   54 FORMAT(4X,'FRAT OR SOR',2X,3(3X,F6.2),5X,F6.2,3X,F6.2,//)
      WRITE(5,25)
      WRITE(5,55)
   55 FORMAT(4X,'THE RESIDENCE OF THE STUDENT,',//)
      LIMR=3
      LIMC=5
      DO56IROW=1,LIMR
      DO56JCOL=1,LIMC
   56 AMX(IROW,JCOL)=ARMX(IROW,JCOL)
      GO TO 99
C-----SUBROUTINE FOR CHI-SQUARE ANALYSIS
C-----CALCULATE EXPECTED MATRIX IF NULL HYPOTHESES IF TRUE.
   99 DO100IROW=1,LIMR
      DO100JCOL=1,LIMC
```

```
C-----CHECK CELLS FOR 5 OR MOR FREQUENCIES.
      IF(AMX(IROW,JCOL)-5)119,100,100
  100 CONTINUE
C-----INITIALIZE ROW TOTALS AND TOTAL OF THE REW TOTALS.
      DO101IROW=1,LIMR
  101 TROW(IROW)=0
      ALLR=0
C-----TOTAL ROWS
      DO103IROW=1,LIMR
      DO102JCOL=1,LIMC
  102 TROW(IROW)=TROW(IROW)+AMX(IROW,JCOL)
C-----TOTAL ALL ROWS
  103 ALLR=ALLR+TROW(IROW)
C-----INITIALIZE COLUMN TOTALS AND TOTAL OF THE COLUMN TOTALS.
      DO104JCOL=1,LIMC
  104 TCOL(JCOL)=0
      ALLC=0
C-----TOTAL COLUMNS.
      DO106JCOL=1,LIMC
      DO105IROW=1,LIMR
  105 TCOL(JCOL)=TCOL(JCOL)+AMX(IROW,JCOL)
C-----TOTAL ALL COLUMNS
  106 ALLC=ALLC+TCOL(JCOL)
C-----CHECK FOR ERROR
      IF(ALLC-ALLR)121,107,121
C-----CALCULATE EXPECTED CELL VALUES
  107 DO108JCOL=1,LIMC
      DO108IROW=1,LIMR
      P(JCOL)=TCOL(JCOL)/ALLC
  108 EMX(IROW,JCOL)=P(JCOL)*TROW(IROW)
C-----WRITE EXPECTED MATRIX
      WRITE(5,109)
  109 FORMAT(22X,'EXPECTED MATRIX IF NULL HYP. TRUE.',//)
      WRITE(5,22)
      WRITE(5,110)((EMX(IROW,JCOL),JCOL=1,LIMC),IROW=1,LIMR)
  110 FORMAT(17X,3(3X,F6.2),5X,F6.2,3X,F6.2,//)
C-----STATE SAMPLE SIZE
      WRITE(5,111)ALLC
  111 FORMAT(4X,'SAMPLE SIZE IS',1X,F4.0,//)
C-----GET CRITICAL VALUE FOR CHI-SQUARE TEST.
      ICDF=(LIMR-1)*(LIMC-1)
      CHICR=CHI(ICDF)
      WRITE(5,112)ICDF,CHICR
  112 FORMAT(4X,'TEST HYPOTHESIS USING CHI-SQUARE AT A 5 PERCENT LEVEL O
     1F SIGNIFICANCE.',//,4X,'THE NUMBER OF DEGREES OF FREEDOM IS',1X,I2
     2,',AND THE CRITICAL VALUE FOR THE TEST IS',1X,F5.2,//)
C-----CALCULATE CHI-SQUARE
      CHISQ=0
      DO113IROW=1,LIMR
      DO113JCOL=1,LIMC
      DIFF2=(AMX(IROW,JCOL)-EMX(IROW,JCOL))**2/EMX(IROW,JCOL)
  113 CHISQ=CHISQ+DIFF2
      WRITE(5,114)CHISQ
  114 FORMAT(4X,'CHI-SQURAE VALUE=',1X,F6.2,//)
C-----COMPARE CRITICAL VALUE WITH CHI-SQUARE VALUE.
      IF(CHISQ-CHICR)115,115,117
  115 WRITE(5,116)
```

```
116 FORMAT(4X,'NO SIGNIFICANT DIFFERENCE AT 5 PERCENT LEVEL BETWEEN AC
   1TUAL',//,4X,'RESULTS AND EXPECTED RESULTS.ACCEPT THE NULL HYPOTHES
   2ES.',//)
    GO TO 123
117 WRITE(5,118)
118 FORMAT(4X,'SIGNIFICANT DIFFERENCE AT 5 PERCENT LEVEL BETWEEN ACTUA
   1L RESULTS',//,4X,'AND EXPECTED RESULTS.REJECT THE NULL HYPOTHESIS.
   2',//)
    GO TO 123
119 WRITE(5,120)
120 FORMAT(4X,'NO CHI-SQUARE TEST POSSIBLE WITHOUT REGROUPING.',//)
    GO TO 123
121 WRITE(5,122)
122 FORMAT(4X,'MATH ERROR.HALT.')
    CALL EXIT
123 CONTINUE
    GO TO 19
130 CALL EXIT
    END

FEATURES SUPPORTED
 ONE WORD INTEGERS
 EXTENDED PRECISION
 IDCS

CORE REQUIREMENTS FOR
 COMMON      0  VARIABLES   1458  PROGRAM   3150

 END OF COMPILATION

// XEQ
```

PROGRAM OF THE T TEST OF RELATIONSHIP BETWEEN THE READING OF A LIBRARY BOOK
OR NOT AND THE SEVERAL CHARACTERISTICS OF THE READER


```
LOG DRIVE    CART SPEC    CART AVAIL   PHY DRIVE
  0000         0008         0008         0000

V2 M06    ACTUAL  8K  CONFIG  8K

// FOR
*LIST SOURCE PROGRAM
*IOCS (CARD,1403 PRINTER,TYPEWRITER,KEYBOARD)
*ONE WORD INTEGERS
*EXTENDED PRECISION
C       T-TEST FOR SIGNIFICANT DIFFERENCES BETWEEN ELTS. IN COLLUMNS AND
C       ELEMENTS IN ROWS TAKING TWO AT A TIME
        INTEGER R,RIDER,RECC
        DIMENSION ASMX(6,7),ALMX(6,7),AYMX(6,7),ARMX(6,7),ANMX(6,7),AMMX(6
       1,7),AAMX(6,7),ATMX(6,7),TROW(6),T(30),AMX(6,7),TCOL(7),P(6,7),Q(6,
       27),RTMX(1,2),RLMX(6,7)
        DATA T/6.31,2.92,2.35,2.13,2.01,1.94,1.89,1.86,1.83,1.81,1.79,1.78
       1,1.77,1.76,1.75,1.74,1.74,2*1.73,3*1.72,3*1.71,5*1.70/
C-----INITIALIZE COUNTERS AND MATRICES
        INTW=0
        RIDER=0
        MATR=0
        RECC=0
        DO1IN=1,6
        DO1JN=1,7
        ASMX(IN,JN)=0
        ALMX(IN,JN)=0
        AYMX(IN,JN)=0
        ARMX(IN,JN)=0
        ANMX(IN,JN)=0
        RLMX(IN,JN)=0
        AMMX(IN,JN)=0
        AAMX(IN,JN)=0
      1 ATMX(IN,JN)=0
      2 READ(2,3)IFORM,INT,I,LIB,K,J,IST,L,N,M,R,AVG
      3 FORMAT(I3,I1,I1,I1,I2,I1,I1,I1,I1,I1,I1,F4.2)
        IF(IFORM)18,18,4
      4 IF(INT-1)2,2,5
      5 INTW=INTW+1
        AYMX(IST+1,J+1)=AYMX(IST+1,J+1)+1
        ASMX(I,J+1)=ASMX(I,J+1)+1
        IF(LIB-5)300,300,301
    300 RLMX(1,J+1)=RLMX(1,J+1)+1
        GO TO 302
    301 RLMX(2,J+1)=RLMX(2,J+1)+1
        GO TO 302
    302 CONTINUE
        IF(IST)13,13,6
      6 RIDER=RIDER+1
        ARMX(R,J+1)=ARMX(R,J+1)+1
        ANMX(N,J+1)=ANMX(N,J+1)+1
        IF(N-5)7,7,13
      7 MATR=MATR+1
        AMMX(M,J+1)=AMMX(M,J+1)+1
        IF(AVG)13,13,8
```

```
    8 RECC=RECC+1
      IF(AVG-2.)9,10,10
    9 AAMX(1,J+1)=AAMX(1,J+1)+1
      GO TO 13
   10 IF(AVG-3.)11,12,12
   11 AAMX(2,J+1)=AAMX(1,J+1)+1
      GO TO 13
   12 AAMX(3,J+1)=AAMX(3,J+1)+1
   13 IF(K-6)14,15,15
   14 ATMX(1,J+1)=ATMX(1,J+1)+1
      GO TO 2
   15 IF(K-11)16,17,17
   16 ATMX(2,J+1)=ATMX(2,J+1)+1
      GO TO 2
   17 ATMX(3,J+1)=ATMX(3,J+1)+1
      GO TO 2
   18 KALL=0
   19 KALL=KALL+1
      GO TO (20,30,40,60,80,90,290,130),KALL
C        LIBRARY BOOK OR NOT SEX
   20 WRITE(5,21)
   21 FORMAT(1H1,22X,'LIBRARY BOOK OR NOT BY SEX OF READER MATRIX',///)
      WRITE(5,22)
   22 FORMAT(20X,'NON-LIBRARY BOOK',4X,'LIBRARY BOOK',//)
      LIMR=2
      LIMC=2
      DO26IROW=1,LIMR
      DO26JCOL=1,LIMC
   26 AMX(IROW,JCOL)=ASMX(IROW,JCOL)
      GO TO 99
C     6IBRARY BOOK OR NOT BY TIME OF WEEK
   30 WRITE(5,31)
   31 FORMAT(1H1,22X,'LIBRARY BOOK OR NOT BY TIME OF WEEK MATRIX',//)
      WRITE(5,22)
      LIMR=2
      LIMC=2
      DO35IROW=1,LIMR
      DO35JCOL=1,LIMC
   35 AMX(IROW,JCOL)=RLMX(IROW,JCOL)
      GO TO 99
C        LIBRARY BOOK OR NOT BY STUDENT OR NOT
   40 WRITE(5,41)
   41 FORMAT(20X,'LIBRARY BOOK OR NOT BY STUDENT READER OR NOT',///)
      WRITE(5,22)
      LIMR=2
      LIMC=2
      DO45IROW=1,LIMR
      DO45JCOL=1,LIMC
   45 AMX(IROW,JCOL)=AYMX(IROW,JCOL)
      GO TO 99
C        LIBRARY BOOK OR NOT BY CLASS YEAR
   60 WRITE(5,61)
   61 FORMAT(20X,'LIBRARY BOOK OR NOT BY CLASS YEAR OF READER',///)
      WRITE(5,22)
      LIMR=4
      LIMC=2
      DO69IROW=1,LIMR
```

334

```
      DO69JCOL=1,LIMC
   69 AMX(IROW,JCOL)=ANMX(IROW,JCOL)
      GO TO 99
C     LIBRARY BOOK OR NOT BY CUM. AVG.
   80 WRITE(5,81)
   81 FORMAT(20X,'LIBRARY BOOK OR NOT BY CUM. AVG. OR READER',///)
      WRITE(5,22)
      LIMR=3
      LIMC=2
      DO86IROW=1,LIMR
      DO86JCOL=1,LIMC
   86 AMX(IROW,JCOL)=AAMX(IROW,JCOL)
      GO TO 99
C     LIBRARY BOOK OR NOT BY TIME OF DAY
   90 WRITE(5,91)
   91 FORMAT(20X,'LIBRARY BOOK OR NOT BY TIME OF DAY READER FOUND',///)
      WRITE(5,22)
      WRITE(5,95)
   95 FORMAT(4X,'BY MORNING IS MEANT 8 00 AM. TO 12 59 PM.,AFTERNOON,1 0
     10 TO 5 59 PM.',//,4X,'AND EVENING,6 00 TO 10 30 PM.',//)
      LIMR=3
      LIMC=2
      DO97IROW=1,LIMR
      DO97JCOL=1,LIMC
   97 AMX(IROW,JCOL)=ATMX(IROW,JCOL)
      GO TO 99
  290 WRITE(5,91)
      WRITE(5,22)
      DO 291 J=1,2
  291 RTMX(1,J)=ATMX(1,J)+ATMX(2,J)
      LIMC=2
      LIMR=2
      DO 294 JCOL=1,2
      AMX(1,JCOL)=RTMX(1,JCOL)
  294 AMX(2,JCOL)=ATMX(3,JCOL)
      GO TO 99
C     SUB-ROUTINE FOR WRITING PERCENT MATRIX WITH RESPECT TO ROWS AND
C     TESTING ELTS. IN ROWS
   99 CONTINUE
C-----INITIALIZE ROW TOTALS AND TOTAL OF THE REW TOTALS.
      DO101IROW=1,LIMR
  101 TROW(IROW)=0
      ALLR=0
C-----TOTAL ROWS
      DO103IROW=1,LIMR
      DO102JCOL=1,LIMC
  102 TROW(IROW)=TROW(IROW)+AMX(IROW,JCOL)
C-----TOTAL ALL ROWS
  103 ALLR=ALLR+TROW(IROW)
C-----INITIALIZE COLUMN TOTALS AND TOTAL OF THE COLUMN TOTALS.
      DO104JCOL=1,LIMC
  104 TCOL(JCOL)=0
      ALLC=0
C-----TOTAL COLUMNS.
      DO106JCOL=1,LIMC
      DO105IROW=1,LIMR
  105 TCOL(JCOL)=TCOL(JCOL)+AMX(IROW,JCOL)
```

335

```
C-----TOTAL ALL COLUMNS
   106 ALLC=ALLC+TCOL(JCOL)
C-----CHECK FOR ERROR
       IF(ALLC-ALLR)550,107,550
   550 WRITE(5,551)
   551 FORMAT(4X,'MATH ERROR.HALT.',//)
       CALL EXIT
C      CALCULATE PERCENTAGES FOR CELLS WITH RESPECT TO ROWS
   107 DO500JCOL=1,LIMC
       DO500IROW=1,LIMR
   500 P(IROW,JCOL)=AMX(IROW,JCOL)/TROW(IROW)
C      WRITE MATRIX
       WRITE(5,560)
   560 FORMAT(4X,'MATRIX BY PERCENTAGES WITH RESPECT TO ROWS.',//)
       WRITE(5,108)((P(IROW,JCOL),JCOL=1,LIMC),IROW=1,LIMR)
   108 FORMAT(2(7X,F5.3),//)
       WRITE(5,109)
   109 FORMAT(4X,'TEST FOR SIGNIFICANT DIFFERENCE BETWEEN ELTS. IN COLUMN
      1',//,4X,'TWO AT A TIME USING T-TEST-ONE TAIL-5 PER.LEVEL.',///)
       WRITE(5,110)
   110 FORMAT(7X,'COLUMN',3X,'ROW',6X,'ROW',6X,'T-VALUE',4X,'CRIT. VAL.',
      16X,'D.F.',5X,'SIGNIFICANT',//)
C      GET THE T-VALUE
       LIMN=LIMR-1
       DO 127 JCOL=1,LIMC
       DO 127 NROW=1,LIMN
       DO 127 IROW=2,LIMR
       IF(IROW-NROW)127,127,111
   111 EST=(AMX(NROW,JCOL)+AMX(IROW,JCOL))/(TROW(NROW)+TROW(IROW))
       S=(P(NROW,JCOL)-P(IROW,JCOL))/(EST*(1-EST)*(1/TROW(NROW)+1/TROW(IR
      1OW)))**.5
C      GET D.F. AND CRITICAL VALUE FOR T-TEST
       IDF=TROW(NROW)+TROW(IROW)-2
       IF(IDF-30)112,112,113
   112 CRITV=T(IDF)
       GO TO 120
   113 IF(IDF-40)114,114,115
   114 CRITV=1.68
       GO TO 120
   115 IF(IDF-60)116,116,117
   116 CRITV=1.67
       GO TO 120
   117 IF(IDF-120)118,118,119
   118 CRITV=1.66
       GO TO 120
   119 CRITV=1.64
   120 CONTINUE
C      TEST FOR SIGNIFICANT DIFFERENCE
       IF(S)121,122,122
   121 IF(S+CRITV)124,123,123
   122 IF(S-CRITV)123,123,324
   123 WRITE(5,125)JCOL,NROW,IROW,S,CRITV,IDF
   125 FORMAT(3(8X,I1),2(8X,F5.2),8X,I3,8X,'NO',//)
       GO TO 127
   124 WRITE(5,126)JCOL,NROW,IROW,S,CRITV,IDF,IROW,NROW
   126 FORMAT(3(8X,I1),2(8X,F5.2),8X,I3,8X,'YES. ROW ',I1,'PERCENTAGE GRE
      1ATER THAN ROW ',I1,//)
```

```
      GO TO 127
  324 WRITE(5,126)JCOL,NROW,IROW,S,CRITV,IDF,NROW,IROW
  127 CONTINUE
      GO TO 129
C     SUB-ROUTINE FOR WRITING PERCENT MATRIX WITH RESPECT TO COLUMNS AND
C     TESTING ELTS. IN ROWS
C     CALCULATE PERCENTAGES FOR CELLS WITH RESPECT TO COLUMNS
  129 DO 400 IROW=1,LIMR
      DO 400 JCOL=1,LIMC
  400 Q(IROW,JCOL)=AMX(IROW,JCOL)/TCOL(JCOL)
C     WRITE MATRIX
      WRITE(5,561)
  561 FORMAT(4X,'MATRIX BY PERCENTAGES WITH RESPECT TO COLUMNS.',//)
      WRITE(5,108)((Q(IROW,JCOL),JCOL=1,LIMC),IROW=1,LIMR)
      WRITE(5,131)
  131 FORMAT(4X,'TEST FOR SIGNIFICANT DIFFERENCES BETWEEN ELTS IN ROWS',
     10/,4X,'TWO AT A TIME USING T/TEST-ONE TAIL-5 PER. LEVEL.',///)
      WRITE(5,132)
  132 FORMAT(7X,'ROW   ',3X,'COL',6X,'COL',6X,'T-VALUE',4X,'CRIT. VAL.',
     16X,'D.F.',5X,'SIGNIFICANT',//)
C     GET T VALUE
      LIMN=LIMC-1
      DO151IROW=1,LIMR
      DO151NCOL=1,LIMN
      DO151JCOL=2,LIMC
      IF(JCOL-NCOL)151,151,133
  133 EST=(AMX(IROW,NCOL)+AMX(IROW,JCOL))/(TCOL(NCOL)+TCOL(JCOL))
      S=(Q(IROW,NCOL)-Q(IROW,JCOL))/(EST*(1-EST)*(1/TCOL(NCOL)+1/TCOL(JC
     10L)))**.5
C     GET D.F. AND CRITICAL VALUE FOR T TEST
      IDF=TCOL(NCOL)+TCOL(JCOL)-2
      IF(IDF-30)134,134,135
  134 CRITV=T(IDF)
      GO TO 142
  135 IF(IDF-40)136,136,137
  136 CRITV=1.68
      GO TO 142
  137 IF(IDF-60)138,138,139
  138 CRITV=1.67
      GO TO 142
  139 IF(IDF-120)140,140,141
  140 CRITV=1.66
      GO TO 142
  141 CRITV=1.64
  142 CONTINUE
      IF(S)143,144,144
  143 IF(S+CRITV)146,145,145
  144 IF(S-CRITV)145,145,149
  145 WRITE(5,147)IROW,NCOL,JCOL,S,CRITV,IDF
  147 FORMAT(3(8X,I1),2(8X,F5.2),8X,I3,8X,'NO',//)
      GO TO 151
  146 WRITE(5,148)IROW,NCOL,JCOL,S,CRITV,IDF,JCOL,NCOL
  148 FORMAT(3(8X,I1),2(8X,F5.2),8X,I3,8X,'YES. COL ',I1,'PERCENTAGE GRE
     1ATER THAN COL ',I1,//)
      GO TO 151
  149 WRITE(5,148)IROW,NCOL,JCOL,S,CRITV,IDF,NCOL,JCOL
  151 CONTINUE
```

337

```
        GO TO 19
    130 CALL EXIT
        END

FEATURES SUPPORTED
 ONE WORD INTEGERS
 EXTENDED PRECISION
 IOCS

CORE REQUIREMENTS FOR
 COMMON        0  VARIABLES   1708  PROGRAM    2562

 END OF COMPILATION

// XEQ
```

PROGRAM OF THE T TEST OF RELATIONSHIP BETWEEN TYPE OF LIBRARY
BOOK BEING READ AND THE SEVERAL CHARACTERISTICS OF THE READER

```
C     T-TEST FOR SIGNIFICANT DIFFERENCES BETWEEN ELTS. IN COLLUMNS AND
C     ELEMENTS IN ROWS TAKING TWO AT A TIME
      INTEGER R,RIDER,RECC
      DIMENSION ASMX(6,7),ALMX(6,7),AYMX(6,7),ARMX(6,7),ANMX(6,7),AMMX(6
     1,7),AAMX(6,7),ATMX(6,7),TROW(6),T(30),AMX(6,7),TCOL(7),P(6,7),Q(6,
     27)
      DATA T/6.31,2.92,2.35,2.13,2.01,1.94,1.89,1.86,1.83,1.81,1.79,1.78
     1,1.77,1.76,1.75,1.74,1.74,2*1.73,3*1.72,3*1.71,5*1.70/
C-----INITIALIZE COUNTERS AND MATRICES
      INTW=0
      RIDER=0
      MATR=0
      RECC=0
      DO1IN=1,6
      DO1JN=1,7
      ASMX(IN,JN)=0
      ALMX(IN,JN)=0
      AYMX(IN,JN)=0
      ARMX(IN,JN)=0
      ANMX(IN,JN)=0
      AMMX(IN,JN)=0
      AAMX(IN,JN)=0
    1 ATMX(IN,JN)=0
    2 READ(2,3)IFORM,INT,I,L,K,LIB,IST,J,N,M,R,AVG
    3 FORMAT(I3,I1,I1,I1,I2,I1,I1,I1,I1,I1,I1,F4.2)
      IF(IFORM)18,18,4
    4 IF(INT-1)2,2,5
    5 INTW=INTW+1
      IF(LIB)2,2,200
  200 CONTINUE
      IF(J-1)2,201,202
  201 ASMX(I,1)=ASMX(I,1)+1
      AYMX(IST+1,1)=AYMX(IST+1,1)+1
      GO TO 204
  202 ASMX(I,2)=ASMX(I,2)+1
      AYMX(IST+1,2)=AYMX(IST+1,2)+1
  204 CONTINUE
      IF(IST)13,13,6
    6 RIDER=RIDER+1
      IF(J-1)2,205,206
  205 ARMX(R,1)=ARMX(R,1)+1
      ANMX(N,1)=ANMX(N,1)+1
      GO TO 207
  206 ARMX(R,2)=ARMX(R,2)+1
      ANMX(N,2)=ANMX(N,2)+1
```

```fortran
  207 CONTINUE
      IF(N-5)7,7,13
    7 MATR=MATR+1
      IF(J-1)2,208,209
  208 AMMX(M,1)=AMMX(M,1)+1
      GO TO 210
  209 AMMX(M,2)=AMMX(M,2)+1
  210 CONTINUE
      IF(AVG)13,13,8
    8 RECC=RECC+1
      IF(AVG-2.)9,10,10
    9 IF(J-1)2,211,212
  211 AAMX(1,1)=AAMX(1,1)+1
      GO TO 13
  212 AAMX(1,2)=AAMX(1,2)+1
      GO TO 13
   10 IF(AVG-3.)11,12,12
   11 IF(J-1)2,213,214
  213 AAMX(2,1)=AAMX(2,1)+1
      GO TO 13
  214 AAMX(2,2)=AAMX(2,2)+1
      GO TO 13
   12 IF(J-1)2,215,216
  215 AAMX(3,1)=AAMX(3,1)+1
      GO TO 13
  216 AAMX(3,2)=AAMX(3,2)+1
   13 IF(K-6)14,15,15
   14 IF(J-1)2,217,218
  217 ATMX(1,1)=ATMX(1,1)+1
      GO TO 2
  218 ATMX(1,2)=ATMX(1,2)+1
      GO TO 2
   15 IF(K-11)16,17,17
   16 IF(J-1)2,219,220
  219 ATMX(2,1)=ATMX(2,1)+1
      GO TO 2
  220 ATMX(2,2)=ATMX(2,2)+1
      GO TO 2
   17 IF(J-1)2,221,222
  221 ATMX(3,1)=ATMX(3,1)+1
      GO TO 2
  222 ATMX(3,2)=ATMX(3,2)+1
      GO TO 2
   18 KALL=0
   19 KALL=KALL+1
      GO TO (20,40,50,60,70,80,90,130),KALL
C-----LIB. BK BY SEX
   20 WRITE(5,21)
   21 FORMAT(1H1,22X,'LIBRARY BOOK BY SEX OF READER MATRIX',///)
      WRITE(5,22)
   22 FORMAT(6X,'SOC. SCI.   OTHER',//)
      LIMR=2
      LIMC=2
      DO26IROW=1,LIMR
      DO26JCOL=1,LIMC
   26 AMX(IROW,JCOL)=ASMX(IROW,JCOL)
      GO TO 99
```

```
C-----LIB. BK BY STUDENT OR NON STUDENT
   40 WRITE(5,41)
   41 FORMAT(1H1,22X,'LIBRARY BOOK BY RIDER STUDENT OR NOT MATRIX',///)
      WRITE(5,22)
      LIMR=2
      LIMC=2
      DO45IROW=1,LIMR
      DO45JCOL=1,LIMC
   45 AMX(IROW,JCOL)=AYMX(IROW,JCOL)
      GO TO 99
C-----LIB. BK. BY RESIDENCE
   50 WRITE(5,51)
   51 FORMAT(1H1,22X,'LIBRARY BOOK BY RESIDENCE OF STUDENT MATRIX',///)
      WRITE(5,22)
      LIMR=3
      LIMC=2
      DO56IROW=1,LIMR
      DO56JCOL=1,LIMC
   56 AMX(IROW,JCOL)=ARMX(IROW,JCOL)
      GO TO 99
C-----LIB. BK BY CLASS YEAR
   60 WRITE(5,61)
   61 FORMAT(1H1,22X,'LIBRARY BOOK BY CLASS OF RIDER READER MATRIX',///)
      WRITE(5,22)
      LIMR=4
      LIMC=2
      DO69IROW=1,LIMR
      DO69JCOL=1,LIMC
   69 AMX(IROW,JCOL)=ANMX(IROW,JCOL)
      GO TO 99
C-----LIB.BK BY MAJOR
   70 WRITE(5,71)
   71 FORMAT(1H1,22X,'LIBRARY BOOK BY MAJOR FIELD OF RIDER READER MATRIX
     1',///)
      WRITE(5,22)
      LIMR=3
      LIMC=2
      DO78IROW=1,LIMR
      DO78JCOL=1,LIMC
   78 AMX(IROW,JCOL)=AMMX(IROW,JCOL)
      GO TO 99
C-----LIB. BK. BY CUM AVE.
   80 WRITE(5,81)
   81 FORMAT(1H1,22X,'LIBRARY BOOK BY CUM. AVG. OF RIDER READER',///)
      WRITE(5,22)
      LIMR=3
      LIMC=2
      DO86IROW=1,LIMR
      DO86JCOL=1,LIMC
   86 AMX(IROW,JCOL)=AAMX(IROW,JCOL)
      GO TO 99
C-----LIB. BK. BY TIME OF DAY
   90 WRITE(5,91)
   91 FORMAT(1H1,22X,'LIBRARY BOOK BY TIME OF DAY MATRIX',///)
      WRITE(5,22)
      WRITE(5,95)
   95 FORMAT(4X,'BY MORNING IS MEANT 8 00 AM. TO 12 59 PM.,AFTERNOON,1 0
```

```
       10 TO 5 59 PM.',//,4X,'AND EVENING,6 00 TO 10 30 PM.',//)
       LIMR=3
       LIMC=2
       DO97IROW=1,LIMR
       DO97JCOL=1,LIMC
    97 AMX(IROW,JCOL)=ATMX(IROW,JCOL)
       GO TO 99
C      SUB-ROUTINE FOR WRITING PERCENT MATRIX WITH RESPECT TO ROWS AND
C      TESTING ELTS. IN ROWS
    99 CONTINUE
C-----INITIALIZE ROW TOTALS AND TOTAL OF THE ROW TOTALS.
       DO101IROW=1,LIMR
   101 TROW(IROW)=0
       ALLR=0
C-----TOTAL ROWS
       DO103IROW=1,LIMR
       DO102JCOL=1,LIMC
   102 TROW(IROW)=TROW(IROW)+AMX(IROW,JCOL)
C-----TOTAL ALL ROWS
   103 ALLR=ALLR+TROW(IROW)
C-----INITIALIZE COLUMN TOTALS AND TOTAL OF THE COLUMN TOTALS.
       DO104JCOL=1,LIMC
   104 TCOL(JCOL)=0
       ALLC=0
C-----TOTAL COLUMNS.
       DO106JCOL=1,LIMC
       DO105IROW=1,LIMR
   105 TCOL(JCOL)=TCOL(JCOL)+AMX(IROW,JCOL)
C-----TOTAL ALL COLUMNS
   106 ALLC=ALLC+TCOL(JCOL)
C-----CHECK FOR ERROR
       IF(ALLC-ALLR)550,107,550
   550 WRITE(5,551)
   551 FORMAT(4X,'MATH ERROR.HALT.',//)
       CALL EXIT
C      CALCULATE PERCENTAGES FOR CELLS WITH RESPECT TO ROWS
   107 DO500JCOL=1,LIMC
       DO500IROW=1,LIMR
   500 P(IROW,JCOL)=AMX(IROW,JCOL)/TROW(IROW)
C      WRITE MATRIX
       WRITE(5,560)
   560 FORMAT(4X,'MATRIX BY PERCENTAGES WITH RESPECT TO ROWS.',//)
       WRITE(5,108)((P(IROW,JCOL),JCOL=1,LIMC),IROW=1,LIMR)
   108 FORMAT(2(7X,F5.3),//)
       WRITE(5,109)
   109 FORMAT(4X,'TEST FOR SIGNIFICANT DIFFERENCE BETWEEN ELTS. IN COLUMN
      1',//,4X,'TWO AT A TIME USING T-TEST-ONE TAIL-5 PER.LEVEL.',///)
       WRITE(5,110)
   110 FORMAT(7X,'COLUMN',3X,'ROW',6X,'ROW',6X,'T-VALUE',4X,'CRIT. VAL.',
      16X,'D.F.',5X,'SIGNIFICANT',//)
       GET THE T-VALUE
       LIMN=LIMR-1
       DO 127 JCOL=1,LIMC
       DO 127 NROW=1,LIMN
       DO 127 IROW=2,LIMR
       IF(IROW-NROW)127,127,111
   111 EST=(AMX(NROW,JCOL)+AMX(IROW,JCOL))/(TROW(NROW)+TROW(IROW))
```

```
      S=(P(NROW,JCOL)-P(IROW,JCOL))/(EST*(1-EST)*(1/TROW(NROW)+1/TROW(IR
     1DW)))**.5
C     GET D.F. AND CRITICAL VALUE FOR T-TEST
      IDF=TROW(NROW)+TROW(IROW)-2
      IF(IDF-30)112,112,113
  112 CRITV=T(IDF)
      GO TO 120
  113 IF(IDF-40)114,114,115
  114 CRITV=1.68
      GO TO 120
  115 IF(IDF-60)116,116,117
  116 CRITV=1.67
      GO TO 120
  117 IF(IDF-120)118,118,119
  118 CRITV=1.66
      GO TO 120
  119 CRITV=1.64
  120 CONTINUE
C     TEST FOR SIGNIFICANT DIFFERENCE
      IF(S)121,122,122
  121 IF(S+CRITV)124,123,123
  122 IF(S-CRITV)123,123,324
  123 WRITE(5,125)JCOL,NROW,IROW,S,CRITV,IDF
  125 FORMAT(3(8X,11),2(6X,F5.2),8X,I3,8X,'NO',//)
      GO TO 127
  124 WRITE(5,126)JCOL,NROW,IROW,S,CRITV,IDF,IROW,NROW
  126 FORMAT(3(8X,I1),2(8X,F5.2),8X,I3,8X,'YES. ROW ',I1,'PERCENTAGE GRE
     1ATER THAN ROW ',I1,//)
      GO TO 127
  324 WRITE(5,126)JCOL,NROW,IROW,S,CRITV,IDF,NROW,IROW
  127 CONTINUE
      GO TO 129
C     SUB-ROUTINE FOR WRITING PERCENT MATRIX WITH RESPECT TO COLUMNS AND
C     TESTING ELTS. IN ROWS
C     CALCULATE PERCENTAGES FOR CELLS WITH RESPECT TO COLUMNS
  129 DO 400 IROW=1,LIMR
      DO 400 JCOL=1,LIMC
  400 O(IROW,JCOL)=AMX(IROW,JCOL)/TCOL(JCOL)
C     WRITE MATRIX
      WRITE(5,561)
  561 FORMAT(4X,'MATRIX BY PERCENTAGES WITH RESPECT TO COLUMNS.',//)
      WRITE(5,108)((Q(IROW,JCOL),JCOL=1,LIMC),IROW=1,LIMR)
      WRITE(5,131)
  131 FORMAT(4X,'TEST FOR SIGNIFICANT DIFFERENCES BETWEEN ELTS IN ROWS',
     10/,4X,'TWO AT A TIME USING T/TEST-ONE TAIL-5 PER. LEVEL.',///)
      WRITE(5,132)
  132 FORMAT(7X,'ROW  ',3X,'COL',6X,'COL',6X,'T-VALUE',4X,'CRIT. VAL.',
     16X,'D.F.',5X,'SIGNIFICANT',//)
      GET T VALUE
      LIMN=LIMC-1
      DO151IROW=1,LIMR
      DO151NCOL=1,LIMN
      DO151JCOL=2,LIMC
      IF(JCOL-NCOL)151,151,133
  133 EST=(AMX(IROW,NCOL)+AMX(IROW,JCOL))/(TCOL(NCOL)+TCOL(JCOL))
      S=(Q(IROW,NCOL)-Q(IROW,JCOL))/(EST*(1-EST)*(1/TCOL(NCOL)+1/TCOL(JC
     1OL)))**.5
```

343

```
C      GET D.F. AND CRITICAL VALUE FOR T TEST
       IDF=TCOL(NCOL)+TCOL(JCOL)-2
       IF(IDF-30)134,134,135
   134 CRITV=T(IDF)
       GO TO 142
   135 IF(IDF-40)136,136,137
   136 CRITV=1.68
       GO TO 142
   137 IF(IDF-60)138,138,139
   138 CRITV=1.67
       GO TO 142
   139 IF(IDF-120)140,140,141
   140 CRITV=1.66
       GO TO 142
   141 CRITV=1.64
   142 CONTINUE
       IF(S)143,144,144
   143 IF(S+CRITV)146,145,145
   144 IF(S-CRITV)145,145,149
   145 WRITE(5,147)IROW,NCOL,JCOL,S,CRITV,IDF
   147 FORMAT(3(8X,I1),2(8X,F5.2),8X,I3,8X,'NO',//)
       GO TO 151
   146 WRITE(5,148)IROW,NCOL,JCOL,S,CRITV,IDF,JCOL,NCOL
   148 FORMAT(3(8X,I1),2(8X,F5.2),8X,I3,8X,'YES. COL ',I1,'PERCENTAGE GRE
      1ATER THAN COL ',I1,//)
       GO TO 151
   149 WRITE(5,148)IROW,NCOL,JCOL,S,CRITV,IDF,NCOL,JCOL
   151 CONTINUE
       GO TO 19
   130 CALL EXIT
       END

FEATURES SUPPORTED
 ONE WORD INTEGERS
 EXTENDED PRECISION
 IOCS

CORE REQUIREMENTS FOR
 COMMON        0  VARIABLES    1576  PROGRAM    2670

 END OF COMPILATION

// XEQ
```

PROGRAM OF THE T TEST OF RELATIONSHIP BETWEEN MAJOR FIELD OF STUDY
OF STUDENT READER AND THE SEVERAL CHARACTERISTICS OF THE READER


```
C    T-TEST FOR SIGNIFICANT DIFFERENCES BETWEEN ELTS.  IN COLLUMS AND
C    ELEMENTS IN ROWS TAKING TWO AT A TIME
         INTEGER R,RIDER,RECC
         DI MENSION ASMX(6,7),ALMX(6,7),AYMX(6,7),ARMX(6,7),ANMX(6,7),AMMX(6
        1,7)AAMX(6,7),ATMX(6,7),TROW(6),T(30),AMX(6,7),TCOL(7),P(6,7),Q(6,
        27)
         DATA T/6.31,2.92,2.35,2.13,2.01,1.94,1.89,1.86,1.83,1.81,1.79,1.78
        1,1.77,1.76,1.75,1.74,1.74,2*1.73,3*1.72,3*1.71,5*1.70/
C-----INITIALIZE COUNTERS AND MATRICES
         INTW=0
         RIDER=0
         MATR=0
         RECC=0
         DO1IN=1,6
         DO1JN=1,7
         ASMX(IN,JN)=0
         ALMX(IN,JN)=0
         AYMX(IN,JN)=0
         ARMX(IN,JN)=0
         ANMX(IN,JN)=0
         AMMX(IN,JN)=0
         AAMX(IN,JN)=0
       1 ATMX(IN,JN)=0
       2 READ(2,3)IFORM,INT,I,M,K,LIB,IST,L,N,J,R,AVG
       3 FORMAT(I3,I1,I1,I1,I2,I1,I1,I1,I1,I1,I1,F4.2)
         IF(IFORM)18,18,4
       4 IF(INT-1)2,2,5
       5 INTW=INTW+1
         AYMX(IST+1,J)=AYMX(IST+1,J)+1
         IF(IST)12,13,6
       6 RIDER=RIDER+1
         IF(N-5)7,7,13
       7 MATR=MATR+1
         ASMX(I,J)=ASMX(I,J)+1
         ALMX(LIB+1,J)=ALMX(LIB+1,J)+1
         ARMX(R,J)=ARMX(R,J)+1
         ANMX(N,J)=ANMX(N,J)+1
         AMMX(M,J)=AMMX(M,J)+1
         IF(AVG)13,13.8
       8 RECC=RECC+1
         IF(AVG-2.)9,10,10
       9 AAMX(1,J)=AAMX(1,J)+1
         GO TO 13
      10 IF(AVG-3.)11,12,12
      11 AAMX(2,J)=AAMX(2,J)+1
```

```
          GO TO 13
       12 AAMX(3,J)=AAMX(3,J)+1
       13 IF(K-6)14,15,15
       14 ATMX(1,J)=ATMX(1,J)+1
          GO TO 2
       15 IF(K-11)16,17,17
       16 ATMX(2,J)=ATMX(2,J)+1
          GO TO 2
       17 ATMX(3,J)-ATMX(3,J)+1
          GO TO 2
       18 KALL=0
       19 KALL=KALL+1
          GO TO (20,30,50,60,70,80,90,130), KALL
C-----MAJOR BY SEX OF READER
       20 WRITE(5,21)
       21 FORMAT(1H1,22X,'MAJOR BY SEX OF READER MATRIX',///)
          WRITE(5,22)
       22 FORMAT(6X,'LIB. ARTS  EDUCATION  BUSINESS',///)
          LIMBR=2
          LIMC=3
          DO26IROW=1,LIMR
          DO26JCOL=1,LIMC
       26 AMX(IROW,JCOL)=ASMX(IROW,JCOL)
          GO TO 99
C-----MAJOR BY KIND OF BOOK
       30 WRITE(5,31)
       31 FORMAT(1HI,22X,'MAJOR BY KIND OF BOOK MATRIX',//)
          WRITE(5,22)
          LIMR=2
          LIMC=3
          DO35IROW=1,LIMR
          DO35JCOL=1,LIMC
       35 AMX(IROW,JCOL)=ALMX(IROW,JCOL)
          GO TO 99
C-----MAJOR BY RESIDENCE OF STUDENT MATRIX
       50 WRITE(5,51)
       51 FORMAT(1H1,22X,'MAJOR BY RESIDENCE OF STUDENT MATRIX',///)
          WRITE(5,22)
          LIMR=3
          LIMC=3
          DO56IROW=1,LIMR
          DO56JCOL=1,LIMC
       56 AMX(IROW,JCOL)=ARMX(IROW,JCOL)
          GO TO 99
C-----MAJOR BY CLASS YEAR
       60 WRITE(5,61)
       61 FORMAT(1H1,22X,'MAJOR BY CLASS YEAR OF STUDENT MATRIX',///)
          WRITE(5,22)
          LIMR=4
          LIMC=3
          DO69IROW=1,LIMR
          DO69JCOL=1,LIMC
       69 AMX(IROW,JCOL)=ANMX(IROW,JCOL)
          GO TO 99
C    MAJOR BY DAY
       70 WRITE(5,71)
       71 FORMAT(1H1,22X,'MAJOR BY DAY OF WEEK OF READING MATRIX',///)
```

```
            WRITE(5,22)
            LIMR=6
            LIMC=3
            DO78IROW=1,LIMR
            DO78JCOL=1,LIMC
         78 AMX(IROW,JCOL)=AMMX(IROW,JCOL)
            GO TO 99
C-----MAJOR BY CUM. AVG.
         80 WRITE(5,81)
         81 FORMAT(1H1,22X,'MAJOR BY CUM. AVG. OF RIDER READER MATRIX',///)
            WRITE(5,22)
            LIMR=3
            LIMC=3
            DO86 IROW=1,LIMR
            DO86JCOL=1,LIMC
         86 AMX(IROW,JCOL)=AAMX(IROW,JCOL)
            GO TO 99
C     MAJOR BY TIME OF DAY
         90 WRITE(5,91)
         91 FORMAT(1H1,22X,'MAJOR BY TIME OF DAY OF LIBRARY READING',///)
            WRITE(5,22)
            WRITE(5,95)
         95 FORMAT(4X,'BY MORNING IS MEANT 8 00 AM. TO 12 59 PM.,AFTERNOON 1 0
           10 TO 5 59 PM.',//,4X,'AND EVENING,6 00 to 10 30 PM.',//)
            LIMC=3
            LIMR=2
            DO97IROW=1,LIMR
            DO97JCOL=1,LIMC
         97 AMX(IROW,JCOL)=ATMX(IROW,JCOL)
            GO TO 99
C     SUB-ROUTINE FOR WRITING PERCENT MATRIX WITH RESPECT TO ROWS AND
C     TESTING ELTS. IN ROWS
         99 CONTINUE
C-----INITIALIZE ROW TOTALS AND TOTAL OF THE ROW TOTALS.
            DO101IROW=LIMR
        101 TROW(IROW)=O
            ALLR=0
C-----TOTAL ROWS
            DO103IROW=1,LIMR
            DO102JCOL=1,LIMC
        102 TROW(IROW)=TROW(IROW)+AMX(IROW,JCOL)
C-----TOTAL ALL ROWS
        103 ALLR=ALLR+TROW(IROW)
C-----INITIALIZE COLUMN TOTALS AND TOTAL OF THE COLUMN TOTALS.
            DO104JCOL=1,LIMC
        104 TCOL(JCOL)=O
            ALLC=0
C-----TOTAL COLUMNS.
            DO106JCOL=1,LIMC
            DO105IROW=1,LIMR
        104 TCOL(JCOL)=TCOL(JCOL)+AMX(IROW,JCOL)
C-----TOTAL ALL COLUMNS
        106 ALLC=ALLC+TCOL(JCOL)
C-----CHECK FOR ERROR
            IF(ALLC-ALLR)550,107,550
        550 WRITE(5,551)
        551 FORMAT(4X,'MATH ERROR.HALT.",//)
```

```
      CALL EXIT
C     CALCULATE PERCENTAGES FOR CELLS WITH RESPECT TO ROWS
  107 DO500JCOL=1,LIMC
      DO500IROW=1,LIMR
  500 P(IROW,JCOL)=AMX(IROW,JCOL)/TROW(IROW)
C     WRITE MATRIX
      WRITE(5,560)
  560 FORMAT(4X,'MATRIX BY PERCENTAGES WITH RESPECT TO ROWS,',//)
      WRITE(5,108)((P(IROW,JCOL),JCOL=1,LIMC),IROW=1,LIMR)
  108 FORMAT(3(7X,F5.3),//)
      WRITE(5,109)
  109 FORMAT(4X,'TEST FOR SIGNIFICANT DIFFERENCE BETWEEN ELTS. IN COLUMN
     1',//,4X,'TWO AT A TIME USING T-TEST-ONE TAIL-5 PER.LEVEL.',///)
      WRITE(5,110)
  110 FORMAT(7X,'COLUMN',3X,'ROW',6X,'ROW',6X,'T-VALUE',4X,'CRIT. VAL.',
     16X,'D.F.',5X,'SIGNIFICANT',//)
C     GET THE T-VALUE
      LIMN=LIMR-1
      DO 127 JCOL=1,LIMC
      DO 127 NROW=1,LIMN
      DO 127 IROW=2,LIMR
      IF(IROW-NROW)127,127,111
  111 EST=(AMX(NROW,JCOL)+AMX(IROW,JCOL))/(TROW(NROW)+TROW(IROW))
      S=(P(NROW,JCOL)-P(I ROW, JCOL))/(EST*(1-EST)*(1/TROW(NROW)+1/TROW(IR
     10W)))**.5
C     GET D.F.AND CRITICAL VALUE FOR T-TEST
      IDF=TROW(NROW)+TROW(IROW)-2
      IF(IDF-30)112,112,113
  112 CRITV=T(IDF)
      GO TO 120
  113 IF(IDF-4D)114,114,115
  114 CRITV=1.68
      GO TO 120
  115 IF(IDF-60)116,116,117
  116 CRITV=1.67
      GO TO 120
  117 IF(IDF-120)118,110,119
  118 CRITV=1.66
      GO TO 120
  119 CRITV=1.64
  120 CONTINUE
C     TEST FOR SIGNIFICANT DIFFERENCE
      IF(S)121,122,122
  121 IF(S+CRITV)124,123,123
  122 IF(S-CRITV)123,123,324
  123 WRITE(5,125)JCOL,NROW,IROW,S,CRITV,IDF
  125 FORMAT(3(8X,I1),2(8X,F5.2),8X,I3,8X,'NO',//)
      GO TO 127
  124 WRITE(5,126)JCOL,NROW,IROW,S,CRITV,IDF,IROW,NROW
  126 FORMAT(3(8X,I1),2(8X,F5.2),8X,I3.8X,'YES.  ROW ',I1,'PERCENTAGE GRE
     LATER THAN ROW ',I1,//)
      GO TO 127
  324 WRITE(5,126)JCOL,NROW,IROW,S,CRITV,IDF,NROW,IROW
 ]27 CONTINUE
      GO TO 129
C     SUB-ROUTINE FOR WRITING PERCENT MATRIX WITH RESPECT TO COLUMNS AND
C     TESTING ELTS. IN ROWS
```

348

```
C          CALCULATE PERCENTAGES FOR CELLS WITH RESPECT TO COLUMNS
      129 DO 400 IROW=1,LIMR
          DO 400 JCOL=1,LIMC
      400 Q(IROW,JCOL)=AMX(IROW,JCOL)/TCOL(JCOL)
C          WRITE MATRIX
          WRITE(5,561)
      561 FORMAT(4X,'MATRIX BY PERCENTAGES WITH RESPECT TO COLUMNS,',//)
          WRITE(5,108)((Q(IROW,JCOL),JCOL=1,LIMC),IROW=1,LIMR)
          WRITE(5,131)
      131 FORMAT(4X,'TEST FOR SIGNIFICANT DIFFERENCES BETWEEN ELTS IN ROWS',
         10/,4X,'TWO AT A TIME USING T/TEST-ONE TAIL-5 PER. LEVEL.',///)
          WRITE(5,132)
      132 FORMAT(7X,'ROW    ',3X,'COL',6X,'COL',6X,'T-VALUE',4X,'CRIT. VAL.',
         16X,'D.F.',5X,'SIGNIFICANT',//)
C          GET T VALUE
          LIMN=LIMC-1
          DO151IROW=1,LIMR
          DO151NCOL=1,LIMN
          DO151JCOL=2,LIMC
          IF(JCOL-NCOL)151,151,133
      133 EST=(AMX(IROW,NCOL)+AMX(IROW,JCOL))/(TCOL(NCOL)+TCOL(JCOL))
          S=(Q(IROW,NCOL)-Q(IROW,JCOL))/(EST-(1-EST)*(1/TCOL(NCOL)+1/TCOL(JC
         1OL)))**5
C          GET D.F. AND CRITICAL VALUE FOR T TEST
          IDF=TCOL(NCOL)+TCOL(JCOL)-2
          IF(IDF-30)134,134,135
      134 CRITV=T(IDF)
          GO TO 142
      135 IF(IDF-40)136,136,137
      136 CRITV=1.68
          GO TO 142
      137 IF(IDF-60)138,138,139
      138 CRITV=1.67
          GO TO 142
      139 IF(IDF-120)140,140,141
      140 CRITV=1.66
          GO TO 142
      141 CRITV=1.64
      142 CONTINUE
          IF(S)143,144,144
      143 IF(S+CRITV)146,145,145
      144 IF(S-CRITV)145,145,149
      145 WRITE(5,147)IROW,NCOL,JCOL,S,CRITV,IDF
      147 FORMAT(3(8X,I1),2(8X,F5.2),8X,I3,8X,'NO",//)
          GO TO 151
      146 WRITE(5,148)IROW,NCOL,JCOL,S,CRITV,IDF,JCOL,NCOL
      148 FORMAT(3(8X,I1),2(8X,F5.2),8X,I3,8X,'YES.  COL  ',I1,'PERCENTAGE GRE
         1LATER THAN COL ',I1,//)
          GO TO 151
      149 WRITE(5,148)IROW,NCOL,JCOL,S,CRITV,IDF,NCOL,JCOL
      151 CONTINUE
          GO TO 19
      130 CALL EXIT
          END

      FEATURES SUPPORTED
       ONE WORD INTEGERS
```

EXTENDED PRECISION
IDCS

CDRE REQUIREMENTS FOR
 COMMON   D   VARIABLES   1576   PROGRAM   2490

END OF COMPILATION

// XEQ

PROGRAM OF THE T TEST OF RELATIONSHIP BETWEEN PLACE OF RESIDENCE
OF THE STUDENT AND THE SEVERAL CHARACTERISTICS OF THE READER

```
C       T-TEST FOR SIGNIFICANT DIFFERENCES BETWEEN ELTS. IN COLLUMNS AND
C       ELEMENTS IN ROWS TAKING TWO AT A TIME
        INTEGER R,RIDER,RECC
        DIMENSION ASMX(6,7),ALMX(6,7),AYMX(6,7),ARMX(6,7),ANMX(6,7),AMMX(6
       1,7),AAMX(6,7),ATMX(6,7),TROW(6),T(30),AMX(6,7),TCOL(7),P(6,7),Q(6,
       27),RTMX(1,3),RRMX(2,3)
        DATA T/6.31,2.92,2.35,2.13,2.01,1.94,1.89,1.86,1.83,1.81,1.79,1.78
       1,1.77,1.76,1.75,1.74,1.74,2*1.73,3*1.72,3*1.71,5*1.70/
C-----INITIALIZE COUNTERS AND MATRICES
        INTW=0
        RIDER=0
        MATR=0
        RECC=0
        DO1IN=1,6
        DO1JN=1,7
        ASMX(IN,JN)=0
        ALMX(IN,JN)=0
        AYMX(IN,JN)=0
        ANMX(IN,JN)=0
        AMMX(IN,JN)=0
        ARMX(IN,JN)=0
        AAMX(IN,JN)=0
      1 ATMX(IN,JN)=0
      2 READ(2,3)IFORM,INT,I,R,K,LIB,IST,L,N,M,J,AVG
      3 FORMAT(I3,I1,I1,I1,I2,I1,I1,I1,I1,I1,I1,F4.2)
        IF(IFORM)18,18,4
      4 IF(INT-1)2,2,5
      5 INTW=INTW+1
        ASMX(I,J)=ASMX(I,J)+1
        AYMX(IST+1,J)=AYMX(IST+1,J)+1
        ALMX(LIB+1,J)=ALMX(LIB+1,J)+1
        IF(IST)13,13,6
      6 RIDER=RIDER+1
        ARMX(R,J)=ARMX(R,J)+1
        ANMX(N,J)=ANMX(N,J)+1
        IF(N-5)7,7,13
      7 MATR=MATR+1
        AMMX(M,J)=AMMX(M,J)+1
        IF(AVG)13,13,8
      8 RECC=RECC+1
        IF(AVG-2.)9,10,10
      9 AAMX(1,J)=AAMX(1,J)+1
        GO TO 13
     10 IF(AVG-3.)11,12,12
     11 AAMX(2,J)=AAMX(2,J)+1
```

```
        GO TO 13
     12 AAMX(3,J)=AAMX(3,J)+1
     13 IF(K-6)14,15,15
     14 ATMX(1,J)=ATMX(1,J)+1
        GO TO 2
     15 IF(K-11)16,17,17
     16 ATMX(2,J)=ATMX(2,J)+1
        GO TO 2
     17 ATMX(3,J)-ATMX(3,J)+1
        GO TO 2
     18 KALL=0
     19 KALL=KALL+1
        GO TO (20,30,50,60,70,80,90,290,130), KALL
C     RESIDENCE BY SEX
     20 WRITE(5,21)
     21 FORMAT(1H1,22X,'RESIDENCE BY SEX OF READER MATRIX',///)
        WRITE(5,22)
     22 FORMAT(6X,'DORMITORY    COMMUTER    FRAT. OR SOR.',//)
        LIMR=2
        LIMC=3
        DO26IROW=1,LIMR
        DO26JCOL=1,LIMC
     26 AMX(IROW,JCOL)=ASMX(IROW,JCOL)
        GO TO 99
C-----RESIDENCE BY KIND OF BOOK
     30 WRITE(5,31)
     31 FORMAT(1H1,22X,'RESIDENCE BY LIBRARY BOOK OR NOT MATRIX',///)
        WRITE(5,22)
        LIMR=2
        LIMC=3
        DO36IROW=1,LIMR
        DO35JCOL=1,LIMC
     35 AMX(IROW,JCOL)=ALMX(IROW,JCOL)
        GO TO 99
C     RESIDENCE BY BY WEEKDAY OR WEEKEND
     50 WRITE(5,51)
     51 FORMAT(1H1,22X,'RESIDENCE OF READER RELATIVE TO WEEK MATRIX',///)
        WRITE(5,22)
        DO251J=1,3
        RRMX(1,J)=ARMX(1,J)+ARMX(2,J)+ARMX(3,J)+ARMX(4,J)+ARMX(5,J)
    251 RRMX(2,J)=ARMX(6,J)+ARMX(7,J)
        LIMR=2
        LIMC=3
        DO56IROW=1,LIMR
        DO56JCOL=1,LIMC
     56 AMX(IROW,JCOL)=RRMX(IROW,JCOL)
C     RESIDENCE BY CLASS YEAR
     60 WRITE(5,61)
     61 FORMAT(1H1,22X,'RESIDENCE OF READER BY CLASS YEAR MATRIX',///)
        WRITE(5,22)
        LIMR=4
        LIMC=3
        DO69IROW=1,LIMR
        DO69JCOL=1,LIMC
     69 AMX(IROW,JCOL)=ANMX(IROW,JCOL)
        GO TO 99
C     RESIDENCE BY MAJOR OR READER
```

```
     70 WRITE(5,71)
     71 FORMAT(1H1,22X,'RESIDENCE OF READER BY MAJOR MATRIX',//)
        WRITE(5,22)
        LIMR=3
        LIMC=3
        DO78IROW=1,LIMR
        DO78JCOL=1,LIMC
     78 AMX(IROW,JCOL)=AMMX(IROW,JCOL)
        GO TO 99
C-----RESIDENCE BY CUM. AVE.
     80 WRITE(5,81)
     81 FORMAT(1H1,22X,'RESIDENCE BY CUM. AVE. OF RIDER READER',///)
        WRITE(5,22)
        LIMR=3
        LIMC=3
        DO86IROW=1,LIMR
        DO86JCOL=1,LIMC
     86 AMX(IROW,JCOL)=AAMX(IROW,JCOL)
        GO TO 99
C-----RESIDENCE BY TIME OF DAY
     90 WRITE(5,91)
     91 FORMAT(1H1,22X,'RESIDENCE BY TIME OF DAY OF LIBRARY READING',///)
        WRITE(5,22)
        WRITE(5,95)
     95 FORMAT(4X,'BY MORNING IS MEANT 8 00 AM. TO 12 59 PM.,AFTERNOON,1 0
       10 TO 5 59 PM.',//,4X,'AND EVENING,6 00 TO 10 30 PM.',//)
        LIMR=3
        LIMC=3
        DO97IROW=1,LIMR
        DO97JCOL=1,LIMC
     97 AMX(IROW,JCOL)=ATMX(IROW,JCOL)
        GO TO 99
    290 WRITE(5,91)
        WRITE(5,22)
        DO291J=1,3
    291 RTMX(1,J)=ATMX(1,J)+ATMX(2,J)
        LIMC=3
        LIMR=2
        DO294JCOL=1,3
        AMX(1,JCOL)=RTMX(1,JCOL)
    294 AMX(2,JCOL)=ATMX(3,JCOL)
        GO TO 99
C       SUB-ROUTINE FOR WRITING PERCENT MATRIX WITH RESPECT TO ROWS AND
C       TESTING ELTS. IN ROWS
     99 CONTINUE
C-----INITIALIZE ROW TOTALS AND TOTAL OF THE REW TOTALS.
        DO101IROW=1,LIMR
    101 TROW(IROW)=0
        ALLR=0
C-----TOTAL ROWS
        DO103IROW=1,LIMR
        DO102JCOL=1,LIMC
    102 TROW(IROW)=TROW(IROW)+AMX(IROW,JCOL)
C-----TOTAL ALL ROWS
    103 ALLR=ALLR+TROW(IROW)
C-----INITIALIZE COLUMN TOTALS AND TOTAL OF THE COLUMN TOTALS.
        DO104JCOL=1,LIMC
```

```
 104 TCOL(JCOL)=0
     ALLC=0
C-----TOTAL COLUMNS.
     DO106JCOL=1,LIMC
     DO105IROW=1,LIMR
 105 TCOL(JCOL)=TCOL(JCOL)+AMX(IROW,JCOL)
C-----TOTAL ALL COLUMNS
 106 ALLC=ALLC+TCOL(JCOL)
C-----CHECK FOR ERROR
     IF(ALLC-ALLR)550,107,550
 550 WRITE(5,551)
 551 FORMAT(4X,'MATH ERROR.HALT.',//)
     CALL EXIT
C    CALCULATE PERCENTAGES FOR CELLS WITH RESPECT TO ROWS
 107 DO500JCOL=1,LIMC
     DO500IROW=1,LIMR
 500 P(IROW,JCOL)=AMX(IROW,JCOL)/TROW(IROW)
C    WRITE MATRIX
     WRITE(5,560)
 560 FORMAT(4X,'MATRIX BY PERCENTAGES WITH RESPECT TO ROWS.',//)
     WRITE(5,108)((P(IROW,JCOL),JCOL=1,LIMC),IROW=1,LIMR)
 108 FORMAT(3(7X,F5.3),//)
     WRITE(5,109)
 109 FORMAT(4X,'TEST FOR SIGNIFICANT DIFFERENCE BETWEEN ELTS. IN COLUMN
    1',//,4X,'TWO AT A TIME USING T-TEST-ONE TAIL-5 PER.LEVEL.',///)
     WRITE(5,110)
 110 FORMAT(7X,'COLUMN',3X,'ROW',6X,'ROW',6X,'T-VALUE',4X,'CRIT. VAL.',
    16X,'D.F.',5X,'SIGNIFICANT',//)
C    GET THE T-VALUE
     LIMN=LIMR-1
     DO 127 JCOL=1,LIMC
     DO 127 NROW=1,LIMN
     DO 127 IROW=2,LIMR
     IF(IROW-NROW)127,127,111
 111 EST=(AMX(NROW,JCOL)+AMX(IROW,JCOL))/(TROW(NROW)+TROW(IROW))
     S=(P(NROW,JCOL)-P(IROW,JCOL))/(EST*(1-EST)*(1/TROW(NROW)+1/TROW(IR
    1OW)))**.5
C    GET D.F. AND CRITICAL VALUE FOR T-TEST
     IDF=TROW(NROW)+TROW(IROW)-2
     IF(IDF-30)112,112,113
 112 CRITV=T(IDF)
     GO TO 120
 113 IF(IDF-40)114,114,115
 114 CRITV=1.68
     GO TO 120
 115 IF(IDF-60)116,116,117
 116 CRITV=1.67
     GO TO 120
 117 IF(IDF-120)118,118,119
 118 CRITV=1.66
     GO TO 120
 119 CRITV=1.64
 120 CONTINUE
     TEST FOR SIGNIFICANT DIFFERENCE
     IF(S)121,122,122
 121 IF(S+CRITV)124,123,123
 122 IF(S-CRITV)123,123,324
```

```
    123 WRITE(5,125)JCOL,NROW,IROW,S,CRITV,IDF
    125 FORMAT(3(8X,I1),2(8X,F5.2),8X,I3,8X,'NO',//)
        GO TO 127
    124 WRITE(5,126)JCOL,NROW,IROW,S,CRITV,IDF,IROW,NROW
    126 FORMAT(3(8X,I1),2(8X,F5.2),8X,I3,8X,'YES. ROW ',(1,'PERCENTAGE GRE
       1ATER THAN ROW ',I1,//)
        GO TO 127
    324 WRITE(5,126)JCOL,NROW,IROW,S,CRITV,IDF,NROW,IROW
    127 CONTINUE
        GO TO 129
C       SUB-ROUTINE FOR WRITING PERCENT MATRIX WITH RESPECT TO COLUMNS AND
C       TESTING ELTS. IN ROWS
C       CALCULATE PERCENTAGES FOR CELLS WITH RESPECT TO COLUMNS
    129 DO 400 IROW=1,LIMR
        DO 400 JCOL=1,LIMC
    400 Q(IROW,JCOL)=AMX(IROW,JCOL)/TCOL(JCOL)
C       WRITE MATRIX
        WRITE(5,561)
    561 FORMAT(4X,'MATRIX BY PERCENTAGES WITH RESPECT TO COLUMNS.',//)
        WRITE(5,108)((Q(IROW,JCOL),JCOL=1,LIMC),IROW=1,LIMR)
        WRITE(5,131)
    131 FORMAT(4X,'TEST FOR SIGNIFICANT DIFFERENCES BETWEEN ELTS IN ROWS',
       10/,4X,'TWO AT A TIME USING T/TEST-ONE TAIL-5 PER. LEVEL.',///)
        WRITE(5,132)
    132 FORMAT(7X,'ROW    ',3X,'COL',6X,'COL',6X,'T-VALUE',4X,'CRIT. VAL.',
       16X,'D.F.',5X,'SIGNIFICANT',//)
C       GET T VALUE
        LIMN=LIMC-1
        DO151IROW=1,LIMR
        DO151NCOL=1,LIMN
        DO151JCOL=2,LIMC
        IF(JCOL-NCOL)151,151,133
    133 EST=(AMX(IROW,NCOL)+AMX(IROW,JCOL))/(TCOL(NCOL)+TCOL(JCOL))
        S=(Q(IROW,NCOL)-Q(IROW,JCOL))/(EST*(1-EST)*(1/TCOL(NCOL)+1/TCOL(JC
       1OL)))**.5
        GET D.F. AND CRITICAL VALUE FOR T TEST
        IDF=TCOL(NCOL)+TCOL(JCOL)-2
        IF(IDF-30)134,134,135
    134 CRITV=T(IDF)
        GO TO 142
    135 IF(IDF-40)136,136,137
    136 CRITV=1.68
        GO TO 142
    137 IF(IDF-60)138,138,139
    138 CRITV=1.67
        GO TO 142
    139 IF(IDF-120)140,140,141
    140 CRITV=1.66
        GO TO 142
    141 CRITV=1.64
    142 CONTINUE
        IF(S)143,144,144
    143 IF(S+CRITV)146,145,145
    144 IF(S-CRITV)145,145,149
    145 WRITE(5,147)IROW,NCOL,JCOL,S,CRITV,IDF
    147 FORMAT(3(8X,I1),2(8X,F5.2),8X,I3,8X,'NO',//)
        GO TO 151
```

```
146 WRITE(5,148)IROW,NCOL,JCOL,S,CRITV,IDF,JCOL,NCOL
148 FORMAT(3(8X,I1),2(8X,F5.2),8X,I3,8X,'YES. COL ',I1,'PERCENTAGE GRE
   1ATER THAN COL ',I1,//)
    GO TO 151
149 WRITE(5,148)IROW,NCOL,JCOL,S,CRITV,IDF,NCOL,JCOL
151 CONTINUE
    GO TO 19
130 CALL EXIT
    END

FEATURES SUPPORTED
 ONE WORD INTEGERS
 EXTENDED PRECISION
 IDCS

CORE REQUIREMENTS FOR
 COMMON     0  VARIABLES  1608  PROGRAM   2704

 END OF COMPILATION

// XEQ
```

PROGRAM OF THE T TEST OF RELATIONSHIP BETWEEN DAY OF WEEK
OF READING AND THE SEVERAL CHARACTERISTICS OF THE READER


```
C     T-TEST FOR SIGNIFICANT DIFFERENCES BETWEEN ELETS. IN COLLUMNS AND
C     ELEMENTS IN ROWS TAKING TWO AT A TIME
      INTEGER R,RIDER,RECC
      DIMENSION ASMX(6,7),ALMX(6,7),AYMX(6,7),ARMX(6,7),ANMX(6,7),AMMX(6
     1,7),AAMX(6,7),ATMX(6,7),TROW(6),T(30),AMX(6,7),TCOL(7),P(6,7),Q(6,
     27)
      DATA T/6.31,2.92,2.35,2.13,2.01,1.94,1.89,1.86,1.83,1.81,1.79,1.78
     1,1.77,1.76,1.75,1.74,1.74,2*1.73,3*1.72,3*1.71,5*1.70/
C-----INITIALIZE COUNTERS AND MATRICES
      INTW=0
      RIDER=0
      MATR=0
      RECC=0
      DO1IN=1,6
      DO1JN=1,7
      ASMX(IN,JN)=0
      ALMX(IN,JN)=0
      AYMX(IN,JN)=0
      ARMX(IN,JN)=0
      ANMX(IN,JN)=0
      AMMX(IN,JN)=0
      AAMX(IN,JN)=0
    1 ATMX(IN,JN)=0
    2 READ(2,3)IFORM,INT,I,J,K,LIB,IST,L,N,M,R,AVG
    3 FORMAT(I3,I1,I1,I1,I2,I1,I1,I1,I1,I1,I1,F4.2)
      IF(IFORM)18,18,4
    4 IF(INT-1)2,2,5
    5 INTW=INTW+1
      ASMX(I,J)=ASMX(I,J)+1
      ALMX(LIB+1,J)=ALMX(LIB+1,J)+1
      AYMX(IST+1,J)=AYMX(IST+1,J)+1
      IF(IST)13,13,6
    6 RIDER=RIDER+1
      ARMX(R,J)=ARMX(R,J)+1
      ANMX(N,J)=ANMX(N,J)+1
      IF(N-5)7,7,13
    7 MATR=MATR+1
      AMMX(M,J)=AMMX(M,J)+1
      IF(AVG)13,13,8
    8 RECC=RECC+1
      IF(AVG-2.)9,10,10
    9 AAMX(1,J)=AAMX(1,J)+1
      GO TO 13
   10 IF(AVG-3.)11,12,12
   11 AAMX(2,J)=AAMX(2,J)+1
```

357

```
              GO TO 13
      12 AAMX(3,J)=AAMX(3,J)+1
      13 IF(K-6)14,15,15
      14 ATMX(1,J)=ATMX(1,J)+1
              GO TO 2
      15 IF(K-11)16,17,17
      16 ATMX(2,J)=ATMX(2,J)+1
              GO TO 2
      17 ATMX(3,J)=ATMX(3,J)+1
              GO TO 2
      18 KALL=0
      19 KALL=KALL+1
              GO TO (20,30,40,50,60,70,80,90,130),KALL
C-----DAY BY SEX MATRIX
      20 WRITE(5,21)
      21 FORMAT(1H1,22X,'DAY BY SEX OF READER MATRIX',///)
              WRITE(5,22)
      22 FORMAT(6X,'MONDAY       TUESDAY      WEDNSDAY     THURSDAY     FRIDAY
       1          SATURDAY     SUNDAY',//)
              LIMR=2
              LIMC=7
              DO26IROW=1,LIMR
              DO26JCOL=1,LIMC
      26 AMX(IROW,JCOL)=ASMX(IROW,JCOL)
              GO TO 99
C---- DAY BY LIB. BK VS. NON-LIB. BK. MATRIX
      30 WRITE(5,31)
      31 FORMAT(1H1,22X,'DAY BY LIBRARY BOOK VS. NON-LIBRARY BOOK MATRIX',/
       1/)
              WRITE(5,22)
              LIMR=2
              LIMC=7
              DO35IROW=1,LIMR
              DO35JCOL=1,LIMC
      35 AMX(IROW,JCOL)=ALMX(IROW,JCOL)
              GO TO 99
C-----DAY BY STUDENT OR NON-STUDENT MATRIX
      40 WRITE(5,41)
      41 FORMAT(1H1,22X,'DAY BY STUDENT VS. NON-STUDENT MATRIX',//)
              WRITE(5,22)
              LIMR=2
              LIMC=7
              DO45IROW=1,LIMR
              DO45JCOL=1,LIMC
      45 AMX(IROW,JCOL)=AYMX(IROW,JCOL)
              GO TO 99
C-----DAY BY RESIDENCE OF STUDENT
      50 WRITE(5,51)
      51 FORMAT(1H1,22X,'DAY BY RESIDENCE OF STUDENT MATRIX',//)
              WRITE(5,22)
              LIMR=3
              LIMC=7
              DO56IROW=1,LIMR
              DO56JCOL=1,LIMC
      56 AMX(IROW,JCOL)=ARMX(IROW,JCOL)
              GO TO 99
C-----DAY BY CLASS YEAR OF RIDER STUDENT MATRIX
```

```
   60 WRITE(5,61)
   61 FORMAT(1H1,22X,'DAY BY CLASS YEAR OF STUDENT MATRIX',//)
      WRITE(5,22)
      LIMR=6
      LIMC=7
      DO69IROW=1,LIMR
      DO69JCOL=1,LIMC
   69 AMX(IROW,JCOL)=ANMX(IROW,JCOL)
      GO TO 99
C-----DAY BY MAJOR OF RIDER READER MATRIX
   70 WRITE(5,71)
   71 FORMAT(1H1,22X,'DAY BY MAJOR OF RIDER READER MATRIX',//)
      WRITE(5,22)
      LIMR=5
      LIMC=7
      DO78IROW=1,LIMR
      DO78JCOL=1,LIMC
   78 AMX(IROW,JCOL)=AMMX(IROW,JCOL)
      GO TO 99
C-----DAY BY CUM. AVERAGE OF RIDER READER MATRIX
   80 WRITE(5,81)
   81 FORMAT(1H1,22X,'DAY BY CUM. AVERAGE OF RIDER READER MATRIX',//)
      WRITE(5,22)
      LIMR=3
      LIMC=7
      DO86IROW=1,LIMR
      DO86JCOL=1,LIMC
   86 AMX(IROW,JCOL)=AAMX(IROW,JCOL)
      GO TO 99
C-----DAY BY TIME OF DAY MATRIX
   90 WRITE(5,91)
   91 FORMAT(1H1,22X,'DAY BY TIME OF DAY OF LIBRARY READING',//)
      WRITE(5,22)
      WRITE(5,95)
   95 FORMAT(4X,'BY MORNING IS MEANT 8 00 AM. TO 12 59 PM.,AFTERNOON,1 0
     10 TO 5 59 PM.',//,4X,'AND EVENING,6 00 TO 10 30 PM.',//)
      LIMR=3
      LIMC=7
      DO97IROW=1,LIMR
      DO97JCOL=1,LIMC
   97 AMX(IROW,JCOL)=ATMX(IROW,JCOL)
      GO TO 99
C     SUB-ROUTINE FOR WRITING PERCENT MATRIX WITH RESPECT TO ROWS AND
C     TESTING ELTS. IN ROWS
   99 CONTINUE
C-----INITIALIZE ROW TOTALS AND TOTAL OF THE REW TOTALS.
      DO101IROW=1,LIMR
  101 TROW(IROW)=0
      ALLR=0
C-----TOTAL ROWS
      DO103IROW=1,LIMR
      DO102JCOL=1,LIMC
  102 TROW(IROW)=TROW(IROW)+AMX(IROW,JCOL)
C-----TOTAL ALL ROWS
  103 ALLR=ALLR+TROW(IROW)
C-----INITIALIZE COLUMN TOTALS AND TOTAL OF THE COLUMN TOTALS.
      DO104JCOL=1,LIMC
```

359

```
      104 TCOL(JCOL)=0
          ALLC=0
C-----TOTAL COLUMNS.
          DO106JCOL=1,LIMC
          DO105IROW=1,LIMR
      105 TCOL(JCOL)=TCOL(JCOL)+AMX(IROW,JCOL)
C-----TOTAL ALL COLUMNS
      106 ALLC=ALLC+TCOL(JCOL)
C-----CHECK FOR ERROR
          IF(ALLC-ALLR)550,107,550
      550 WRITE(5,551)
      551 FORMAT(4X,'MATH ERROR.HALT.',//)
          CALL EXIT
C     CALCULATE PERCENTAGES FOR CELLS WITH RESPECT TO ROWS
      107 DO500JCOL=1,LIMC
          DO500IROW=1,LIMR
      500 P(IROW,JCOL)=AMX(IROW,JCOL)/TROW(IROW)
C     WRITE MATRIX
          WRITE(5,560)
      560 FORMAT(4X,'MATRIX BY PERCENTAGES WITH RESPECT TO ROWS.',//)
          WRITE(5,108)((P(IROW,JCOL),JCOL=1,LIMC),IROW=1,LIMR)
      108 FORMAT(7(7X,F5.3),//)
          WRITE(5,109)
      109 FORMAT(4X,'TEST FOR SIGNIFICANT DIFFERENCE BETWEEN ELTS. IN COLUMN
         1',//,4X,'TWO AT A TIME USING T-TEST-ONE TAIL-5 PER.LEVEL.',///)
          WRITE(5,110)
      110 FORMAT(7X,'COLUMN',3X,'ROW',6X,'ROW',6X,'T-VALUE',4X,'CRIT. VAL.',
         16X,'D.F.',5X,'SIGNIFICANT',//)
C     GET THE T-VALUE
          LIMN=LIMR-1
          DO 127 JCOL=1,LIMC
          DO 127 NROW=1,LIMN
          DO 127 IROW=2,LIMR
          IF(IROW-NROW)127,127,111
      111 EST=(AMX(NROW,JCOL)+AMX(IROW,JCOL))/(TROW(NROW)+TROW(IROW))
          S=(P(NROW,JCOL)-P(IROW,JCOL))/(EST*(1-EST)*(1/TROW(NROW)+1/TROW(IR
         1OW)))**.5
C     GET D.F. AND CRITICAL VALUE FOR T-TEST
          IDF=TROW(NROW)+TROW(IROW)-2
          IF(IDF-30)112,112,113
      112 CRITV=T(IDF)
          GO TO 120
      113 IF(IDF-40)114,114,115
      114 CRITV=1.68
          GO TO 120
      115 IF(IDF-60)116,116,117
      116 CRITV=1.67
          GO TO 120
      117 IF(IDF-120)118,118,119
      118 CRITV=1.66
          GO TO 120
      119 CRITV=1.64
      120 CONTINUE
C     TEST FOR SIGNIFICANT DIFFERENCE
          IF(S)121,122,122
      121 IF(S+CRITV)124,123,123
      122 IF(S-CRITV)123,123,324
```

```
      123 WRITE(5,125)JCOL,NROW,IROW,S,CRITV,IDF
      125 FORMAT(3(8X,I1),2(8X,F5.2),8X,I3,8X,'NO',//)
          GO TO 127
      124 WRITE(5,126)JCOL,NROW,IROW,S,CRITV,IDF,IROW,NROW
      126 FORMAT(3(8X,I1),2(8X,F5.2),8X,I3,8X,'YES. ROW ',I1,'PERCENTAGE GRE
         1ATER THAN ROW ',I1,//)
          GO TO 127
      324 WRITE(5,126)JCOL,NROW,IROW,S,CRITV,IDF,NROW,IROW
      127 CONTINUE
          GO TO 129
C         SUB-ROUTINE FOR WRITING PERCENT MATRIX WITH RESPECT TO COLUMNS AND
C         TESTING ELTS. IN ROWS
C         CALCULATE PERCENTAGES FOR CELLS WITH RESPECT TO COLUMNS
      129 DO 400 IROW=1,LIMR
          DO 400 JCOL=1,LIMC
      400 Q(IROW,JCOL)=AMX(IROW,JCOL)/TCOL(JCOL)
C         WRITE MATRIX
          WRITE(5,561)
      561 FORMAT(4X,'MATRIX BY PERCENTAGES WITH RESPECT TO COLUMNS.',//)
          WRITE(5,108)((Q(IROW,JCOL),JCOL=1,LIMC),IROW=1,LIMR)
          WRITE(5,131)
      131 FORMAT(4X,'TEST FOR SIGNIFICANT DIFFERENCES BETWEEN ELTS IN ROWS',
         10/,4X,'TWO AT A TIME USING T/TEST-ONE TAIL-5 PER. LEVEL.',///)
          WRITE(5,132)
      132 FORMAT(7X,'ROW    ',3X,'COL',6X,'COL',6X,'T-VALUE',4X,'CRIT. VAL.',
         16X,'D.F.',5X,'SIGNIFICANT',//)
C         GET T VALUE
          LIMN=LIMC-1
          DO151IROW=1,LIMR
          DO151NCOL=1,LIMN
          DO151JCOL=2,LIMC
          IF(JCOL-NCOL)151,151,133
      133 EST=(AMX(IROW,NCOL)+AMX(IROW,JCOL))/(TCOL(NCOL)+TCOL(JCOL))
          S=(Q(IROW,NCOL)-Q(IROW,JCOL))/(EST*(1-EST)*(1/TCOL(NCOL)+1/TCOL(JC
         1OL)))**.5
C         GET D.F. AND CRITICAL VALUE FOR T TEST
          IDF=TCOL(NCOL)+TCOL(JCOL)-2
          IF(IDF-30)134,134,135
      134 CRITV=T(IDF)
          GO TO 142
      135 IF(IDF-40)136,136,137
      136 CRITV=1.68
          GO TO 142
      137 IF(IDF-60)138,138,139
      138 CRITV=1.67
          GO TO 142
      139 IF(IDF-120)140,140,141
      140 CRITV=1.66
          GO TO 142
      141 CRITV=1.64
      142 CONTINUE
C         TEST FOR SIGNIFICANT DIFFERENCE
          IF(S)143,144,144
      143 IF(S+CRITV)146,145,145
      144 IF(S-CRITV)145,145,149
      145 WRITE(5,147)IROW,NCOL,JCOL,S,CRITV,IDF
      147 FORMAT(3(8X,I1),2(8X,F5.2),8X,I3,8X,'NO',//)
```

```
      GO TO 151
146 WRITE(5,148)IROW,NCOL,JCOL,S,CRITV,IDF,JCOL,NCOL
148 FORMAT(3(8X,I1),2(8X,F5.2),8X,I3,8X,'YES. COL  ',I1,'PERCENTAGE GRE
   1ATER THAN COL ',I1,//)
      GO TO 151
149 WRITE(5,148)IROW,NCOL,JCOL,S,CRITV,IDF,NCOL,JCOL
151 CONTINUE
      GO TO 19
130 CALL EXIT
      END

FEATURES SUPPORTED
 ONE WORD INTEGERS
 EXTENDED PRECISION
 IOCS

CORE REQUIREMENTS FOR
 COMMON      0  VARIABLES   1576  PROGRAM   2594

 END OF COMPILATION

// XEQ
```

INDEX

DATE DUE

Withdrawn From
Ohio Northern
University Library

GAYLORD   PRINTED IN U.S.A.

HETERICK MEMORIAL LIBRARY
028.7 D132l   onuu
Daiute, Robert Jame/ Library operations r

3 5111 00060 5570